T0168617

A Call for
Heresy

A Call for
Heresy

Why Dissent Is Vital to Islam and America

ANOUAR MAJID

UNIVERSITY OF MINNESOTA PRESS

MINNEAPOLIS • LONDON

A major part of chapter 1 is also published as "The Postcolonial Bubble,"
in Revathi Krishnaswamy and John C. Hawley, eds., *The Postcolonial and the Global*
(Minneapolis: University of Minnesota Press, 2007).

Published by the University of Minnesota Press
111 Third Avenue South, Suite 290
Minneapolis, MN 55401-2520
http://www.upress.umn.edu

Library of Congress Cataloging-in-Publication Data

Majid, Anouar, 1960–
A call for heresy : why dissent is vital to Islam and America / Anouar Majid.
p. cm.
Includes bibliographical references and index.
ISBN: 978-0-8166-5127-6 (hc alk. paper)
ISBN-10: 0-8166-5127-2 (hc : alk. paper) 1. East and West. 2. Civilization, Islamic—21st century.
3. United States—Civilization—21st century. 4. Islamic countries—Relations—United States.
5. United States—Relations—Islamic countries. I. Title.
CB251.M284 2007
909′.09767—dc22
2007019401

Printed in the United States of America on acid-free paper

The University of Minnesota is an equal-opportunity educator and employer.

12 11 10 09 08 07   10 9 8 7 6 5 4 3 2 1

It comes about, therefore, that we find precisely among the heretics of all ages men who were inspired by this highest religious experience; often they appeared to their contemporaries as atheists, but sometimes also as saints. Viewed from this angle, men like Democritus, Francis of Assisi, and Spinoza are near to one another.

—ALBERT EINSTEIN

CONTENTS

PREFACE

I started thinking about this project in 2003, inspired, partly, by the attempt to shift the global debate away from the customary "us versus them" binary—however this binary is conceived—to one that highlights common trends and perils in the Islamic world and the United States. It was clear to me that both nations, or *ummas,* if you will, were endangered by forces darker and more insidious than the ones they were fighting with guns and bombs. Sometimes all we need is a different perspective to untie knotty problems, loosen the climate of suspicion, and, if all works well, increase the possibilities for dialogue and thoughtful collective action. By looking at the fortunes of Muslim and American societies together, we may perhaps recognize the futility of armed conflict and consider solutions that address underlying causes, rather than exacerbate anger and confusion.

Readers familiar with my previous academic work will find a different rhetorical approach in this book. My goal here is to address scholars and general readers from any discipline, culture, religion, and (if translated) language who want to understand how Muslims and Americans are trapped in the nightmares of their own histories. Although specialized knowledge designed for fellow academics is vital for the well-being of any society, scholarship must sometimes step over the boundaries of its sheltered environment and jealously guarded conventions to reframe questions and help create better conditions for broad, democratic dialogue.

The task of undertaking such a project was daunting, not least because I am quite aware of the emotions it could stir among traditionalists in both camps, and also because of the vast scope of my inquiry. It is always a bit of a gamble to examine well-established traditions critically, for to question their foundations is akin, in some ways, to undoing the structures of our identities and communities. However imperfect they may be, traditions, whether national, religious, or both, are the ties that bind us together; to imagine a world without them is to see oneself falling into some kind of existential abyss. The scriptures of our cultures (such as the Bible, Qur'an, or the Declaration of Independence) may be the work of humans in history, often carried out in messy and complicated circumstances and therefore open to critique and reevaluation, as this work will suggest; still, doing so doesn't really take away from the frightening prospects such questioning engenders. Where would we be without our communities, anchored as they are in beliefs that rarely withstand the scrutiny of modern knowledge and which, moreover, contain the seeds of violence that continue to undermine our quest for peace? It is a question yet to be fully and rigorously addressed, but for now I limit myself to opening up our myths and scriptures for more capacious visions and practices, even when such practices go against the pillars of the faith.

Long after this book had gone into production, and therefore too late to discuss in the main text, I read two new books that wrestled with this issue and offered different solutions to the crisis of religion in the postmodern world. In his best-selling book *God Is Not Great: How Religion Poisons Everything,* the noted columnist Christopher Hitchens announces that modern sciences have so thoroughly dethroned the intellectually unconvincing postulates of religious thought that only the finest works of Western literature and music could compensate for the spiritual uplift that traditional religions have so far offered. Such a secular attachment to the cultural aesthetic is not exactly the answer of the once devout Catholic and now atheist French philosopher André Comte-Sponville. In his *L'esprit de l'athéisme: Introduction à une spiritualité sans Dieu,* published in 2006, Comte-Sponville is aware of the urgency to struggle for the freedom of the irreligious, and he also wrestles with the issue of spirituality in a world without Western religions (Judaism, Christianity, and Islam). In the end, however, he comes out convinced that one can indeed experience a sense of immanence and plenitude without having to subscribe to the dogma of a monotheistic creed or to read the classics of the Western literary canon. To be aware of the immensity of the creation, to experience what the French writer Romain Rolland called "the oceanic feeling" is, as Sigmund Freud himself recognized in a letter to Rolland in 1929, to go beyond the limits of ordinary psychology and to do away with our little selves, our obstructionist egos caught firmly in the lowest degree of experience. Perhaps this is why Alexandre Kojève wrote in his *Essai d'une histoire raisonnée de la philosophie païenne* that "every authentic mystical experience is more or less atheistic." So thoroughly convinced is Comte-Sponville of the truth of this perspective that he concludes his examination of God, religion, and the spiritual life by reminding those of us who are apt to forget that "We are already in [God's] kingdom."

While the question of faith in a postmonotheistic world order has yet to receive the widespread and sustained attention it deserves, I limit myself in this work to opening up our myths and scriptures for more capacious visions and practices, even when such practices go against the pillars of the faith—any faith, whether that faith be in the gods of religion, politics, or the economy. I am far more interested in emphasizing the vital need of criticism and the right to difference in any society or faith than in imagining new and better models of communal life, since all systems, however liberating they may at first appear, have a natural tendency to harden into dogmas and various degrees of illiberalism over time. In a thoughtful article for the May 21, 2007, issue of the *New Yorker* magazine, Anthony Gottlieb, commenting on the recent trend of accusing religions for all our ills, suggested that the absence of religion from our lives would in no way guarantee a more peaceful coexistence, since the people who use religion to make mischief could surely devise other ways to achieve the same goal. Atheism, in other words, is no panacea for people trying to live together. All systems and ideas can stand to be humanized through constant questioning and friendly amendments, as major figures of the Enlightenment knew. As the veteran historian and essayist Tzvetan Todoror noted in *L'esprit des Lumières* (2006), the well-calibrated critical spirit that is essential to the maintenance of an enlightened community is now seriously undermined by some of the global economic, cultural, and political forces discussed in the course of this book.

I cannot overstate how crucial the support and encouragement of Jason Weidemann, my editor and first-rate interlocutor at the University of Minnesota Press, was to this project. Jason knew instantly what I was trying to do. Through his agency and courteous exchange, the manuscript has been substantially improved. In addition to his own extensive list of probing questions and comments, I was able to obtain several readings of the manuscript, each one reflecting its author's perspectives and suggesting valuable improvements. Most helpful, too, were the comments conveyed to me from several faculty board members. Jason's steadfast support, along with the enthusiasm and professionalism of the entire staff at the press, has made the publication process a truly exceptional experience. To all these accomplished professionals from the vanguard state and press of Minnesota, and to Robert J. Allison, who, from the heartland of Puritans, continues to share his grace with this Moroccan pilgrim farther to the north, my undying gratitude.

I only wish my friend the historian Jacques Downs was still among us to read this book and ground my ideas in his typical Franklinesque common sense. But he is gone to where Franklin, Jefferson, and, most probably, Paine have preceded him. If we, who are still on their trail, don't "have it in our power to begin the world over again," then perhaps we can console ourselves with the knowledge that we tried to keep their legacy—and the legacy of their Muslim predecessors in embracing enlightened views about humans and their gods—alive.

Saints in Peril

A Virtuous heretic shall be saved before a wicked Christian.

—BENJAMIN FRANKLIN

The atheist staring from his attic window is often nearer to God than the believer caught up in his own false image of God.

—MARTIN BUBER

This book is both an attempt to treat Islam over and beyond the confines of the familiar extremist/moderate dichotomy and an extension of my reflections on ways to divert Muslim and other cultures toward more progressive formulations. In the past I called for a progressive interpretation of Islam and its canons, urged both Muslims and Westerners to question their orthodoxies, and argued for a polycentric world of "neoprovincials" questioning dogmas at home, reaching out to progressive elements in other cultures, and forging global alliances in the building of a genuinely multicultural human civilization, one in which economies are integrated into the broader aspirations of nations, not ruling over them like ruthless, insatiable deities. Here I am taking the discussion to its outer limits, calling on both Muslims (who consider their religion to be God's final word in history) and Americans (who often think of themselves as having received a special dispensation from the Creator) to embrace heretical thought, or freethinking, as the only life-saving measure left to avoid an apocalyptic future.

By asking Muslims and Americans to examine their histories, traditions, and cultures critically, I am not, obviously, assuming a perfect symmetry between Islam and America, for, technically speaking, Muslims are members of a faith, while Americans are members of a nation. (That nationalism is another form of religion is another matter.)[1] Neither am I positing that Islam is monolithic in its effects, as many are wont to object anytime the word *Islam* is used to describe the experience of people in sprawling and diverse parts of the globe. I could have used Marshall Hodgson's adjective *Islamicate* to refer to the broader set of complex cultural practices one finds in Islamdom (lands of Islam) and thus dissociate the religion proper from its cultural effects, or from the non-Islamic customs on which the faith was grafted;[2] but since the word *Islam* as a signifier is heavily used by both Muslims and non-Muslims, by scholars and nonscholars, in the current global environment, I think it would be better to use it—instead of a series of more technically accurate designations for each particular occasion—in order to intervene more meaningfully in the discussion about Islam in the world.

Suffice to say that while Islam, as a set of precepts and obligations, is universal, the practice of Islam varies from one cultural milieu to the next. I grew up in Tangier, Morocco, a city more famous for its beaches, cafés, bars, and nightclubs than for its mosques and minarets. In such a place, one could talk about God and good wine in the same breath, although the spheres of the sacred and the profane are carefully kept apart, so as not to take away from the inherent quality of each. One may not find this social experience in Saudi Arabia, Pakistan, or Iran, where absolutism in matters of faith is taken more seriously than in my native country and city. Yet even in Morocco today, there is a serious attempt to throw Saudi Arabia's homegrown puritanical ideology, known as Wahhabism, on the country's liberal attitudes, increasingly seen by Islamists as unacceptably hedonistic. One hopes that such an outcome never comes to be, not because I want to defend hedonism (although, obviously, a serious philosophical argument could be made for it) but because all societies are diminished when multiple ways of being are eroded by self-appointed, single-minded guardians of authenticity. The drive for purity, in the end, results in terror and genocide. The coexistence of different lifestyles within a polity is a testament to the community's ability to live with real difference, an experience that is becoming increasingly rare in Muslim societies. Pluralism is essential to any conversation, and without it Muslims in Muslim societies will keep sliding deeper into the dark tunnel of monologues and self-congratulatory pronouncements.

Just as I hope that the reader will keep a nuanced understanding of Islam, I also want her to remember that *America* is an equally slippery notion, standing as it is for a whole continent (which is not how it is used in this book) and for a religiously, racially, and culturally diverse society. America is a set of ideals blending a Puritan worldview with the philosophies of eighteenth-century European liberalism. It is a nation struggling to be secular and Christian at once, and so is infused with a strong but tortured missionary streak that seeks to convert the unconverted at home (often the newly arrived, non-English-speaking immigrant) and bring the light to the rest of the world. In fact, the United States itself could be defined as a form of religion—with its scripture (Declaration of Independence), Ten Commandments (Bill of Rights), and chosen people—that has inaugurated a new era in the history of freedom, human rights, and government. The reverence for the aforementioned documents, all encased in a heavily guarded "shrine" at the National Archives in Washington, D.C., is now a commonplace of American consciousness and political discourse, although the sacralization of what were initially working blueprints for change, as with all the founding texts of monotheistic religions, developed over time, reaching their pinnacle, in the case of the Declaration, in their consecration by Abraham Lincoln, following his own mythical rise to the status of Founding Father. With such sacred foundations, the chosen nation of America considers those who do not benefit from its principles (nowadays dubbed as a "way of life") as slaves laboring in the darkness of tyranny, and therefore in need of redemption. This outlook is a significant yet often overlooked element in American foreign affairs. Following the military intervention in Iraq in 2003, the British columnist George Monbiot, relying on a book by Clifford Longley, declared that "the United States is no longer a nation. It is now a religion." So collapsed are the categories that to question American nationalism is to commit blasphemy; it makes one "anti-American."[3]

That the United States is akin to a religion made up of the dual but intersecting strains of Protestant fundamentalism and republican notions of liberty is well known. But what is relatively less known, as Timothy Marr, building on the groundbreaking work done by Robert J. Allison, among others, has argued, is that Islamic despotism was the foil against which the new republic's national identity was defined and, through wars against North Africans and Malays, consolidated. "Muslim ascendancy in the Mediterranean, and elsewhere in Africa and Asia," writes Marr, who has coined the term *islamicism* to define the particular brand of American attitudes toward Islam, "challenged American global aspirations for expanding its blend of democratic principles and Christian values. Cultural negotiations of islamicist despotism comprised a key but critically neglected part of the construction and consolidation of early American nationalism." It was not surprising at all that in 1787, John Jay, the U.S. Secretary of Foreign Affairs, would threaten New Yorkers that if they didn't ratify the new Constitution, "Algerians could be on the American coast and enslave its citizens who have not a single sloop of war." Oriental and Islamic despotism, a theme that came to America by way of Baron de Montesquieu's influential *The Spirit of the Laws* (1748), justified American moral superiority and what Marr calls an "imperialism of virtue." In plays and action, Americans prided themselves in their willingness to die fighting such a mighty foe. In a five-act play called *The Young Carolinians, or, Americans in Algiers,* published in 1818, a young gambler is redeemed by taking up the cause of rescuing captive sailors, declaring that "our sailors shall make the crescent bend to our fixed stars." By fighting Muslims in North Africa, and through the trumpeted exploits of Stephen Decatur and William Eaton, the Navy was "transformed into an emblematic instrument of national honor" and smoothed fears about its threat to American liberties.[4]

The fusion of a Christian eschatological imaginary, making the removal of Ottomans and Muslims from the Holy Land essential to the fulfillment of millennial prophecies, and the drive to spread liberty around the world turned Islam into a power of darkness to be defeated. "Because American political ideology was opposed to extracontinental colonization, the religious vision through which the divine will orchestrated the universal success of Protestant aspirations became a strong cultural means of consolidating national power and pride," explains Marr.[5] Protestant theology and American nationalism were thus blended into a super-ideology of expansionism and conversion, one that is too colossal not to be seriously considered a religion in its own right. In short, the American nation saw itself as the antithesis of Islam, even though Islam is a religion, not a nation, in the narrow political sense:

> Since the beginnings of the settlement of what is today the United States, the Islamic world has formed an extrahemispheric horizon that Americans have engaged to define the cultural contours of their changing sense of worldliness. The cultural discourse of islamicism dislocated Islam from its

diverse everyday practices and recalibrated it into an imaginary resource for articulating local, regional, and national situations within a broader planetary perspective.[6]

One could, therefore, reasonably claim that because of the strong universalist drives that Islam and America (or Americanism) generate, both could be treated as rivals in the struggle to shape minds and souls across the globe. Sometimes, as we shall see in the course of this book, Europeans see Islamic fundamentalism and American commercial expansionism as allies in the war against European liberalism, so much so that in 1997, only four years before 9/11, Marc Anna (better known as Alexandre Del Valle), a right-wing author, christened this alliance "Islamerica." The conservative American author Dinesh D'Souza has imagined another kind of alliance between America and Islam, one that brings together America's conservative agenda and those of traditional Islam to fight a common war against Muslim extremists, European liberals, and American leftists. I will say more about the similarities between America and Islam in a later chapter, but for now, the point to retain is that despite the missionary ideologies that animate Muslims and Americans, I am interested primarily in the ways in which both peoples, each in their separate historical and cultural spheres, are increasingly being subjected to religious, political, and economic orthodoxies that suppress the intellectual legacies that once gave both traditions, however briefly, their greatest cultural élans. Thus, Islamic cultures, long in a state of decline, are fighting a nation whose ideals are fast losing ground to the same reactionary forces that have condemned Islam to a state of stagnation.

That Islam has rarely been as challenged to deal with its contradictions as it has in the post–9/11 period is now quite obvious. The day after 9/11, when the world was still in shock, Sam Harris, a young scholar and graduate student at Stanford University, started writing an attack on Islam and all monotheistic religions that would burst out into the publishing scene in 2004 and 2005, complete with endorsements from leading intellectual figures in the United States and Britain, and eliciting a tremendous amount of attention and debate. Such a remarkable publishing debut was due in no small measure to the author's ability to alert readers of the world that by sugarcoating religious nonsense and overlooking the fairy tale dimensions of all religions, humans are forsaking reason, our only hope in a world awash with all forms of unreason. Sam Harris's *The End of Faith* struck a chord and issued a challenge that we may as well address, if our quest for understanding and peace is not to be held captive by foggy logic.[7]

Dismayed by the fact that people in the twenty-first century still believe in the "untestable propositions" of ancient religions, Harris blames the so-called moderates (failed fundamentalists, he describes them at one point) who continue to abet beliefs in obsolete creeds and the sacredness of scriptures that are no less fantastical than ancient Greece's mythical gods, long discarded for what they are: mere fables. He chastises towering scientists like the late Stephen Jay Gould for indulging in this form of political correctness and points out that, as a result of our "failure to criticize the unreasonable (and dangerous) certainty of others," we live in "a country in which a person cannot get elected president if he openly doubts the existence of heaven and hell."[8] While Harris understands that humans "cannot live by reason alone,"[9] using this phrase shouldn't mean accepting the dictates of people who lived thousands of years ago as articles of faith, or as indispensable guides to a future that could not have been imagined by people who lived two hundred, let alone two thousand, years ago.

Harris is harshest on Muslims, quoting from the Qur'an selectively and relying almost exclusively on the authority of Bernard Lewis and a couple of other scholars to show that it sanctions violence (although Lewis's reading of Islam is far more nuanced). He dismisses University of Chicago professor of political science Robert A. Pape's scholarly findings on suicide bombers and singles out the latter for his ire because it is, in his view, Islam that motivates them to commit violence and atrocities against their enemies, as if religion here were less inspirational than, say, family, tribe, or nation. Not only does Harris downplay the context in which such acts happen, but he doesn't seem to realize that people do not always kill, or even commit large-scale atrocities, for, or in the name of, God. Dogma, which he invokes, would have been a safer category to emphasize. Still, it is true that Muslim extremists seem to worry about "contamination" (a crucial ingredient in Kwame Anthony Appiah's system of "new cosmopolitanism")[10] and seem unable to shake out their sense of "humiliation,"[11] but then again, this is due to a more complex global phenomenon.[12]

To Harris, who provides a scientific analysis of belief, one cannot reason with people of faith—that is, people inhabited by delusions legitimized by the rubric of religion—and so it is perfectly legitimate to kill Muslim extremists in self-defense. For "the men who committed the atrocities of September 11 . . . were men of faith—*perfect* faith."[13] That religious people do a lot of good doesn't make faith necessary, Harris repeats throughout.[14] The bloody record of religion doesn't compensate for the horrors executed in its name. Religions are simply wired to be intolerant and ultimately violent. The Holy Inquisition, to take one instance, started with the attempt to wipe out the "popular movement of Catharism" (a form of Manichaeanism founded by Mani, who also was "flayed alive at the behest of Zoroastrian priests in 276 CE") in 1184, by deploying the most elaborate forms of torture to punish heretics, as the following description chillingly illustrates:

> The condemned are then immediately carried to the Riberia, the place of execution, where there are as many stakes set up as there are prisoners to be burnt. The negative and relapsed being first strangled and then burnt; the professed mount their stakes by a ladder, and the Jesuits, after several repeated exhortations to be reconciled to the church, consign them to eternal destruction, and then leave them to the fiend, who they tell them stands at their elbow to carry them into torments. On this a great shout is raised, and the cry is, "let the dogs' beards be made"; which is done by thrusting flaming bunches of furze, fastened to long poles, against their beards, till their faces are burnt black, the surrounding populace rending the air with the loudest acclamations of joy. At last fire is set to the furze at the bottom of the stake, over which the victims are chained, so high that the flame seldom reaches higher than the seat they sit on, and thus they are rather roasted than burnt. Although there cannot be a more lamentable spectacle and the sufferers continually cry out as long as they are able, "Pity for the love of God!" yet it is beheld by persons of all ages and both sexes with transports of joy and satisfaction.[15]

And it is this murderous certitude that turned people into witches and Jews into blood-sucking monsters preying on holy Christian blood eligible for torture and some of the most degrading treatment ever experienced by human beings. Of course, the Jews' dogma of chosenness didn't make things easier for them, but the Christian demonization of Jews for refusing to believe in tenets such as Mary's virginity (almost certainly the result of the Greek mistranslation of the Hebrew word *alma,* meaning young woman) gave way to the secular vilification of Jews as they turned into a degraded race ineligible for the redeeming powers of baptism. And their fate, one might note, served as a well-tried template for the treatment of Muslims, whether converted or not, in Catholic Spain after 1492. For being non-Christian, the Jews would pay a heavy price indeed![16]

Yet even in the midst of such a barbaric record, Muslims, according to Harris, are the worst offenders, alone among the aggrieved of the world to resort to "terrorism of the sort that has become so commonplace among [them]."[17] It's an inextricable feature of their faith, just as their inability to acknowledge their own imperialist history or to seriously challenge apostasy laws expresses the practical inexistence of truly moderate, critical Muslims. "Within the House of Islam, the penalty for learning too much about the world—so as to call the tenets of faith into question—is death. If a twenty-first-century Muslim loses his faith, though he may have been a Muslim only for a single hour, the normative response, everywhere under Islam, is death."[18] And though the House of Islam was generally better for Jews than Christendom was, the Jews, as were Christians, let alone members of nonrecognized faiths, were still persecuted. As if it were irrefutable proof, Harris piles up more than five pages of quotations from the Qur'an to prove that Islam's holy book, unlike the Bible, teaches an exclusivist and intolerant ideology to its adherents.[19]

To Harris, there is very little, if anything at all, to like in Islam. The Muslim paradise "resembles nothing so much as an al fresco bordello," and if democracy were to be implemented in the Muslim world today, it would be "little more than a gangplank to theocracy."[20] Moreover, because of the unwillingness of Muslims to desacralize their faith, the main discourse in such societies is "currently a tissue of myths, conspiracy theories, and exhortations to recapture the glories of the seventh century."[21] These are societies that are morally and politically inferior to "our own," Harris adds matter-of-factly, wasteful of human and natural resources, without a civil society that allows people to speak their minds about rulers, divine and temporal. And so, once again, he sees no solution to a moderate alternative, one that is daring, not wishy-washy.

To be sure, a medieval mind-set also prevails in the U.S. government and in American culture as a whole, where wars are declared on nonviolent drug use and consenting adult sexuality; the state kills criminals who are themselves victims of "bad genes, bad parents, bad ideas, or bad luck"; funding for condoms is prohibited in poor countries; and research on life-saving "human embryonic stem cells" is banned by Congress.[22] But Harris is no typical liberal. After reflecting on the science of good and evil (and providing some interesting insights into the nature/ethics debate), he ends up criticizing relativists and pragmatists like Richard Rorty, and pacifists, including Gandhi (he had already taken Edward Said, Jean Baudrillard, and Noam Chomsky to task for failing to ascribe incomparable villainy to Muslims), while agreeing with Alan Dershowitz's provisional sanction for the torture of (Muslim) terrorists to extract life-saving information. Torture, in this sense, is no less ethical than "collateral damage," for, after all, torture targets particular people, such as the "rather scrofulous young men" at Guantánamo Bay,[23] and doesn't, like Muslim suicide bombers, kill civilians indiscriminately. While the United Nations Commission on Human Rights came to condemn the treatment of prisoners at Guantánamo Bay,[24] Harris says that whoever accepts war must also accept torture and collateral damage.

Harris, "who was raised by a Jewish mother and a Quaker father," and doesn't mind having a small Christmas tree in his house (a concession to his wife, he said in an interview),[25] doesn't call himself an atheist, or anything, for that matter. But while exploring the nature of the self and the "I," the consciousness that stands over and above the self, creating the object (self)/subject ("I") split, he clearly extols Eastern spirituality, including aspects of monotheistic mysticism, as the only way we have to attain the "loss of self" and collapse the dangerous duality (object/subject) that has kept the world's religions and cultures at each others' throats. For in a world of six billion selves, we need a spirituality that erodes this duality, this sense of separateness—and in this area, the East, as always, with its long traditions of meditation, refined almost to a science that helps people transcend their disabling sense of dualism while keeping consciousness alive, has much to teach a West that is hostage to monotheistic ethic and "religious traditions [that] are intellectually defunct and politically ruinous."[26] "Buddha, Shankra, Padmasambhava, Longchenpa, and countless others down to the present have no equivalents in the West. In spiritual terms, we appear to have been standing on the shoulders of dwarfs."[27] Only mystical trends within the three religions, such as Sufism ("itself influenced by Buddhism, Hinduism, Zoroastrianism, and Christian monasticism")[28] and the rare occasional luminary from a monotheistic creed, like the thirteenth-century Muslim mystic Rumi (virtually the only Muslim who looks good in Harris's account), seem to be able to escape the iron grip of dualistic faith. Harris quickly adds that "the existence of such spiritual luminaries, however, suggests nothing about the adequacy of the Bible and the Koran as contemplative manuals."[29]

Thus, Harris concludes the "God of Abraham" is "unworthy of . . . man," let alone the vastness and immensity of the creation. It is far better to recognize the ways in which we are bound to one another, to take stock of our interdependence and help each and every one of us flourish. Religions with their uncompromising dualist ideologies simply cannot promote tolerance and peace. It is not in the nature of their DNA. So the path is laid out in front of us: mysticism, which increasingly has everything to recommend it, including scientific research, is the way out of our dysfunctional faiths.

In the end, in order to address the twentieth-century atrocities committed by totalitarian regimes in the name of secular ideologies, Harris still manages to find elements of religious thinking and the abdication of reason in the face of such beliefs, or the connection between some of these ideologies and a residual religious outlook. One could argue, for instance, that Nazism can be traced back to the Inquisition itself and the Catholic Church's long history of vilifying Jews. Harris, however, is on safer ground when he reiterates in the afterword to the 2005 paperback edition that the faith he addresses in the book is really the "problem of dogma itself"; the problem occurs when Reason inexplicably forfeits its right for evidence in the face of irrational and, what's worse, rigid and dangerous mythologies.[30]

There is no doubt at all that Sam Harris's eloquent, scathing, and occasionally humorous demolition of religion, particularly of Islam, is a challenge to all scholars interested in global peace. For instance, while Harris's book was a best seller in the United States, a similar case against monotheism was being made in France by Michel Onfray, a philosopher of ethical hedonism who wants to carry on the program of "atheology." This concept, first enunciated by the philosopher and writer Georges Bataille in 1950, builds on the traditions of the Enlightenment by giving physical shape to the metaphysical and deconstructing Judaism, Christianity, and Islam, which together have inaugurated and perpetuated millennia of false

convictions, irreconcilable textual contradictions, and relentless dehuman-
ization, and nurtured cultures of hatred and war, all in the name of a God
that never speaks for him- or herself. To hold on to such a legacy as our
ticket to a better world in the heavens only delays the building of a more
harmonious human civilization on earth, one that would make us more
palpably aware of the finitude of our lives and the importance of seeing
ourselves merely as humans, denuded of the abstract ideologies that recast
our perceptions of one another.[31]

Since the disposition of all three religions is inherently problematic, to
say the least, moderation in matters of monotheism, according to Harris,
only legitimizes the drive toward extremism. It makes "dupes" of otherwise well-meaning people.[32] One might certainly agree that moderation in
Muslim societies hasn't done much to broaden the field of intellectual
inquiry, because Islam, like other religions, could only exist by upholding
its superior theology of infallible truth; but Harris's canvas of dogmatism
is rather small and selective, choosing to focus on monotheistic religions
and the persistent medievalism in American politics and cultures, without
reaching out for a more inclusive, more panoramic view of extremism in
the world today. One doesn't find much about the effects of unexamined
nationalism and cutthroat capitalism, both causing, as we shall see in the
next chapter, incalculable deaths and damage to the human patrimony.
One might, therefore, argue that the supreme deity of the United States
right now, the absolute and absolutist god that broaches no dissent, is not
Jesus or his increasingly vociferous defenders, but capitalism. In fact, religious fundamentalism, as with all other forms of fundamentalism, doesn't
happen in a cultural vacuum but emerges in response to a sense of threat
to one's being or core beliefs. Fundamentalism is often situational; it
always expresses itself in relation to a contending force. Even if one were
to take Harris's reading of the Bible and the Qur'an at face value, both
documents were written in particular historical contexts, thereby reflecting the sense of siege befalling the emerging faiths. This doesn't exonerate
the faiths, by any means, but reveals that identity is always construed
in relation to somebody else's, the Other's, and can only be surpassed, in
Harris's own estimation, by the erasure of the duality embedded in our
worldviews and the adoption of Eastern forms of meditation. Thus religious fundamentalism today may be caused by an entirely different set of
conditions from those in effect during, say, the birth of Islam. Similarly,

the current wave of Christian fundamentalism in the United States may be a response to a failed social model, not the expression of loyalty to early Puritan settlers who fled Europe to establish different communities of faith in America.

We must, therefore, add all these elements to Harris's canvas, even while addressing his intellectual challenge regarding the failure of Islam today. We need to examine the history of Islamic fundamentalism, the Muslim intellectuals' attempt to challenge it, why the United States can but has failed to help Muslims break out of their historic impasse, how the United States itself is undergoing an identity crisis similar to the one expressed in Muslim lands, and why Harris's message, if broadened and recalibrated, could offer promising possibilities, not just to Muslims but also to Americans and the rest of the world, including nations that gave birth to Buddhism and Confucianism—India and China. It is also important to realize that jihadism, however irrational and violent it appears in news bulletins and in the popular imagination, is not inexplicable or an anomaly within the more encompassing blanket of globalization. It makes far better sense to postulate that a skewed model of human development is one of the primary causes of most of the violence in the world today, including, sometimes, the violence that appears shrouded in the cover of religion.

While Muslim scholars have been examining their traditions critically for centuries, their work has yet to get the public attention it deserves. It needs to be better known, if only to prove to progressive forces around the world that Muslims are as capable of self-criticism as are the members of more mature democratic polities. There has never been a better time to cast aside unexamined tribal attitudes and reach for enlightened commitments that enrich the mind and soul together, not impoverish one at the expense of the other. The need for such emancipation was impressed on me during talks I gave in 2004 and 2005 in my native Morocco and in Turkey, two liberal societies where most topics are freely debated, except for the sensitive issue of religion. I found very little inclination to see Islam as one truth among many, or to accept that Islam has had as bloody a history as any other major community or nation. With minor exceptions, much silence surrounds the issues of slavery, racism, social relations, past imperial reach, or any object or person deemed sacred by the canons of the faith or the hallowed pages of history. To raise such topics is to discover that the Muslim individual is governed, as Malek Chebel put it, by a list of proscriptions (*interdits*) that stigmatizes critical thinking and frames the individual's life with carefully delineated norms.[33] Such forms of self-censorship, intellectual solipsism, or historical amnesia are typical in any society that considers itself to be above others, but they cannot endure in a world of free-flowing communication and higher levels of education. Sooner or later, the passion of the mind will come clashing against the taboos of the faith. And it is my contention that such a process is long overdue, if only to reinvigorate the great intellectual traditions of the distant Islamic past.

To call for a radical openness in the Islamic imagination is not an invitation for Muslims to adopt other cultural traditions by superimposing them onto their own or by renouncing their memory. Both are impossible for any culture or human being to achieve, at least not in the short term. The goal, in the case of Islam, is to reimagine modernity not as a package of imported goods from the West but as a method of inquiry, whether it appears in the form of heresy or in the Aristotelian approach of the twelfth-century Moorish philosopher Averroës, a Muslim infidel so admired in Christian Europe that Dante spared him his inferno and kept him, together with another Muslim philosopher, Avicenna, in limbo. But as the luster of Islamic thought was strangled by the cold hand of orthodoxy, and as Muslims were shocked into realities not of their own design, they have embraced very tightly the belief that they, and they alone among the world's religions, possess the final truth, the only possession left them and to which their nonbelieving oppressors cannot accede. Having done so, they froze inquiry into the tenets of the faith, often the work of humans in history, not the outcome of miraculous revelations.

That the holy is often more human than not was obvious to Islam's early dissidents, the scholars who questioned revelation, engaged in lively soirees of poetry and pleasure, philosophized intently about the meaning of life and death, worked diligently to cure the sick, and bravely faced persecution for their different views. Thus, after I show the limits of moderate Islamic thought, I point to these radicals and progressives as a model, if not to emulate, then to seriously consider. It is worth recalling that at a time when the West simply didn't exist, at least not as a serious force in history, Muslim heretics, or the *zanadiqa,* chose not to abide by the monotone and lifeless dictates of religious orthodoxy, often the handmaiden of political despotism, bravely resolving to rely on their God-given talents and intellects to make sense of their own destiny and place in the universe. The *zanadiqa* were not lackeys of alien conniving colonialists (although Manichaeans and non-Arabs certainly resented Arab imperialism), but members of a rising nation and original thinkers who reflected deeply on the welfare of human beings and defended their views with vigor. Any Muslim who is grateful to the Western radicals who consistently defend minorities and rely on their critical faculties and natural intelligence to question the cultural and political consensus in their societies must certainly extend that gratitude to their Muslim ancestors who did the same hundreds of years ago. Islam has its tradition, however neglected and tentative, of dissent, and the revival of such a legacy may well be the answer to the long-simmering crisis in the Muslim world. The instauration of *dissensus,* a term first used by Jacques Rancière and adopted by a new collective of self-declared insubordinates (*insoumis,* in French) of what the psychoanalyst Fethi Benslama has called "islamessence," or the tendency of Islamism to coerce all Muslims into submission, is now a matter of life or death for the culture of Islam.[34]

Clearly, then, regime change, whether through military intervention, economic sanctions, or even friendly bank loans and grants is not the answer to Islam's long-enduring impasse. The only way out from the Muslims' intellectual crisis, which is at the heart of all the ills plaguing Muslim societies, is through the adoption of new forms of inquiry and protocols of discussion in a vibrant culture of ideas. Yet the burden of change and critical self-examination doesn't fall on Muslims alone, but on the world's people as a whole, since by now the entire planet is threatened with massive damage, or, rather, premature extinction, if our ways don't change, and change radically as well. And because the United States defines much of the world's economic and political agendas, I am arguing here that the saintly community of Americans, the other chosen people of modern history, is now facing the same daunting challenge Muslims face, namely, the retrieval of their progressive heritage to counter the corrosive effects of rampant commercialism, accompanied as it is by a cacophony of orthodoxies, ranging from religious fundamentalism to political messianism.

The brave voices of American dissent—and the birth of the United States, like the emergence of Islam itself, was the ultimate act of dissent—have been silenced by the loud cheering for the virtues of unbridled capitalist globalization. It really doesn't take much to find out that the great republic founded to enshrine equality and freedom is adrift in a world both of and not of its making, unable to renew its old covenants or infuse more energy and passion into its revolutionary principles. One laments the bad timing for such a lapse, too, because no tradition can be more helpful to Muslims than that of America's revolutionary generation. Many of the problems facing Muslims today, especially the place of religion in public life, were worked out successfully in eighteenth-century America. They were not perfect, but they pointed the way and managed to keep the two realms delicately separated, while (also imperfectly) granting equal respect to all faiths to this day.

At a time when the U.S. government is trying all sorts of propagandistic approaches to reach the hearts and minds of the global Muslim community, Muslims remain largely ignorant of America's earth-shaking revolution, with its own gospel, nicely conveyed by Jon Meacham, blending faith and liberty, honoring people's religious experiences while keeping them away from the machinery of government in order not to privilege any one faith or discriminate against another. How would Muslims react if they knew that Thomas Jefferson, while a hawk on the war against North African Muslims, had labored hard to grant equal rights to Muslims in the United States before the U.S. Constitution was drafted? Or that George Washington saw America as a place of refuge for persecuted "Mohametans, Jews or Christians of any sect" and "atheists"? Or that in July 1843, President John Tyler affirmed America's revolutionary principle of plurality of beliefs and faiths by saying that "the Mohammedan, if he were to come among us, would have the privilege guaranteed to him by the constitution to worship according to the Koran," and finished his thoughts by saying that "such is the spirit of toleration inculcated by our political institutions"? Or that in late June 1957, President Eisenhower and his wife removed their shoes for the inauguration of the Islamic Center in Washington, D.C., and repeated what Thomas Jefferson and James Madison had enshrined and Tyler had affirmed? Speaking extemporaneously, President Eisenhower assured his Muslim friends that

> under the American Constitution, under American tradition, and in American hearts, this center, this place of worship, is just as welcome as could be a similar edifice of any other religion. Indeed, America would fight with her

whole strength for your right to have here your own church and worship according to your conscience. This concept is indeed part of America, and without that concept we would be something else than what we are.[35]

This is the America that Muslims need to know about; instead, what Muslims see and hear are the purveyors of market dogmas and triumphalist doctrines, not the views of pioneers whose rebellious tenacity culminated in the fall of colonial despotism and a new age of freedom for the world's downtrodden. Critics of U.S. foreign policy might be impressed by America's revolutionary view on the role of government, conveyed by Abraham Lincoln through his ambassador, Charles Francis Adams, to Karl Marx in January 1865:

> The Government of the United States has a clear consciousness that its policy neither is nor could be reactionary, but at the same time it adheres to the course which it adopted at the beginning, of abstaining everywhere from propagandism and unlawful intervention. It strives to do equal and exact justice to all states and to all men and it relies upon the beneficial results of that effort for support at home and for respect and good will throughout the world.
>
> Nations do not exist for themselves alone, but to promote the welfare and happiness of mankind by benevolent intercourse and example.[36]

Nations, in other words, are but their ideas and visions; the nobler and grander ones are the ones that earn the sympathy of the world and embellish the pages of history.

I find heresy (or *zandaqa,* in the case of Islam) a particularly useful concept (certainly a more expansive one than the much-advocated notion of *ijtihad,* or intellectual effort) because it is almost invariably an indigenous alternative to, not just an improvement on, mainstream thinking. It acknowledges difference as part of a community's history and does not punish innovative thought as *bid'a* (a sort of transgression), *kufr* (disbelief), or a crime against the state, as theologians and politicians are wont to do with views that don't match their own. It was not for no reason that Al-Jahidh, the great ninth-century Arab philosopher, remarked that "the piety of theologians consists of hastening to denounce dissidents as unbelievers."[37] As the case of Gnosticism (made popular more recently by the publication of the *Gospel of Judas*) during the early phase of Christianity makes abundantly clear, heretical thought is simultaneously part and not part of a community's main ideology; in its positive or progressive form (which is the only one I am interested in, since dissent can also take on reactionary tones), it espouses a break with orthodoxy only to bring into sharper focus the finer aspects of the faith. Great figures in American history, such as Thomas Jefferson, not to speak of the blasphemous pamphleteer of the American Revolution, Tom Paine, or the quietly radical scholar Ralph Waldo Emerson, elevated the potential divinity embedded in the human over and above the spiritually and intellectually alienating rituals of the Church. As with the Christian Gnostics before them, Muslim heretics made similar observations, hundreds of years before the Enlightenment. The divine, they all said, in one way or another, reveals itself equally to all those who seek its blessings. Inspiration is a universal right, not the privilege of a few chosen prophets.

The practice of heresy is not an intellectual luxury for a few contrarians; it has now become an imperative for anyone who cares about the future of the world. While the United States and Islam are fighting over which way of life is better, it is no longer an exaggeration to say that such disputes, including those that explode into armed conflict, distract us from the more urgent task of rescuing the planet, the only known human habitat, from disaster. With the arsenal of knowledge at its disposal, one would have expected human civilization to be in a radically different state at the dawn of the twenty-first century from that which it had been in previous millennia. Yet what we see is a titanic fight for national supremacy and corporate profits, accompanied by all sorts of nativist ideologies, many of them based on the worldviews of Middle Eastern realities that have long ceased to exist. (Any practicing Jew, Christian, or Muslim in the United States is, in some sense, influenced by people from the Middle East.) To think that we haven't devised philosophies that are better suited to humanity's aspirations in the twenty-first century, or that we haven't been able to overcome the blinding parochialisms of old, is a testament to the failure of our systems of knowledge and social organization. Muslims who think of only what is good for Muslims, Christians for Christians, Jews for Jews, or Americans for America are bound to perpetuate the hatreds of a past that didn't have a fraction of the knowledge and science humans nowadays possess. It baffles the mind, as the celebrated Spanish writer Juan Goytisolo once lamented, to know that all our cultural institutions haven't lessened our pain or given us an advantage over more primitive societies: "The selfishness, corruption, cruelty, quest to accumulate wealth and power, arrogance, and insensitivity to the misfortunes of others are the same ones described by Sophocles, Shakespeare, and Fernando de Rojas, author of *Celestina* (1499)."[38]

Actually, in many ways, one might even argue that the scale of suffering and human tragedies has become worse. Only rarely is one reminded of how much we could accomplish through the wealth of information at our disposal, as when, during much of 2004, I observed people in the cancer wing of a children's hospital in Portland, Maine, struggle to save young lives in the face of what only a few decades ago were impossible odds. From that safe house of sorrow and hope, a place where artificial social rankings were eclipsed by the higher honor of being merely human (as the great Spanish poet Antonio Machado once proclaimed), the world appeared darkly surreal and tragically flawed, as news of political mudslinging and war filtered in to remind us that the old furies are still awaiting us. Here were people frantically trying to repair endangered bodies, while out there, in the realm of the healthy, people were tirelessly producing casualties of pain and despair. Yet I knew it doesn't take much to mend our ways. One line from the Hippocratic oath and one from its modern variant, the Declaration of Geneva, is all the ideology we really need to lay the foundations of a truly humane world order.

Thus, while this book seeks to push the boundaries of acceptable thought in Islam, it situates such an undertaking in a series of interconnected phenomena, such as the unfolding drama of the slipping influence and prestige of the United States and the rise of a bewildering form of globalization. Although Muslims and Americans see themselves as favored by God, they seem to have lost control over the content of their destiny, and may very well have become passive witnesses, if not willing agents, in the making of ungodly regimes. The saints, in other words, are in peril because they preempted the progressive renewal of their cultures by silencing their heretics and freethinkers, and by allowing the tsunamic power of the market to assert itself as the indomitable deity of our age. By presenting this point of view, the book doesn't seek to undermine or trivialize people's cherished beliefs, nor does it try to address the vexing conundrum of how to build communities without the false consciousness and violence embedded in most foundational acts; at best, it invites readers to ponder whether we have misdiagnosed our ills and miscalculated our priorities, and whether the Islamic and American traditions are not better served by paying more attention to the faded voices of their heretics and free-thinkers, and by daring to envision structures of fulfillment that are more adequate to a world of teeming billions.

chapter 1

Death in Cancún

And upon seeing the wound of Cuba
I entrusted myself to fate
Together with the suffering patria
And I bid farewell to life
And went in search of death.

—LUIS VICTORIANO BETACOURT, "A mi madre"

In fact, this new brand of supranational neo-fundamentalism is more a product of contemporary globalization than of the Islamic past.

—OLIVIER ROY, "Neo-Fundamentalism"

To understand this Danish affair, you can't just read Samuel Huntington's classic, *The Clash of Civilizations.* You also need to read Karl Marx because this Muslim rage is not just about some Western insult.

—THOMAS L. FRIEDMAN, "Empty Pockets, Angry Minds"

In more ways than one, the world has entered a phase of terror that seems to have no end under the prevailing economic conditions. The proliferating cult of the suicide bomber in the Middle East is part of a continuum of global violence that is affecting every sphere of life and cannot be read except as the cultural expression of a failed global system and civilizational model. And it is merely one form of suicide. According to the World Health Organization, the global death toll of suicide in 2001 exceeded those of homicide and war combined, and now accounts for about a million fatalities a year, costing billions of dollars. In 2003, more than 50 percent of violent deaths in Virginia were caused by suicide, including by men older than sixty-five and by veterans of the armed forces, while across the United States, "50,000 suicides and homicides are committed" each year. Among the causes listed for such grim statistics, the World Health Organization cites poverty, unemployment, personal loss, breakdown in human relations, and work problems—all features of capitalism, commonly known as globalization.[1] "Terror," Arjun Appadurai wrote in a recent book dealing with the "fear of small numbers" and the "geography of anger," is "the nightmarish side of globalization" and "the rightful name for any effort to replace peace with violence as the guaranteed anchor of everyday life."[2] In fact, the past few decades are marked by the growing attention of jurists, economists, and health professionals to violence. As if it needed proof, the authors of a study funded by the World Bank found a strong correlation between income inequality and crime,[3] while another study by Paul Collier, director of the Development Research Group in the World Bank, showed that economists such as H. I. Grossman tend to see insurgents as "indistinguishable from bandits or pirates" and concludes that "dependence on primary exports, low average incomes, slow growth and large diasporas" are a toxic mix when it comes to the stability of country or region.[4] And in a first report of its kind ever, the World Health Organization reported in 2002 that violence is one of the leading causes of death and injury in the world.[5] It is in this context that one can make sense of the mounting despair of the non-Western poor and the death toll it generates, a picture too grim to be explained away by the failure of Islam or other monotheistic religions.

No other event brought this reality more forcefully to the world's attention than the suicide of a humble South Korean farmer in the Mexican resort of Cancún. On September 16, 2003, the *New York Times* displayed a moving image that, at first sight, could have fooled even the best culturally trained eye. Twelve men or so, shoulder to shoulder, were photographed kneeling down on a small carpet, their shoes taken out and placed behind them, and bowing down in Muslim-like fashion. A second closer look quickly shows that these men were not facing toward Mecca (although the room in which the picture was taken could have easily passed for any of the makeshift mosques that dot the Western landscape) but toward the white-and-yellow photograph of Lee Kyung Hae, a gentle-looking man with a blue jacket and tie, surrounded by two elegantly knotted green ribbons, the picture sitting in an altar filled with white and green bouquets, the whole surrounded by elegant Korean script. The photograph produced an eerie impression, briefly collapsing two different cultural and religious traditions (Korean and Islamic) into a common ritual. For what makes this Korean ceremony of mourning similar to the ones being held for other Muslim "martyrs" is that Kyung Hae was a fifty-six-year-old farmer and president of the Korean Advanced Farmers Federation who had gone to Cancún to attend the Fifth World Trade Organization (WTO) Ministerial Conference held between September 10 and 14, 2003, with the determined purpose to commit suicide. On the day the WTO conference opened (coinciding with the Korean Thanksgiving holiday of Chusok and around the second anniversary of 9/11), Kyung Hae climbed the steel barricades separating protesters from officials and stabbed himself to death, thus concluding a long attempt (including a self-stabbing in Geneva a decade earlier) to bring the world's attention to the destructive impact of globalization on South Korean and, by extension, all the world's farmers. Before he killed himself, he distributed a handout denouncing the devastating impact of globalization on South Korea's rural communities: "I am crying out the words to you that have boiled so long time inside my body," he wrote.[6]

Kyung Hae was now a hero in his rural community of Jangsu, much like many terrorists and suicide bombers become heroes in their native slums or barren suburbs.[7] Indeed, Kyung Hae immediately acquired the status of a global martyr since his suicide was in fact quite common among the world's poor farmers struggling against agribusiness monopolies. That bloody moment in the sunny Mexican resort brought the world's attention to the plight of farmers around the world. Christine Ahn of the Food First/Institute for Food and Development Policy reported that in one year alone in India (1998–99), more than a thousand farmers committed suicide. One Indian activist told marchers in Cancún that "650 farmers committed suicide [in India] in just one month," a tragic statistic foreshadowing the catacombs of 2003, when 17,107 farmers, reeling from the combined effects of debt and shame at not being able to make ends meet, ended their lives, some by drinking pesticide. So desperate is the situation of Indian farmers that the celebrated writer Arundhati Roy declined "the prestigious Sahitya Akademi Award" in early 2006 to highlight their plight. And such tragic conditions are not the lot of India alone: even in prosperous Britain and Canada suicide rates are much higher among farmers than in the rest of the population.[8]

Farmers are not alone. Miners and indigenous people, still brutally exploited in Latin America and Australia, are also blowing themselves up in protest against the antisocial policies of globalization. In March 2004, a miner blew himself up in Bolivia's congress, killing two people and injuring many others, capping a list of grievances ranging from the privatization of Bolivia's "vast reserves of gold and other mineral deposits" to the vanishing benefits for the working class.[9] Bolivia, like the rest of Latin America, suffers from some of the highest forms of inequality in the world, and its people had just forced out Gonzalo Sánchez de Lozada, a president who had planned a $5 billion pipeline scheme to transport gas through Chile to the United States and Mexico. To Bolivia's indigenous people, globalization is a mere smokescreen for the same policy of dispossession that they have been subjected to since the Spaniards came looking for silver and gold about five hundred years ago. A foreign aid official in Bolivia reported in 2005 that Indians were still subjected to a "pigmentocracy of power," a system of apartheid that still bars them—the majority of the country's population—from some swimming pools and keeps most of them in abject poverty.[10] In Chile, Latin America's poster-country for prosperity and stability, the one-million strong Mapuche Indians, whose medicinal powers are being increasingly recognized, are being persecuted under terrorism laws and charged with "generating fear among sectors of the population" for standing up for their historic rights and reclaiming their lands that are being exploited and polluted by the timber industry. One Mapuche leader, exhausted by the government's stalling maneuvers, bluntly said, "We have the right to recover what was stolen from us, even if that means incorporating violence within our struggle."[11]

Globalization didn't spare once-prosperous and rather egalitarian Argentina, either. By 2003, that country had spiraled down into shocking levels of poverty. According to statistics issued in January of that year, "at least 60 percent of the country's 37 million people [were living] in poverty, defined as an income of less than $220 a month for a family of four. That [was] nearly double the number toward the end of 2001. Even more alarming, more than a quarter the population [was] classified as 'indigent,' or living on less than $100 a month for a family of four." So bad had the situation become that Argentine doctors were "treating patients with kwashiorkor, a disease caused by lack of protein and characterized by its victims' distended bellies and reddish hair." It was only after Argentina's government chose to default on its more than $100 billion debt and defy the economic orthodoxy of the U.S.-controlled International Monetary Fund that the country regained its momentum and renewed the confidence of its citizens, who now poured more of their money into their economy, giving it the impetus to grow at the rather exceptional rate of 9 percent per annum. The economist Mark Weisbrot, commenting on the spectacular outcome of breaking away from global economic common sense, deemed Argentina's comeback "a remarkable historical event, one that challenges 25 years of failed policies." (Argentina's economic recovery did not, however, narrow the gap between the rich and the working classes.)[12] Brazil, of course, has always been a study in gross class divisions. Income inequalities in this joy-exuding, samba-happy country have given rise to a mainstream culture of kidnapping, one in which average middle-class people could be ransomed for as little as $500. Trying to explain this routine form of business, one professor said that the socially excluded are refusing to be docile, and that "daily, well-structured acts of violence are no longer just the tools of the rich." The situation is so dire that a news magazine published a kidnapping "survival guide" in one of its issues. And whether fueled by poverty or not, drug gangs in Mexico are beheading people and dumping severed heads in bars to instill terror in rival gangs and government officials alike.[13]

Class disparities and poverty levels have become so bad in Latin America that leaders are being ousted in violent protests, politicians are being lynched by angry mobs, and people would rather have an honest tyranny than a democracy that serves as cover for plundering the people's resources.[14] (The drift toward authoritarianism is noticeable in Russia, too.)[15] No wonder the "Negro e Indio" (Black and Indian) Bolivarian president of Venezuela, Hugo Chávez, keeps overcoming its well-organized and financed middle-class opposition to his attempt to improve the lot of the overwhelming Negro e Indio landless and hopelessly poor majority of that country. At the Sixth World Social Forum held in Caracas in January 2006, Chávez, who called President Bush "Mister Danger" and the United States a "perverse, murderous, genocidal, immoral empire," heralded the rise of indigenous peoples across America and proclaimed the rebirth of a new socialism and the defeat of U.S. imperialism. "There will be nothing beyond the 21st century if we don't change," he announced to an international crowd. The choice, he said, is between socialism and the extinction of the human species.[16]

And he is not alone to espouse such views. In 2004, Dr. Tabaré Vázquez, a socialist oncologist from a working-class background opposed to U.S.-backed free market policies, won the presidency of Uruguay, supported by a coalition of progressives that included former Tupamaro guerilla fighters.[17] By the end of 2005, when Eva Morales—a forty-six-year-old Aymara Indian, a former herder of llamas who lost four siblings in childhood, a promoter of coca farming, a foe of globalization, a leader of the Movement Toward Socialism, and a champion of "communal socialism"—was given the mandate to run Bolivia, he immediately declared war on imperialism and the "neoliberal" economic model (also known as the Washington consensus). On the day before he was sworn in as president in the Bolivian Congress, Morales, barefoot and dressed in the costume of an ancient indigenous civilization, underwent a purification ceremony at the sacred site of Tiwanaku, about fourteen thousand feet above sea level in the presence of tens of thousands of Aymara and Quechua Indians, and vowed to end five hundred years of exploitation. "Today begins a new era for the indigenous peoples of the world, a new life of justice and equality," he announced. The following day, he told supporters that his "democratic, cultural fight is part of the fight of our ancestors. It is the continuity of the fight of Che Guevara." Soon after, Morales appointed a cabinet of Indians, Marxist intellectuals, and union members, then slashed his and their salaries by more than 50 percent, so that the president of Bolivia now makes less than $2,000 a month (the minimum wage in Bolivia is slightly more than $56 a month). On May 1, 2006, Bolivia became the first country in the twenty-first century to nationalize its hydrocarbon resources, until then scandalously exploited by foreign companies, and secured a majority of the revenues of all exploited gas fields. And by late November of that same year, Morales managed to confiscate unproductive private land to redistribute among the country's indigenous population. As a result of such measures, Bolivia quickly posted hundreds of millions of dollars in additional revenue and Morales presided over the best economy in forty-five years.

To his credit, David Brooks, the *New York Times* columnist, had seen this coming. When the United States was engrossed in the National Security Agency's spying on American citizens in late 2005, Brooks offered a Christmas gift to his readers by noting that the election of Morales "illustrated many of the combustible phenomena we'll be dealing with for the rest of our lives. It demonstrated that economic modernization can inflame ethnic animosity, that democracy can be the enemy of capitalism and that globalization, far from bringing groups closer together, can send them off in wild and hostile directions." Brooks wrote about how Bolivia's white elites, enriched through globalization schemes, had dispossessed most of the native Indians, and why the toxic mixture of race, ethnicity, and inequality in emerging democracies is likely to cause "ever-growing resentments and flare-ups."[18]

Not long after this dramatic victory of indigenous rights in a continent long bathed in the blood of the natives, Michelle Bachelet, a fifty-four-year-old single mother, pediatrician, agnostic, and socialist, won the presidency of Chile, defeating her billionaire opponent, owner of Chile LAN airlines, vowing to seek "change with continuity" and to work for women and the poor people's rights. And she didn't wait to declare her intention to work with Chávez and Morales, whom she considers legitimate "presidents elected by their peoples." By the time Bachelet was sworn in as president of her conservative country on March 11, 2006, she had appointed a cabinet equally divided between men and women.[19] Around the same time in Mexico, the fifty-two-year-old Andrés Manuel López Obrador (known as AMLO) of the Party of Democratic Revolution, the "plain-spoken and direct" son of a shopkeeper from the state of Tabasco, a former social worker and uncompromising leftist inspired by the legacy of the nineteenth-century Zapotec president Benito Juárez, running on a popular campaign to root out corruption, to cut down the privileges of elites, including slashing the salaries of government officials, to redistribute wealth and resources, and to stand up to Mexico's northern neighbor, was ahead of his two rivals in the presidential campaign. (He lost the election amid highly contested ballot counts.) Yet even this fiery politician was not convincing to significant segments of the downtrodden in Mexican society. On January 1, 2006, the enigmatic rebel/poet of Mexico, the ski-masked, pipe-smoking Subcomandante Marcos emerged from his Zapatista stronghold in the Lacandonian jungle of Chiapas to launch his own educational anticapitalist campaign, one powered not by big money and PR ads but by the *viento de abajo* (wind from below), and challenge the Mexican left, including Obrador, to live up to its principles. Naming himself Delegate Zero, his message in the words of the *Los Angeles Times* was simply, "Capitalism is bad. Globalism is bad. Racism is bad. All politicians, all parties are the same—bad. The rich get all the breaks; the young and poor are ignored." Meanwhile, Mexicans who live in slums and make a living outside of the law are giving up on the country's traditional saints and creating their own, ones that sympathize with their plight. Thus, Santa Muerte, or Saint Death, "a scythe-wielding skeleton with a blood-curdling grin," a *cabrona,* or bitch, who prefers mariachi music, has appeared to lend succor to growing numbers of people living "on the fringes of a society besieged as much by renegade cops and corrupt politicians as by crime."[20]

In Peru, the forty-three-year-old nationalist caudillo Ollanta Humala, campaigning on a platform against globalization and elitism, and aligning himself with Latin America's leftist leaders, was the front-runner in that country's 2006 presidential race.[21] Haiti's endemic poverty and violent political culture may not inspire much hope in the future, but there, too, sixty-three-year-old René Préval, once a bakery owner, the "twin brother" of Jean-Bertrand Aristide, the exiled "fiery slum priest who could command this country's poor masses as firmly as Moses did the Red Sea," won an election despite avowed opposition from that country's elite.[22] In November 2006, when American voters were in the process of giving majorities in both houses of the U.S. Congress to Democrats, the Sandinista Daniel Ortega, long the leftist nemesis of U.S. administrations, won the presidential election in his country Nicaragua and wasted no time denouncing the U.S. military intervention in Iraq and vowing to work with Fidel Castro and Hugo Chávez. A few days later, Rafael Correa, a leftist forty-three-year-old mestizo who speaks Quechua, the main indigenous language of the country's Indians, and who counted Chávez as a friend, won the presidency of Ecuador, easily defeating a banana tycoon and promising radical changes in favor of the dispossessed. Like Michelle Bachelet of Chile, Correa immediately transformed the face of Ecuadorian politics, appointing seven women to his cabinet, including to the ministry of defense. Hugo Chávez, too, won a landslide reelection in early December 2006, giving further impetus to the Bolivarian revolution he had started. At his inauguration ceremony for another six-year term on January 10, 2007, he consolidated his pantheon of socialist leaders by adding Jesus Christ to the list. Jesus, he said, perhaps in reply to the Catholic Church's opposition to his socialist agenda, is "the greatest socialist in history."

And so, as the year 2006 was coming to a close, the rise of champions of the poor and dispossessed all over Latin American continued unabated, giving the southern hemisphere a political life and dynamism rarely witnessed in the world's major capitalist centers. "Five centuries after the European conquests," writes Noam Chomsky, "Latin America is [finally] reasserting its independence." Chomsky's enthusiasm is well justified, for when do full-blooded indigenous people or single, agnostic mothers ever have the chance to win the presidency in the more advanced north?[23] Or, as Hugo Chávez had commented on the outcome of earlier elections in Brazil, Bolivia, Chile, and his own country, "In Latin America, you have a laborer becoming president, that's Lula; an Indian, Evo, has arrived; a socialist woman; and a soldier—that's me, a revolutionary soldier—building a new South American project that is vital for the salvation of our people." Chávez may be dismissed in the U.S. media as a ranting ideologue, but many Latin Americans, as the Argentine novelist Luisa Valenzuela has noted, feel empowered by his politics.[24]

Is it, then, surprising that when Chávez's fortune was ascending and Morales was elected in Latin America on populist platforms promising better lives for the poor and the indigenous, and vowing to face down the United States, the forty-nine-year-old Mahmoud Ahmadinejad, the son of a blacksmith, was elected president of Iran on a similar platform, defeating the much savvier, millionaire Ayatollah Ali Akbar Hashemi Rafsanjani? Although many Iranians are chafing under clerical cultural edicts, and businessmen tried to keep the socialist candidate out of the president's office, most Iranian people in 2005 were, in the end, more interested in securing a living and providing for their families. The economic policies of the outgoing President Mohammed Khatami, often praised in the West as a moderate, had benefited the upper classes while the condition of the poor and middle classes kept deteriorating. Ahmadinejad was elected because he denounced the "mafia of the rich" and promised a better life to the working poor. "People have been talking about head scarves and TV shows and music. Wonderful," opined a thirty-year-old Iranian, "but what about talking about having enough to eat or raise a family?" An exit poll, the *Washington Post* reported, "found many voters were motivated by anger over the gap between rich and poor. Even after the ultraconservative man who calls the United States "world oppressor" had become the object of satire in his own country and earned the fear and loathing of the West for his pernicious remarks on the Holocaust and his dogged pursuit of a nuclear agenda, he was still being appreciated throughout Iran, particularly in the long-neglected provinces, as the spokesman for the masses. He looked familiar to an eighteen-year-old bakery worker who said, "TV showed us his house. It was very simple. He is making these efforts for the people and all he wants is Iran's dignity." President Ahmadinejad's strong sense of social justice was revealed in his famous eighteen-page letter to President George W. Bush on May 8, 2006. After defending the rights of all the oppressed people in the world, the Iranian president said that "the people are protesting the increasing gap between the haves and the have-nots and the rich and poor countries." Even the Iranian activist and 2003 Nobel laureate, Shirin Ebadi, once the target of assassination by the clerical regime's henchmen, declared that, in case of U.S. military intervention, "we will defend our country till the last drop of blood."[25]

The Korean Kyung Hae's death signaled yet another reversal. Twenty-one of the world's developing nations (known as G-21), such as India, Malaysia, Brazil, and South Africa, joined hands with even poorer nations in what was reported as an "attack" on the West by refusing to compromise on what a Senegalese delegate called their survival.[26] The collapse of WTO talks in Cancún was considered an epoch-making event, the first major triumph of the colonized at the negotiations table. John Cavanagh and Robin Hood later wrote that the failure of the summit was "a turning point in the increasingly contentious globalization debate" because "for the first time in decades of globalization negotiations, democracy trumped narrow elite interests."[27]

Of course, this fiasco could have been avoided. Almost two months earlier, the *New York Times* had warned about such an outcome. In an exceptionally long editorial (covering its entire editorial space) warning against the consequences of the onslaught on the world's farmers (96 percent of whom reside in developing and poor countries) through rich state subsidies to agribusinesses, it condemned such practices as "morally depraved." Such subsidies (at the rate of $2 per cow a day, double the income of about one billion people) allow the rich to dump their products at below cost in poor countries' markets, thereby undermining the world's struggling small farmers. "In the aftermath of 9/11," the *Times* continued, "Americans have desperately been trying to win the hearts and minds of poor residents of the Muslim world," but in countries like the Philippines, where farmers have suffered grievously since joining the WTO in 1995, Al-Qaeda is making inroads among the groups that are suffering the most (such as in the corn-producing region of the Mindanao island). "The United States and its wealthy allies will not eradicate poverty—or defeat terrorism, for that matter—by conspiring to deprive the world's poor farmers of even the most modest opportunities. And the threat of a devastating antiglobalization backlash set off by widespread resentment of 'northern' trade practices is enormous."[28]

In one brilliant editorial move, the *Times* managed to insert terrorism and Islamic extremism into the larger culture of despair produced by capitalism (termed euphemistically in all public discourse as "globalization"). It had put its finger on one of the primary causes of terror through acts of suicide. By charging the current economic regime with the rise of terror, it, in effect, mutatis mutandis, suggested that religion is less important than it appears in the rise of what one could only call the politics of suicide. The influential *New York Times* columnist and champion of globalization Thomas Friedman, writing after the collapse of trade talks in Cancún, began his column, "The U.S. war on terrorism suffered a huge blow last week—not in Baghdad or Kabul, but on the beaches of Cancún" and blamed U.S. trade policies and double standards.[29] In fact, Joseph Stiglitz, the Nobel prize laureate in economics, has shown that while the United States puts pressure on the poor to privatize, the United States supports new technologies and subsidizes farming, for it knows from experience that the role of government in developing the country is crucial. The International Labor Organization (ILO), then chaired by the presidents of Finland and Tanzania, and whose board members included the head of Toshiba, saw globalization as not only having failed but, according to Stiglitz, as contributing to "social distress." "Premature capital market liberalization" and "unbalanced intellectual property provisions" are dangerous to so-called developing countries. Even a Pentagon report on countering terrorism, part of which was released in February 2006, recommended encouraging "economic prosperity abroad" as one of the strategies to overcome the insidious trend of terrorism.[30]

Two months after the exceptional *New York Times* editorial was published, Robert A. Pape (whose thesis is dismissed in Sam Harris's *The End of Faith*) wrote for the same paper confirming, through research he had conducted between 1980 and 2001 and the data he had collected, that "religion is rarely the root cause" of suicide bombings, since the movement that is the leading instigator (75 out 188 incidents in the period covered by Pape) is Marxist-Leninist and opposed to religion—the Tamil Tigers in Sri Lanka. As if to confirm Pape's thesis, in the course of two days in October 2006, two Tamil suicide bombers were responsible for killing more than 110 people and wounding at least another 150 for the sake of their nationalist cause.

Religion is used as a strategy of recruitment, but the main (and secular) goal of Muslims and non-Muslims alike is the liberation of their territory from what they perceive as foreign occupation. Pape's findings helped explain, too, the futile attempt to destroy the Lebanese organization and militia Hezbollah in the summer of 2006, as Israel had hoped to do through military intervention in Lebanon. Examining the records of Hezbollah's suicide bombers in the 1980s, Pape's researchers were shocked to find out that out of thirty-eight identified suicide attackers, "only eight were Islamic fundamentalists. Twenty-seven were from leftist political groups like the Lebanese Communist Party and the Arab Socialist Union. Three were Christians, including a high-school teacher with a college degree. All were born in Lebanon." Hezbollah, despite its religious rhetoric, was, in other words, an umbrella organization akin to the "multidimensional American civil-rights movement" of the 1960s. (On the same day that Pape's article on Hezbollah appeared in the *New York Times,* the *Chicago Tribune* wrote on the raging popularity among all social classes, faiths, and denominations of Hezbollah's leader, Sheikh Hassan Nasrallah, in the Arab and Muslim worlds, confirming Pape's thesis that religious rhetoric often masks what are essentially political disputes. By the time the cease-fire was mandated in August, the *Times* reported that Hezbollah and its leader, with their unambiguous Islamic ideology, were widely celebrated as heroic resistance fighters restoring Arab dignity.) Following the publication of the Iraq Study Group in December 2006, Pape strongly recommended that "American combat forces" leave Iraq because "more than 95 percent of all suicide terrorist attacks around the world have been caused by the presence of foreign combat forces on territory the terrorists value."

In a recent book, Mike Davis, the renowned scholar of cities and urban life, traced the history of suicide bombings to the earlier decades of the twentieth century, when all sorts of political movements used car bombs— a device inadvertently perfected by the Provisional Irish Liberation Army in 1972—to fight back against stronger states. It's hard to believe, but Wall

Street was the target of terrorists in September 1920, when Italian anarchist Mario Buda, intent on avenging his comrades Nicola Sacco and Bartolomeo Vanzetti, packed his horse-drawn carriage with explosives, parked it near J. P. Morgan's offices, and walked away. His target, J. P. Morgan, was in Scotland, but the blast killed forty people and wounded more than two hundred.[31]

"Suicide bombing as a tool of stateless terrorists," legal scholar Noah Feldman writes, "was dreamed up . . . by European anarchists immortalized in Joseph Conrad's *Secret Agent*" and "became a tool of modern terrorist warfare only in 1983, when Shiite militants blew up the U.S. Marine barracks in Lebanon." According to Alan B. Krueger and Jitka Malecková, writing in the *Chronicle of Higher Education,* the rise of terrorism is "a violent, inappropriate form of political engagement," a "response to political conditions and longstanding feelings of indignity and frustration that have little to do with economic circumstances."[32] Michael Shermer, reviewing a crop of books on suicide and suicide bombing, found out that religion and poverty play a minor role (if at all) in this troubling phenomenon, ranking behind political tyranny, a sense of hopelessness, and loyalty to preexisting bonds. Shermer coined the word *murdercide* to describe suicide bombers who seek death by maliciously plotting the death of others (in the United States some choose what's called "suicide by cop," putting themselves in a situation to be shot at by police officers). As the psychologist Thomas Joiner phrased it in his 2006 book *Why People Die by Suicide,* "people desire death when two fundamental needs are frustrated to the point of extinction; namely, the need to belong with or connect to others, and the need to feel effective with or to influence others." Nichole Argo, a graduate student and former freelance journalist for the *Jerusalem Post* in the Palestinian territories (from 2003 to 2004), found no convincing correlation between an irrational faith and suicide bombing, after both experiencing the situation on the ground and reviewing current scholarly works. (Argo thinks a more apt description of suicide bombers is "human bombs," since humans turn themselves into bombs to fight back.) The preliminary findings of a two-year Gallup poll in eight Muslim countries (published in May 2006) revealed that "fear of U.S. domination, not religious fanaticism" is what explains the rise of extremism, even in historically West-oriented nations like Morocco and Turkey. Soon after the fifth anniversary of 9/11, U.S. intelligence agencies found that the U.S. invasion of Iraq had made terrorism worse. Most important, though, "according to neuroscientific studies, ritual effects do not require religion" since "any social ritual, where people are brought together in repetitive acts imbued with meaning, will do."[33]

In Cuban culture, suicide is so deeply embedded in the national psyche and ideology that it has practically become a fact of life, an idiosyncrasy that also explains Cuba's remarkable resistance to its mighty northern neighbor for almost five decades. "For more than 150 years," writes Louis A. Pérez Jr., "the rate of suicide has ranked consistently among the highest in the world." Cuba's national anthem, "La Baymesa" (1868), straightforwardly states that "To die for the patria is to live" (Morir por la Patria es vivir), a notion that survived in the twentieth-century revolutionary slogan "Patria o muerte."[34] The motif of Cuban resistance fighters sounds eerily similar to the language of Muslim suicide bombers. In a poem titled "De la madre al hijo," a mother enjoins her son to choose death over indignity:

Although I am your mother and love you
    as son of the blood of my heart,
I prefer to see you dead in campaign
    than to see you slave.
Act like a warrior,
    for whom death does not frighten:
The dangers of war
    have been made for who is a man.
And if you want to make a name for yourself
    go fight for your land.[35]

It is this same sense of indignity among ghettoized and socially dispossessed African Americans that is the cause of the perplexing rise in murders over petty disputes in the United States, young people killing each other over "mean mugging," code for dirty looks, or simply a perceived slight. For the downtrodden and hopeless, dignity is the last line of defense. The same thing is happening in class-divided France. A recent report found that gratuitous violence against individuals, triggered by nothing more than an argument over cigarettes or using the wrong word, is on the rise, even as general crime rates are declining.[36]

Ian Buruma, the coauthor of *Occidentalism: The West in the Eyes of Its Enemies* (2004), pointed out in an op-ed article that "history shows that the forceful imposition of even decent ideas in the claim of universalism tends to backfire—creating not converts but enemies who will do anything to defend their blood and soil." After explaining to a seemingly mystified audience of readers that "the main fault line crossing most Muslim societies isn't even between secularists and religionists, but between Muslims with different ideas about the proper role of religion," Buruma warned that Western military intervention (in Muslim societies) only strengthens the hand of extremists.[37] (Ironically, on the day Buruma's op-ed piece appeared in the *New York Times,* the same newspaper reported on the newest poll by the Pew Research Center for the People and the Press, conducted before the terrorist attacks on Madrid in March 11, 2004, showing the continued decline of the U.S. image abroad.)[38]

The rise of political Islam in Iraq, Palestine, and across much of the Islamic world only proves that religion is the refuge of the oppressed. "History shows," explains Dilip Hiro, "that when an ethnic, racial, or social group is persecuted or overly oppressed, it tends to turn to religion to find solace. In the Americas, this was true, for instance, of the Africans brought in as slaves. It is not accidental that today African-Americans are still more religious than white Americans." When the Palestinian political party Hamas—designated as a terrorist organization by the United States—shocked the world with its landslide victory in the legislative council elections of January 25, 2006, a taxi driver from Ramallah was quoted in the *New York Times* as saying that he favored Hamas because "it has clean hands, puts the poor before the rich and will resist the occupier." Meanwhile, the recourse to terrorism in Iraq had become so common after the U.S. invasion in 2003 that the Iraqi insurance industry, a surprisingly successful business even in the chaos of war and insurgency, was the first in the world to cover that risk.[39]

An injurious form of globalization, underwritten by the increasing militarization of diplomacy and international affairs (the sort of solution Sam Harris recommends for intractable Muslims), is, I am arguing, the main producer of extremism and violence in the world today. One need only recall that even an ideology as odious as Hitlerism was justified by Germany's rejection of globalization. As Doug Henwood noted in *Wall Street:*

How It Works and for Whom, Hitler sounded deceptively progressive in *Mein Kampf* (1943) when he wrote that

> the task of the state toward capital was comparatively simple and clear; it only had to make certain that capital remain the handmaiden of the state and not fancy itself the mistress of the nation. This point of view could then be defined between two restrictive limits: preservation of a solvent, national, and independent economy on the one hand, assistance of the social rights of the workers on the other. . . . The sharp separation of stock exchange capital from the national economy offered the possibility of opposing the internationalization of the German economy without at the same time menacing the foundations of an independent national self-maintenance by a struggle against all capital. The development of Germany was much too clear in my eyes for me not to know the hardest battle would have to be fought, not against hostile nations, but against international capital.[40]

That globalization is running roughshod on the world's traditions and cultures, dehumanizing rich and poor, making life untenable for the latter, and fueling violent reactions and the politics of terror, is a condition that has not changed much in the past hundred years or so, regardless of the political status of newly developed nations, or the class membership of citizens in rich societies.

The despair generated by the classic capitalist syndrome of dire poverty in the midst of excess and waste is the reigning condition today. By the end of 2004, a report by the United Nations Children's Fund (UNICEF) drew the world's attention to the ravages of poverty among a billion children across the world, including in the advanced economies of the West. Noting that global military spending was $956 billion, while the cost of effectively combating poverty could range from $40 to $70 billion, one would think that the UNICEF report was a clear challenge to the global community to set its priorities straight. Even while the United States and Britain were fighting for more freedoms in the Middle East, child mortality in both nations was the worst recorded in twenty-four developed nations, according to a British study published in 2007. Children just seem to be another unfortunate casualty of capitalism.[41]

Take a look at the figures provided by the Worldwatch Institute in its 2004 report to gauge the severity of the global condition. Not only is the misery of the poor intensifying, but the world's 1.7 billion members of the "consumer class" are literally consuming themselves—and our planet—out of existence.[42] (Before it was recycled by spin doctors in the last part of the twentieth century, the word *consumption* itself had long been associated with violence, illness, and death.)[43] Although family sizes are shrinking, houses are getting bigger. By 2006, a whole industry had emerged to organize the ever-expanding garages of befuddled homeowners, while an increasing number of full-time American workers, priced out of one-bedroom apartments, were turning their cars into residences.[44] More than one billion people worldwide, according to the latest report from the Earth Policy Institute, do not have access to safe water supplies, yet bottled water, often no better than tap water, is now a $100 billion industry, one that adds to the world's pollution substantially and takes away from the resources needed to provide clean water for all.[45] Soda, meanwhile, is the world's third favorite beverage, after tea and milk. "Luxury foods" with "marginal nutritional value" are doing a brisk business: "The $57-billion trade in coffee, cocoa, wine, and tobacco is worth more than international trade in grain," and depending on how it is defined, the "chocolate business is worth $42–60 billion annually," according to the same Earth Policy Institute report.[46] (In 2004, during a recovering economy with persistent unemployment and low-paying jobs, luxury products such as Porsche cars sold very well, as did merchandise at the elite stores Neiman Marcus, Nordstrom, and Saks Fifth Avenue, outpacing sales even at Wal-Mart, Sears, and Payless Shoes.)[47]

Despite the promise of computer technology, the consumption of paper has never been as high as it is today. Semiconductors are "more materials-intensive than most 'traditional' goods. A single 32-megabyte microchip requires at least 72 grams of chemicals, 700 grams of elemental gasses, 32,000 grams of water, and 1,200 grams of fossil fuels. Another 440 grams of fossil fuels are used to operate the chip in its typical life span." Welcome to the era of e-waste. Not that we are doing better with old-fashioned solid refuse. People in rich countries are producing so much of it (basically, 560 kilos of municipal waste per person per year) that the cost of America's contribution alone was calculated in the mid-1990s to be "at least $2 trillion." Waste and pollution work in tandem. The plastic bag, scourge of the world's landscape, has been christened the "national flag" in Ireland and the "national flower" in South Africa, and while it doesn't make it out of the recycling bin or trash can in the United States, "Americans throw away 100 billion plastic grocery bags each year."[48] And now that poorer countries are racing to catch up with the United States and the West, the situation will only get worse. Who will fuel China's (whose pollution levels are frightening) and India's meteoric growth when oil production is on course to shrink in the coming decades? In fact, nothing less than the fate of the world rests on what developmental model these emerging giants choose to pursue. According to the 2006 edition of *State of the World*, "if China and India were to consume resources and produce pollution at the current U.S. per-capita level, it would require two planet Earths just to sustain their two economies." These two countries' need for fresh water, oil fuel, grain, soybeans, and wood products far outstrips available resources, while their reliance on "coal-dominated energy systems" is directly affecting global climate change through the emission of high quantities of carbon dioxide. The Worldwatch Institute may see a glimmer of hope in these two nations' pursuit of sustainable models of development,[49] but their feeble attempt may well be too little too late.

James Lovelock, the British scientist who coined the term *Gaia* in the 1970s to describe how the Earth keeps itself fit for life and "conceived the first wholly new way of looking at life on Earth since Charles Darwin," shocked public opinion in early 2006 by asserting that we have passed the point of no return in damaging our habitat, and the best we can hope for now is a soft landing and a concerted effort to live with fewer resources in an ailing planet. The eighty-six-year-old environmental scientist was not a man given to alarmist statements, since in the 1970s he thought the Earth could take care of itself forever. But now he was warning that unless we do our best to make amends with our environment immediately, we will most likely end up in a dystopian world "led by brutal war lords." Soon after Lovelock's views were made public, no less than Britain's prime minister, Tony Blair himself, contributed the foreword to a new study titled *Avoiding Dangerous Climate Change*, accepting and warning of the impending prospect of disruptive climate change in this century. "It is now plain," Blair wrote, "that the emission of greenhouse gases, associated with industrialization and economic growth from a world population that has increased six-fold in 200 years, is causing global warming at a rate that is unsustainable."[50]

The development of more efficient technologies—another mantra of progress—is only accelerating the current human catastrophe. "Modern industrial workers [can] now produce in a week what took their eighteenth-century counterparts four years," reports the *State of the World 2004*. A Toyota plant in Japan "rolls out 300 completed Lexuses per day, using only 66 workers and 310 robots." Supertrawler fishing vessels "can process hundreds of tons of fish per day. They are part of the reason that communities of many oceanic fish have suffered declines on the order of 80 percent within 15 years of the start of commercial exploitation." In fact, if present patterns of fishing continue unmodified, scholars in late 2006 predicted a "global collapse" of all marine species by the middle of this century. And yet corporations continue to spend heavily on advertising. In 2002, global spending on advertising reached $446 billion, more than half of which was spent in the United States. Even when the state restricts access to harmful products, advertisers find creative ways to reach consumers. For instance, according to the *State of the World,* "smoking is three times more prevalent in the movies than in the actual U.S. population."[51]

Ever since the salesman King Camp Gillette came up with the idea of disposable razor blades, a culture of "planned obsolescence" has taken root and is now financed primarily through debt. By 2002, the average outstanding balance on an American's credit card was $12,000, which at an average interest rate of 16 percent would cost the cardholder "about $1,900 a year in finance charges—more than the average per capita income (in purchasing power parity) in at least 35 countries."[52] By the end of 2005, annual U.S. household savings were at their lowest since the Great Depression, with Americans spending $42 billion more than they earned and owing "$800 billion in credit card debt," while more than 2 million people applied for bankruptcy that same year. Much the same is happening in Britain, which by the end of 2005 accounted for two-thirds of the European Union's credit card debt, while France's consumer credit is getting worse. And the number of insolvent Britons was expected to grow from "around 20,000 in 2005 to more than 100,000 by the end of the decade."[53]

Needless to say, the political economy of globalization is directly responsible for the amounts of violence that terrorizes the world today. (So accustomed have Americans become to violence that New York City at the end of 2005 celebrated the low murder toll of 537, a figure that compared quite favorably with 649 deaths in 2001 and 2,245 in 1990!)[54] According to the director of the department of injuries and violence prevention at the

World Health Organization, more than a million people, mostly in poor or middle-income countries, "die in road accidents, and 20 to 50 million are injured and survive, often with disabilities for the rest of their lives." Despite the decline in smoking, "tobacco-related medical expenditures and production losses cost the United States more than $150 billion" in 1999.[55] While a recent report in the UK-based *Food Magazine* shows that intensive farming is depleting our vegetables, fruits, meat, and dairy products of minerals,[56] obesity is now a global epidemic, with *National Geographic* giving it front-cover attention in its August 2004 issue, as if confirming that human evolution had entered a new phase with the ballooning sizes of our malnourished bodies. So many children are becoming obese that health officials are expecting this generation of children to die before their parents. Yet if people ate less ice cream, used less makeup, and spent less on pet food, the world's poor could be provided adequate food, clean water, and basic education.[57]

A casual reading of any newspaper would reveal the depths to which our civilization is descending in the name of antiquated economic and political philosophies, yet the silence on such horrors is as deafening as Harris's loud condemnation of religion as the main culprit of violence in the world today. When people are literally leasing or even permanently selling their foreheads as spaces for advertising and buying life insurance policies to resell to investors to collect profits upon their death, glaciers are melting and lakes are evaporating at a rapid pace,[58] and entire nations are struggling to keep up with a destructive way of life, isn't it time to widen our perspective and raise questions about the future of the planet itself? Just as many Muslims are unable to be self-critical or to think beyond their zone of comfort, so are the champions of capitalism, whether it be the Anglo-Saxon model, supply-side economics, or the Keynesian approach unwilling to open the pages of their newspapers and periodicals to a robust, nonpartisan discussion of the reigning economic system. Those who are inclined to oppose adventurous wars in faraway lands somehow remain indifferent to the violence generated by the precarious social conditions of billions of people worldwide. Just as with the environment, such an approach is ruinous to winners and losers alike in the long run. The sooner we adopt that broader perspective, the better our chances for surviving and, perhaps, developing a more harmonious form of globalization.

It is in this context that the conflict between the world of Islam (which consists mostly of poor countries) and the West must be read, if we are looking for serious solutions to this global crisis. Religion is used as an ideology by many Muslims as much as other nations use patriotism and the defense of liberty to change their citizens' tendency toward disengagement and indifference and rally them to an old-style nationalism. It is true that the much-discussed Huntingtonian notion of the "clash of civilizations" seems to be justified by current events, that Islam seems to be on an ongoing course of collision with a Judeo-Christian West; but as I described above, that is clearly not the case, and the divisions are not that neat. Even the notion that the West is roughly the domain of Christianity not only is a profoundly erroneous and misleading belief, but it also occludes the new schisms within Christianity itself, and how such schisms are further polarizing the world in unpredictable ways.

Philip Jenkins's thorough study of the New Christendom irrefutably proves that Christianity, not Islam, is the fastest-growing religion in the world. Basing his numbers on current estimates, Jenkins predicts that there will be around 2.6 billion Christians by 2025, and three Christians to every two Muslims in the world by 2050.[59] The faithful of all major churches (mainstream and alternative) will be overwhelmingly southern and poor. In Africa, where Christians outnumbered Muslims for the first time in the 1960s, and now form roughly one-half of the continent's population, Christian growth was phenomenal in the twentieth century. At least in Africa, the twentieth century was indeed a Christian Century.

Though often introduced by Europeans or Americans, Christianity in the South—not just Africa—quickly assumed messianic, millenarian, utopian, charismatic, prophetic, anticolonial, activist overtones, a trend that fit well with the expansion of Pentecostalism (the most successful movement in the twentieth century). As Laurie Goodstein explains,

> The world's fastest growing religion is not any type of fundamentalism, but the Pentecostal wing of Christianity. While Christian fundamentalists are focused on doctrine and the inerrancy of Scripture, what is most important for Pentecostals is what they call "spirit-filled" worship, including speaking in tongues and miracle healing. Brazil, where American missionaries planted Pentecostalism in the early 20th century, now has a congregation with its own TV station, soccer team and political party.[60]

Much like medieval Europe, the separation of state and church, or the Western notion of secularism, doesn't make any sense to this rising Christianity. The spheres of the temporal and the spiritual are one and the same. Sermons focusing on prayers for worldly success fill giant churches and stadia. In the Philippines, "El Shaddai followers raise their passports to be blessed at services, to ensure that they will get visas they need to work overseas. Many open umbrellas and turn them upside-down as a symbolic way of catching rich material blessings they expect to receive from on high,"[61] notes Philip Jenkins. Much as Christianity developed in its infancy,[62] the next Christendom is fired not simply by biblical truths but also by a response to poverty and alienation in the world system:

> One common factor is that various Southern churches are growing in response to similar economic circumstances. Their success can be seen as a by-product of modernization and urbanization. As predominantly rural societies have become more urban over the past thirty or forty years, millions of migrants are attracted to ever larger urban complexes, which utterly lack the resources or infrastructure to meet the needs of these "post-industrial wanderers." Sometimes people travel to cities within the same nation, but often they find themselves in different countries and cultures, suffering a still greater sense of estrangement. In such settings, the most devoted and fundamentalist-oriented religious communities emerge to provide functional alternative arrangements for health, welfare, and education. This sort of alternative social system has been a potent factor in winning mass support for the most committed religious groups, and is likely to become more important as the gap between popular needs and the official capacities to fill them becomes ever wider.[63]

And this surge in Christian fundamentalism is spelling trouble for co-existence among faiths and between the South and the secular West. "Evangelical Christians [now] speak of the great missionary territory of the future as 'the 10–40 window,' a vast and densely populated rectangle stretching across Africa and Asia, from 10 degrees north to 40 degrees north of the equator." This is the "Resistant Belt" of Islam. Given this missionary zeal, the West should be as worried about a new "crusade" as it is about jihad. And Muslims won't be the only targets: in due time, the secular, capitalist, underpopulated North will be facing "the flags not of red revolution, but of ascendant Christianity and Islam." As it turns in disgust against this new Christianity, what some Westerners see as a "jungle religion," the West will come to be seen as "the final Babylon," the real "Heart of Darkness," ripe for conversion and overtaking.[64] Already, African missionaries are preaching in New York and other parts of the United States, while entire segments of the Episcopal Church USA are seceding from their liberal dioceses in the United States to join more conservative affiliates in Africa and Latin America. By the end of 2006, Archbishop Peter J. Akinola, leader of the Anglican Church in Nigeria, famous for his condemnation of homosexuality, was "the spiritual head of 21 conservative churches in the United States."[65] The Nigeria-based Redeemed Christian Church of God is ministering in what has until recently been the whitest areas in Texas, such as Hunt County, and the Church's proclaimed goal is nothing less than "to establish parishes within five minutes' driving distance of every family in every city and town in the United States."[66]

The clash between secularism and religion may be escalating, a clash in which poor literalist Christians from the Southern Hemisphere are rushing to the rescue of their wealthier brethren in the North, but the prognosis for relations between this southern Christianity and Islam is getting worse (even though both are fighting the same demons of poverty and tyranny). Potential hot spots include Indonesia (where people asserted their Islamic identity during the Cold War to avoid the charge of communism), the Philippines (mostly Catholic but with a Muslim separatist group), Nigeria, Sudan, and even Kenya and the Ivory Coast.[67]

There is also no avoiding a proper accounting of the material conditions that undergird the proliferation of violence, extremism, and the clash of civilizations if we are to think our way out of this deadly impasse. Recent economic analyses have shown clearly that the global capitalist system has entered a phase of decline and crisis that is being reflected in global social and cultural breakdowns, including the rise of nativism across cultures. Not only is it abundantly clear that the rich are getting richer since the "financialization" of capital in the 1970s, but according to Giovanni Arrighi, the capitalist system that emerged in Renaissance Italy in an attempt to overcome the chaos that preceded it is itself breaking down, partly because the United States is unwilling to cede the torch to the next major capitalist player, East Asia.[68] Even as the power of the nebulous middle class in high capitalist societies is getting more precarious than ever (without a social or class consciousness to awaken it to its plight), the state's recourse to debt places it even more firmly in the grip of capitalist interests, thereby ensuring the longevity of the global dysfunctional system. It is, in fact, the booming trade in credit that is perpetuating class and global divisions, reflecting at once the usurious exploitation of the poor (through loans to the masses who are made to believe that they can borrow their way out of poverty) and the benefits of a "legal form of graft" (bailing out the state through the purchase of government and tax-exempt municipal bonds in exchange for tax subsidies and reductions that also punish the poor through austerity measures that always reduce benefits to the poor).[69] Indeed, as Robert Brenner notes, the rise of private credit (household and corporate) is a counter-Keynesian move since it shifts the onus of the burden from the public to the private sector: "Crudely put, rising equity prices [by the second half of the 1990s] were now enabling US economic growth to depend for its expansion to an ever-increasing extent on the growth of US private indebtedness."[70]

Hence the contradictions of capitalism are, once again, becoming glaringly apparent: while, as Marx once put it, "the ultimate reason for all real crises always remains the poverty and restricted consumption of the masses, in the face of the drive of capitalist forces as if only the absolute consumption capacity of society set the limit to them,"[71] capitalist ideology is growing more socially ruinous. Instead of addressing the global problem of "over-capacity and over-production in manufacturing, in which competition had over-ridden complementarity and redundant production had prevailed over mutually beneficial specialization,"[72] the stress is falling on individuals to address the fundamental flaw in capitalism—that is, how to spread the wealth generated by production, while, at the same time, insisting on extracting maximum profit from a declining base of consumers. The United States, once a net exporter of durable and nondurable goods, has lost significant share value in both to foreigners, increasingly relying on specialized, nonexportable services (such as recreation and health care) and some high-tech manufacturing. "We are becoming a nation of advisers, fixers, entertainers and high-tech engineers," wrote Daniel Altman in early 2006, "with a lucrative sideline in treating our own illnesses." It is not only the United States that is losing its manufacturing base. The lack of complementarity in international manufacturing (resulting in a sort of rich man's race to the bottom, or an unstoppable decline in the rate of profit) is having such a deleterious effect on societies and businesses that the *Economist* suggested in early 1999 that the world may well be entering a phase similar to the one of the 1930s.[73]

In fact, scholars have long been predicting the resurgence of premodern conflict within the dual processes of globalization and waning state power—a period of "turbulence," in James Rosenau's expression.[74] Because the United States is unwilling to let go of its hegemony to new capitalist centers (in East Asia, for instance) by appropriating "through force, cunning, or persuasion the surplus capital that accumulates in the new centers and thereby terminate capitalist history through the formation of a truly global empire," escalating violence in the post–Cold War period may very well be a sign of the collapse of the system that regulated capitalism since its inception in Renaissance Italy and the return to the chaos that it tried to overcome. In other words, we may be talking about the end of capitalism, if not, more ominously, the end of humanity itself in the furnace of an overarmed world.[75] The sleep of reason produces monsters indeed!

In the world briefly sketched above, wealth and wretchedness, peace and terror can coexist in the same location or across geographical divides. We are not witnessing the clash of cultures as much as their implosion. When Billy Graham, America's legendary evangelical preacher and pastor to a succession of presidents, was asked in June 2005, on the eve of a new crusade in New York, if he believed in the clash of civilizations (his son, William Franklin Graham III, had called Islam "a very wicked and evil religion" in 2002), the eighty-six-year-old preacher replied, "I think the big conflict is with hunger and starvation and poverty."[76] In a world where, according to the International Labor Organization, "at least 12.3 million people worldwide work as slaves [including sexual slavery] or in other forms of forced labor,"[77] and cows are better provided for by states than two billion humans, prospects for peace just don't look promising.

In my introduction, I discussed Sam Harris's thesis about the danger of faith in irrational religions, particularly the violence-prone religion of Islam, and suggested that it would have been far better for him if he had included religion in a larger constellation of fundamentalisms, each one provoking the other, in a never-ending vicious circle of economic self-interest, political tyranny, and violence. It is true that Islam, like all seemingly self-enclosed ideologies, contains its own limitations, for one definition of faith is transcendence of the here and now, the historical and the biological, which is why it is always problematic to engage believers in a rational discussion. As I hope to show in the next chapter, Islam has always been aware of the competition—previous monotheistic religions, for instance—and thus formulated its identity in a context of rivalry and fear. The drive for autonomy, in this case, is already a drive to extremism. But then one could say the same thing about nationalism, or any "ism" for that matter, since nationalism, or in the case of the United States, Americanism, always develops in relation to another ism, or at least with the awareness of a difference against which the self defines itself. And so there is very little reason—from a theoretical point of view—to see nationalism as any less dangerous (or beneficial) than religion. Both provide a sense of identity and motivate the struggle for the preservation of community. When commenting on the situation of Iraq for the *New York Times* in late 2005, Ian Buruma said that "when worldly authority becomes intolerably oppressive, . . . religion is often the only base of resistance. Such was the case in Poland under Communist rule, when the Catholic Church provided a source of dissent." Later on, and after citing a few disastrous experiments of leaders trying to impose a revolution on a people from above—such as in modern Turkey and Iran—Buruma explained that the result was "not democracy but militarism, absolute monarchy, fascism and variations of Stalinism." To which the response has been political Islam.[78] Islam, with its iconography and myths, is the foundation of an identity that is no less real than nationalism.

Saying this, however, does not exonerate scholars from challenging Islam to open up to all forms of inquiry without threatening members of the community with charges of blasphemy, or *zandaqa,* as heretics, or freethinkers, have been known to be throughout much of Islamic history. The renowned cognitive psychologist Daniel Dennett is right to see religious moderates, no matter how well intentioned and ecumenical, as ultimately ineffective in the struggle against absolutism. "Moderate Muslims have so far been utterly unable to turn the tide of Islamic opinion against Wahhabist and other extremists," he writes, "but moderate Christians and Jews and Hindus have been equally feckless in countering the outrageous demands and acts of their own radical elements." Those who defer judgment on serious moral issues to their spiritual leaders (rabbis, priests, and imams) and don't subject faith to the test of reason (as Harris recommends) should in fact be excluded from any moral conversation, since many will obstruct the social good through the abdication of their own independent decision-making ability, and because, ultimately, "no God pleased by displays of unreasoning love is worthy of worship."[79]

Actually, I will posit that Islam's future well-being may well rest with the restoration of the challenging and troubling freethinking championed by heretics, or *zanadiqa,* like Ibn al-Rawandi and Abu Bakr Razi in the early years of Islam. Not to allow for the separate spheres of philosophy and religion to coexist, or to state that humans in their natural states (what Islam calls *fitra*) are Muslim, is to impose an implacable determinism on historical diversities and condemn Islamic thought to renounce free inquiry. It is only by allowing serious intellectual and theological dissent to coexist in the same polity with orthodoxy that the mind grows gradually unshackled and a new emergence (not the longed-for *nahda,* the Arabic word for Renaissance, which evokes notions of righteous ancestors and the golden past) is possible. "It is through revision that heresy accomplishes what is probably its most historic function in relation to orthodoxy," writes Roberto Giorgi in his exploration of *zandaqa,* even though such change may lead to yet another orthodoxy.[80]

Nothing has saddened me more over the course of my intellectual career than the Muslims' inability to deal with their own religion and history critically, to admit that Muslims were, yes, imperialists, slave owners, racists, despots, and, even though the faith calls for compassion and tolerance, avengers. Heretics and Sufis were executed; blacks in Africa were hounded and sold in markets by Muslim Arabs; and although Muslims are accustomed to seeing themselves as victims, they were equally responsible for the depredations of the Crusades, since Islam was born to rival previously "revealed" religions, particularly Christianity, carving out its domains in relentless military cavalcades, thereby fueling the spirit of reconquest and retribution among its rivals. Does admitting this make Islam inferior to its rival religions or any other ideology for that matter? Not at all. It only shows that Muslims have reached a level of intellectual and emotional maturity to confront their own contradictions, that their confidence is robust enough to allow for troubling questions to be raised (persecution is ever the mark of insecurity).

Equally lamentable is the reluctance of Muslim intellectuals (and by *Muslim* here I mean those who are born into the Islamic culture) to examine their faith in light of modern knowledge, to see how both our concepts of the sacred that broaches no dissent, our notions of TheGod (that is, nameless god, for that is the literal meaning of Allah—*al-ilah*),[81] infallible prophets and scriptures, and apocalyptic views of the future are human constructions, shaped by cultural borrowings and adapted to the particular need of a people without their own book. As we shall see in the course of this book, some of the greatest minds and Sufis of Islamic history had no trouble proclaiming the superiority of the mind and soul over legalistic doctrines and narrow conceptions of the faith. The great thirteenth-century theosophist Ibn 'Arabi, for instance, believed that the Creator is created in the image of humans, not vice versa.[82] After all, Christians have been unveiling the myths of their faith for more than a century now, leading biblical scholars to conclude that Christianity is now a dangerous archaism, that the biblical God "is frankly too small" and outdated, and that the Bible is nothing more than a collection of legends and propaganda.[83] But to say that Muslims cannot deal rationally with their history is to perpetuate their intellectual dependence on the West; it allows learning and cultural centers in non-Muslim societies to outshine those in the Islamic world, including in the study of Islam itself. Memorization of old truths doesn't lead to intellectual breakthroughs; it merely enshrines ancient ones. As the next two chapters will show, Muslims have been grappling with the challenge of modernity for a long time without coming to any resolution whatsoever, partly because they have excluded the possibility of irreligion (in the sense presented by Harris) as an option at all, and often because they don't pay adequate attention to the global economic context in whose drift we are all helplessly floating.

There is no doubt that the United States, with its rich heritage, could lend a helping hand to Muslim societies struggling to break out of this stalemate, but the success of such an endeavor depends on which aspect of the American legacy is deployed for such a purpose. Capitalism? Political liberalism? The intriguing synthesis of religious zeal and the republicanism of the Enlightenment? Or the legacy of the American Revolution and the spirit of America's Founding Fathers? Because this question has not been posed and debated with the seriousness that it deserves, especially on the eve of the conquest of Iraq, regime change in that country, and in Afghanistan, is unlikely to yield much of a positive transformation in Muslim societies and will most likely strengthen the very features that have hindered genuine progress in the Islamic world. I will say more about this later in this book, but then by that time, we may well find out that the United States itself is in the throes of a disabling crisis and may well need to recover those aspects of its own past that Muslims need most now.

Following my discussion of the problematic of change in Muslim societies and within Islamic traditions, the failure of the American policy of regime change in the Middle East, and the rise of a troubling illiberal culture in America itself, I will make the case that what both convinced ideologues and dogmatic believers need is a healthy culture of freethinking, a tradition of heresy, or *zandaqa,* that would help the indoctrinated see past their convictions and toward a future that opens the wider gate of the common good, not squeeze us through the tunnel of narrow interests and the end of life. For there is no reason not to heed the warnings of scientists and environmentalists that unless we change our ways radically, our days on earth are numbered. There is no option to a humanity bound together by the solid ties of solidarity and love, or *mahabba,* as a late-eighteenth-century Moroccan envoy to France addressed his French correspondents;[84] for what else could legitimize globalization more than the ability to bring people into the fold of a common family, to see others as we see ourselves, and to forgive ourselves for the sins of our traditions and entrenched mental habits? We could imagine a new global order based on human solidarity and the equitable sharing of the world's natural and human resources, a system that would dramatically reduce the causes of conflict and violence. Utopian, you might think, but what else justifies what we do, particularly those of us in academia? If the past has an implacable hold on us—if traditions, much like biology, rarely go away—the best we can do is broaden its scope of tolerance and push it to include innovative thought without punishing humans for daring to imagine life-saving alternatives.

Specters of Annihilation

There is a geology of human relationships which it is unwise to neglect.

—RICHARD FLETCHER, *The Cross and the Crescent: The Dramatic Story of the Earliest Encounters between Christians and Muslims*

Fundamentalism thus begins as an internal dispute, with liberalizers or secularists within one's own culture, or nation.

—KAREN ARMSTRONG, *Islam: A Short History*

Soon after he got out of prison in 1972, Mohammed Qutb, brother of the executed Sayyid Qutb (1906–1966), often described as the intellectual mastermind of Islamic extremism and terrorism in the world today, was welcomed into Saudi Arabia and given the means to publicize his brother's theses while inspiring Saudi Arabia's *sahwa* (religious awakening), a hybrid brand of Islamism that combines his brother's philosophy and Wahhabi doctrines.[1] He also published what Sadik J. al-Azm called "a famous Islamist classic," a sort of compendium of his brother's summa theologica.[2] The book, a cri de coeur about Islam as the last stronghold against the *jahiliyya,* the tendency toward decadence that has plagued and destroyed human societies throughout history, includes a chapter titled "Why Do They Hate Islam?!" It was an unsettling question to read in the post–9/11 political climate, particularly since it uncannily preempts the charge that Muslims hate the United States for its freedoms and way of life.

But Mohammed Qutb goes further than America's complaint, stating that all forms of decadence throughout history have been implacable foes of Islam, simply because Islam is Islam, and no one was more vicious in its hatred than twentieth-century *jahiliyya,* since it has been the most successful in driving people away from God. The Qur'an cites several cases of nations whose prophets were ignored and who later perished because of their refusal to heed the good message, but the contemporary *jahiliyya* (modernity) "hates Islam and cannot stand it. It hates whoever calls people to it and tries to take him out or to destroy him," all in the name of freedom of opinion and belief. Over and over again, Mohammed Qutb emphasizes modern *jahiliyya's* enmity toward Islam and its crusade to destroy it. It's an evil project that joins Eastern and Western Europe, the United States, Arab and Muslim rulers (since sovereignty is God's alone), intellectuals, artists, novelists, TV personalities, cinematographers, and the so-called liberated woman (a project deemed most crucial by a Jewish American scholar, Morroe Berger, author of *The Arab World Today*), and even the masses who, when they don't hate Islam, prefer to have fun, watch (belly) dancing in the movies, and listen to music. Islam, with its prayers and fasting, to them is too hard and strenuous an exercise in self-restraint. Thus, international crusaders, financed by Jewish interests, are the allies of most Muslims, since all are united in destroying or marginalizing Islam. Who, then, is left to stand up for Islam and is willing to counter the juggernaut of this genocidal *jahiliyya?* wonders Qutb. Only a few and often powerless real Muslims scattered across the Islamic world.

Such views, mixing the quest for unsullied purity and the resistance to the corrupting influence of other, ungodly cultures, are the quintessential expression of martyrology that inspires Muslim jihadists today. It's part of a discourse that is not specific to Islam, or monotheism, for that matter, for many a politician and scientist has attributed the ills that bother a community to the exposure of that community to alien ideologies and microbes, thereby joining the cause for self-purification with the denunciation of the stranger. The impulse is at the heart of all nativist movements, whether such movements are heaven-bound (as in the case of religion) or earthbound (as in the case of a biological or ethnic essence). Very often, as will be shown in a discussion of Karen Armstrong below, the attempt to infuse the ideal, which is always exclusively in the realm of the imagination, into the real, our condition in the here and now, leads to the violence that besets the world today. Because the attempt to recover an essence cleansed from the corruption of history is what unites ardent nationalists and zealous believers, or the two together, as is not infrequently the case in the world of Islam and the United States, it was not really surprising to hear the eerie echo of Mohammed Qutb's question about the world's hatred of Islam repeated in America after 9/11.

"Why Do They Hate Islam?!" crystallizes a set of recurring arguments throughout the book, beginning with Qutb's attempt to rescue the meaning of *jahiliyya* from good and bad interpreters alike, the first because they restrict its meaning to its pre-Islamic, Arabian context, and the second because they try to show that pre-Islamic Arabs were not backwards and had a dynamic civilization. But Qutb, relying on verses from the Qur'an, says that this is not the Islamic meaning of the term, since it is nowhere stated in the Qur'an that this condition is limited in time and place; on the contrary, the condition of *jahiliyya* is a feature of history; it is the general condition of any nation or people who don't abide by the absolute sovereignty of God, particularly Islam. Which is why twentieth-century *jahiliyya* is the worst and most vicious: through its deceptive ideologies of science, research, and progress, it has managed to drive the widest wedge between human beings and their god, and has therefore caused the most damage. Qutb is aware that his book can't do much, yet he takes comfort in the fact that the (printed) word is never lost, though it may be forgotten every now and then, and he is optimistic that, despite the overwhelming darkness of the *jahiliyya,* one may still glimpse a silver lining of hope. He knows that many skeptics would welcome this kind of *jahiliyya,* the one that brings science and progress, but he is determined to forge ahead and show how mistaken they are.

The *jahiliyya* is a fact of life, part of human nature and its duality since Adam and Eve were created. Just as there is good and evil, there is also Islam and *jahiliyya.* To obey God and be guided by His teachings is the only way to avoid such a condition. This duality structures principles and virtues and has nothing to do with the state of science and progress. One is either Muslim or a *jahili* (in a state of decadence). Thus, Europe, and its extension, the United States, are the products of a series of *jahiliyyas* beginning with ancient Greece and moving through the Roman empire and the Christian Middle Ages, then, after benefiting from contact with Islamic science and knowledge, through the Reformation and Enlightenment, until we reach the nineteenth century and the rise of the industrial revolution, capitalism, and Darwinism. In Qutb's reading, the leitmotif of Greek civilization is the conflict between humans and gods, with Zeus taking his revenge on Prometheus (who showed a soft spot for humans and gave them the sacred fire) by dispatching Pandora and her box of evil, which was opened by her husband, Prometheus's brother. In Greek culture, humans fought the gods to assert their agency and independence, privileged "reason" over soul as the source of knowledge, then fell into sexual chaos and were destroyed. Qutb notes over and over again that *jahiliyya* doesn't mean that *jahili* cultures haven't produced refined legacies and contributed to human civilization, or that they don't have their virtues and advantages. It simply means that cultures go wrong when they reject divine guidance. The same goes for the Romans, who were masters of administration and organization but were also fiercely materialistic at the expense of spirit, and whose leaders were despots who sought pleasure in extreme brutality. This sort of *jahiliyya* was followed by the mixture of paganism and Christianity imposed on the Romans by Emperor Constantine, a fact, like many others repeated throughout the book, that characterized the European Church during the Middle Ages, an extremist institution that launched war against the Muslims, who nevertheless still taught Christians nation building and the value of human rights. The Crusades defined Europe's relation with Muslims, while the corrupt church drove Europeans, step by step, into secularism. The Renaissance didn't do much better, since it resurrected the paganism of ancient Greece and the barbarism of Rome, and making these long-forgotten, non-Semitic cultures the foundation of a new European civilization. Thus, according to Mohammed Qutb, by the nineteenth century, brutal capitalism and Darwinism, both orchestrated by Jews and abetted by Marx, Freud, and Durkheim, dealt the mortal blow to whatever was left of religion.

Qutb concedes that democracy, with its rights and protections, has conferred relative freedoms; yet the tyranny and inhumanity of capitalism (whose grounds were laid by the abolition of usury, a practice controlled by Jews), manifested in its most grotesque form in the United States, where captains of industry assassinated John F. Kennedy in broad daylight to protect their economic interests, reign despotically over people's lives, sucking their life force and subjecting them to *"total terrorism."*[3] The answer to this economic terrorism is not Communism, of course, but Islam. Writing during the Cold War period, Qutb saw both capitalism and Communism, or West and East, as hopelessly decadent since the hegemony of capital is countered by the equally malevolent dictatorship of the proletariat, one that totally subjects the individual to the tyranny of the state.

To Qutb, the crude materialism of the capitalist mode of production that affects the quality of the human experience is not determined by blind forces, but by human choices and lack of belief. He notes that people in capitalist societies may be nice, but they are ultimately driven by self-interest, while selfless values—such as devotion and honesty—that were learned from Muslims during the Crusades or from Christian ethics have become rare indeed. To him, divorcing values from faith has led to Machiavellianism, colonialism, capitalist alienation, sexual decadence, the exploitation of women, the delinquency of Western youth (recognized by European, American, and Soviet leaders alike), and the breakdown in gender relations (all of which, again, were instigated by Jews in their quest for global domination). The liberation of women and free sex have trivialized sexuality, led to the rise of divorce, the pain and suffering of children, the banality of eroticism, and the drive toward homosexuality. In short, in a remarkable echo of Albert Einstein's famous ultimatum "socialism or barbarism," Qutb asserts that the choice now is between "Allah or destruction" (*imma allah . . . wa imma al-inhiyar*).[4] Islam unites all the spheres of human life—the material and the spiritual, the social and the cultural—into a way guided by God's sovereign principles of mercy, moderation, and compassion. Islam is thus the alternative to the decadent humanism of Greek and Roman civilizations, whose apogee is expressed in twentieth-century cultures, the ne plus ultra of *jahiliyyas*. Citing verse after verse from the Qur'an in brilliant rhetorical moves, Qutb affirms the indispensability of Islam as the only solution to this global malaise. To take but a random example in which Mohammed Qutb follows his discussion of the Islamic concept of love, which is in sync with the divine, rational order:

Yes. Islam is a realistic path . . . it's the path that says: "Had Allah not pushed people against each other, the earth would have been rotted" (2:251). And He says, "O Man! You are forever striving to meet your Lord—and you shall" (84:6). And He says, "We have created Man into toil" (90:4).

Allah does not promise an idealized paradise on earth! And He doesn't tell a human being that he will find favor and abundance [*an-na'eem*] under his feet in this world! What He tells him is that life is strife, toil, pushing, and struggle.[5]

Remarkably, despite his obsession with Jewish conspiracies, wholesale condemnation of Western civilization, and contempt for bad Muslims, Mohammed Qutb denounces extremism as "proof of false religiosity, for the truly religious never falls into extremism, but is guided by God."[6] Through a careful reading of texts, particularly of the Qur'an, the liberal use of exclamation marks, and frequent use of paragraph-long sentences or even phrases, and the journal-like quality of the prose, he displays a moving sense of victimization and martyrdom, making it clear that Islam is under siege, although God will not abandon his people, because a new generation will rise to defend His sovereignty. The tone is that of a man who, with the support of a few friends, is working against overwhelming odds, in a world that's rushing into disaster. It's more of a monkish voice, a saint's warning to a deluded world, very much in the tradition of his older brother, Sayyid Qutb, whose "fiery style was capable of provoking great emotions of dignity, solidarity, unity, universality, and similar feelings and could, for instance, uplift the reader to the greatness of Islam."[7]

Mohammed Qutb's book also encapsulates brilliantly his brother's philosophy and makes it available in one volume to those who are not inclined to labor through Sayyid's forty published books, thirty unpublished ones, and hundreds of articles. For it was Sayyid Qutb, borrowing from the South Asian scholar Abul 'Ala' Mawdudi (1903–1979), who used the *jahiliyya* as an "epistemological device" to reject all non-Islamic philosophies, practices, ideologies, and ways of life. Sayyid Qutb had led a monastic existence (he never married) of scholarship, anticolonial (broadly defined) intellectual activism, and serious interest in politics. Not unpredictably, it was during his two-year visit to the United States on a scholarship to find out about new theories of pedagogy, beginning in 1948, that his first major book on fundamentalism, *al-'adala al-ijtima'iyya fi al-islam* (Social justice in Islam), was published, and the stay itself was one of the major catalysts that led him to reject Western civilization. Later, in a 1951 essay titled *"amrika allati ra'aytu"* ("The America I Have Seen"), he described good people living in a technologically advanced society but who were spiritually bereft and had no clue as to what fraternity meant. Everything, even prayer, was experienced as entertainment and romance.[8] Ironically, Qutb found support in *War or Peace,* a book published in 1950 by none other than John Foster Dulles, the U.S. Secretary of State, who at least recognized that the American way of life could appear as an ominous threat to other cultures:

We can talk eloquently about liberty and freedom, and about human rights and fundamental freedoms, and about the dignity and worth of the human personality, but most of our vocabulary derives from a period when our own society was individualistic. Consequently, it has little meaning for those who live under conditions where individualism means premature death. Also, we can talk eloquently about the material successes we have achieved, about the marvel of mass production, and about the number of automobiles, radios, and telephones owned by our people. That materialistic emphasis makes some feel that we are spiritually bankrupt. It makes others envious and more disposed to accept communist glorification of "mass" efforts to "develop the material life of society."[9]

Qutb was in the United States when Israel was created (an event that left him embittered at America and the West's betrayal of the Arabs) and the leader of the Muslim Brothers was assassinated. Upon his return to Egypt, he joined the Muslim Brothers and stuck to an uncompromising position, refusing to dilute the purity of Islam by joining the government. Never having enjoyed good health, persecution and torture had an adverse effect on him. He was hanged on August 29, 1966, despite numerous interventions on his behalf.

Despite his refutation of Marxist determinism, atheism, and Communism, and although he wanted to regulate capitalism, not undo it, Sayyid Qutb's economic agenda is liberal, one that includes provisions for the protection of the poor and provides equal opportunities and resources to children.[10] In Qutb's regime of the *hakimiyya* (God's sovereign realm, the opposite of the human-created *jahiliyya*), all ownership ultimately (at least theoretically) reverts back to God.[11] In fact, as Sayyid Qutb put it, "Islam does not only secure complete social justice in the large Islamic countries for its adherents alone but also serves all its inhabitants regardless of their religion, race, language. . . . And this is one of its [Islam's] humane characteristics which other ideologies do not achieve."[12] To achieve this state of justice, a shaking up (*zalzala*) of the old regime is necessary, with a vanguard (*tali'a*) engaged in a long-term, four-step jihad process, ranging from basic education to the unhindered freedom to preach Islam worldwide.[13]

Zalzala, indeed, is what the world has been experiencing since 9/11, or as, Gilles Kepel, probably the foremost journalist analyzing the Islamist movement today, termed it in his book, *fitna*—chaos, political turmoil—

akin to the *fitna al-kubra* (Great Upheaval) that followed the death of the prophet and divided the Muslim community into sometimes violently murderous factions.[14] Yet the thing to remember is that today Islamic fundamentalism, like other forms of "militant piety," is a modern movement, the expression of what Karen Armstrong called the new Axial Age of European modernity—the first Axial Age (700–200 B.C.) saw the emergence of all major religions, such as Buddhism, Hinduism, Confucianism, Taoism, monotheism, and rationalism—in which mythos (the way people make sense of the past and purpose in life) and logos ("the rational, pragmatic, and scientific thought that enabled men and women to function in the world"), hitherto kept strictly separate and generally understood to have different functions, are dangerously conflated by fundamentalists who try to translate, or bring down to earth, myth into an agenda that could be instituted in real life. This is, of course, not merely a monotheistic problem: imperial nationalistic ideologies are often driven by the missionary zeal of remaking the world in the image of their founding myths, even if such myths are not inspired directly from religion. One would be hardpressed to find examples of U.S. intervention in the world for purposes other than to make things better, to redeem the world's oppressed, and to protect the sacred flow of commerce; yet the amount of violence and tragedies generated by such good intentions remonstrates us again and again that the world, and its people, do not bend easily—if at all—to lofty ideological aspirations. The righteous, in all cultures and places, often end up causing more darkness than light.

The Qutb brothers' tone, then, is part of the besieged believers fighting for the "survival of their faith." Armstrong even speculates that some of the 9/11 hijackers who drank and flirted before the attacks went beyond even the most extreme fringes of fundamentalism to engage in "holy sin," a radical theology developed in the seventeenth century by the likes of the Jewish (and later Muslim) Shabbetai Zevi and his disciple Jacob Frank.[15] That Armstrong finds explanations to the behavior of Muslim fundamentalists and terrorists in Jewish history opens the way to a wider survey of all three monotheistic faiths after 1492. It shows how Judaism, Islam, and Christianity developed apocalyptic views of what the Qutbs called *jahiliyya.*

Nineteen-forty-two, the year the last stronghold of Islam was defeated in Spain, marks the moment when the old Axial Age came to an end; it was the time when Jews and Muslims were subjected to Christian persecution. (Jewish converts, the *conversos,* would be known as *marranos* [pigs] by Spaniards, while Muslims allowed to remain under Christian rule in Spain would be known as *mudéjar.*)[16] Caught in a European-wide culture of anti-Semitism, some Jews, such as the Ashkenazic Isaac (Yitzhak) Luria (1534–1572) developed the doctrine of Zimzum, or withdrawal, complete with its new myth of creation and a violent beginning that mirrors the tribulations in Jewish history.[17] (In October 2005, Luria appeared in the news when Israeli rabbis strongly condemned the singer Madonna, a devotee of the Kabbalah, and prophesied that she would be divinely punished for commercially exploiting Luria's name in "Isaac," a song on the album *Confessions on a Dance Floor.*)[18] Meanwhile, some members of the Diaspora in Europe, such as Juan Prado and Baruch Spinoza, started rethinking the validity of the Bible altogether, developing notions of secularism *avant la lettre;* Spinoza would, in fact, become "one of the first secularists in Europe."[19] Shabbetai Zevi of Smyrna, Turkey, declared himself Messiah in 1665 and prophesied the defeat of the Ottoman Sultan, the return to the Holy Land, and the submissions of gentile nations to his rule;[20] but when he was defeated by the Sultan, he committed "holy sin" by embracing Islam. He later studied the *sharia* and saw himself as a bridge between all three monotheistic religions. Thus, the Jews, persecuted minorities everywhere, developed a range of responses to their alienation—Lurianic Kabbalah; embryonic forms of secularism; messianism; Shabbateanism, or the doctrine of "holy sin" (harking back to the Marrano experience in Spain, akin the Muslim Shiite concept of *taqiyya,* or dissimulation); even, as in the case of the Polish Jacob Frank (1726–1791), a theology of immorality and violent attacks on all religions.

The new Axial Age of Reason was also the age of violence: witch hunts, wars, antinomianism, and religious awakenings (religion, Armstrong wisely reminds us, often guides people through radical changes).[21] Even the Enlightenment was not, initially, kind to the Jews. Baron d'Holbach (1723–1789), "one of the first avowed atheists of Europe," described them as "the enemies of the human race,"[22] while Voltaire (1694–1778) called them "a totally ignorant nation." In response to these conditions, various reformist Jewish movements, such as the Hasidim, the Misnagdim, and the Maskilim, arguing among each other, appeared to make sense of their place in the new world. The Maskilim, combining Judaism with the Enlightenment, would eventually influence the birth of Reform Judaism, which found eager adherents in the United States. A new science of Judaism allowed scholars to consider the Halakha as "man-made." But all tendencies have a common anxiety about the future of Judaism and the Jewry:

> Both the Reformers and the scholars of the Science of Judaism were pre-occupied with the survival of their religion in a world that seemed, how-ever benevolently, bent on destroying it. As they watched their fellow Jews rushing to the baptismal font, they were deeply concerned for the future of Judaism and were desperate to find ways of ensuring that it continued to exist. We shall find that many people in the modern world have shared this anxiety. In all three of the monotheistic faiths, there has been recur-rent alarm that the traditional faith is in deadly danger. The dread of annihilation is one of the most fundamental of human terrors, and many of the religious movements that have arisen in the modern world have sprung from this fear of extinction. As the secular spirit took hold and as the prevailing rationalism became more hostile to faith, religious people became increasingly defensive and their spirituality more embattled.[23]

Napoleon's conquest of Egypt in 1798 was experienced by Egyptians as a cataclysmic event akin to the European conquests of the Americas.[24] As a response, Mohammed Ali (1769–1849) launched Egypt on a violent, rather Stalinist process of modernization, including the "ethnic cleansing" of the Mamluks. Yet this modernization, led by Westernized elites, was a shallow form of mimicry that simply produced a profoundly divided society. As the role of the *ulema* (Islam's religious scholars, the traditional defenders of the community) was diminished, Ali's descendants couldn't do any better, nor could they stem the decline of their increasingly indebted country. The end result was colonialism: "The whole experience of modernization was crucially different in the Middle East: it was not one of empowerment, autonomy, and innovation, as it had been in Europe, but a process of deprivation, dependence, and patchy, imperfect imitation."[25]

In Iran, Sayyid Ali Mohammed (1819–1850), influenced by Islam, partic-ularly the Shiite tradition of the messiah-like figure of the Hidden Imam, announced in 1844 that he was the "gate" (*bab*) to the divine. Like Joseph Smith, the founder of Mormonism in the United States, he "produced a newly inspired scripture, the Bayan" and abrogated previous holy books.

His messianic message appealed to the masses, who rallied to his eman-cipatory, revolutionary, feminist message. But when his disciples were defeated by the Iranian government after they had revolted, and the *Bab* was executed in 1850, they developed the Baha'i religion, embracing many of Europe's Enlightenment ideals. Still, as Karen Armstrong explains,

> the Babi revolution had shown that religion could help people to appro-priate the ideals and enthusiasms of modernity, by translating them from an alien secular idiom into a language, mythology, and spirituality that they could understand and make their own. If modernity had proved difficult for the Christians of the West, it was even more problematic for Jews and Muslims. It required a struggle—in Islamic terms, a *jihad,* which might sometimes become a holy war.[26]

By the mid–nineteenth century, modernity appeared as soulless and, given the deadliness of wars, apocalyptic, to many European writers and thinkers. It was also discredited by huge class divisions and atrocious liv-ing conditions for the poor. In the United States, Protestants mobilized against Darwinian theories, and in 1886, the revivalist Dwight Moody (1837–1899) founded the Moody Bible Institute in Chicago to combat the teachings of the "Higher Criticism." Like the Jewish Yeshiva developed in Eastern Europe, the Bible Institute (a precursor to many Christian col-leges and home schooling) was meant to be a "safe and sacred enclave in a godless world, which would prepare a cadre for a future counteroffensive against modern society." (The following year, the American Protective Society was formed to confront the "Catholic threat.")[27]

In Europe, the target—this time in the name of scientific racism—was once again the Jew. In a renewed climate of hate and vilification, pogroms reappeared in Russia, pushing the Jews of that country into a hostile West-ern Europe, the United States, and Palestine. The Habad Hasidim, a movement out of Lubavitch, Russia, blamed secular Jews (Zionists, social-ists) for their ills. Zionism, a product of this climate, was seen as an enemy of Judaism, but the Zionists were bent on creating a new Jewish identity without having to bother much about the finer details of the faith, thus lay-ing the ground to the yet-unresolved debate between secular nationalists imbued by the spirit of the Enlightenment and the traditional, orthodox Jews whose goal was and is to preserve the mythos of the faith.

Muslims, meanwhile, were experiencing secularism as imperialism, and so the main reaction to it was one of fear, even though early Egyptian travelers in Europe expressed admiration and sought reform in Egypt. The Persian Shiite Jamal al-Din al-Afghani (1839–1897) agitated against the threat of the West to Muslim identities and seems to have started the futile quest to adapt modernity to the Qur'an. Al-Afghani was an ideologue deeply worried, as were many Jews, about the annihilation of Islam, even condoning terrorism to fight his enemies in the Muslim world. Later Mohammed Abdu (1849–1905), who became Mufti of Egypt, and Qassim Amin (1865–1908), among others, also tried to reconcile Islam and modernity but kept stumbling. The quest proved elusive:

> A living civilization had been transformed by the colonialists into a dependent bloc, and this lack of autonomy induced an attitude and habit of subservience that was profoundly at odds with the modern spirit. Inevitably, the earlier love and admiration of Europe, epitomized by Tahtawi and the Iranian reformers, soured and gave way to resentment.[28]

Egypt and Iran were mostly under secular nationalists (shahs or presidents), but the birth and growing strength of the Muslim Brothers in Egypt, founded in 1928, and the rise of Qum in Iran as a stronghold for Shiite scholars—including young Khomeini—meant that religion was once again poised to challenge the status quo.[29] Under assault from secular ideologies—experienced in Islam as imperialism, in Israel as secular Zionism, and in the United States as "secular humanism"—fundamentalists launched counteroffensives and mobilized to defend their imperiled identities. It was in this general climate that Abul 'Ala' Mawdudi decried democracy as a form of *shirk* (disbelief through association), announced the sovereignty of God, and issued a "call to arms," a jihad against the *jahiliyya,* an ideology embraced by the Qutb brothers, as we have seen above. As Sayyid Qutb saw it in his magnum opus, *fi dhilal al-Qur'an* (In the shadow of the Qur'an), the culture of modernity is an affront to human dignity and the sacred purpose of life:

> Humanity today is living in a large brothel! One has only to glance at its press, films, fashion shows, beauty contests, ballrooms, wine bars, and broadcasting stations! Or observe its mad lust for naked flesh, provocative

postures, and sick suggestive statements in literature, the arts and the mass media! And add to all this, the system of usury, which fuels man's voracity for money and engenders vile methods for its accumulation and invest-ment, in addition to fraud, trickery, and blackmail dressed up in the garb of law.[30]

Qutb established Mohammed's life as an ideal to be emulated and pro-claimed high and loud the sovereignty of God as the best way to achieve independence.[31] Khomeini in Iran echoed the same sentiment, and in an innovative and controversial move, entrusted the *ulema* with the guard-ianship of Islam and the Qur'an. So did religious Zionists in Israel, the Gahelet, who combined Zionism with orthodoxy. "We accept upon our-selves the entire Torah, its commandments and ideas," explained one Pinchas Rosenbluth. "We want to carry out the Torah all the time and in every area, to grant [Torah] and its laws sovereignty in the life of the individual and the public."[32] In this view, the law of Eretz Israel is holy, including the promised biblical lands, the West Bank and Gaza.

Meanwhile in the United States, beginning in the 1960s, industrialization, demographic shifts, and contact with the liberal North gave the South a higher profile. The New South emerged more fundamentalist. Christians retreated into enclaves—such as evangelical schools and home schooling. Like all fundamentalists, the "Pro-Family Forum" declared a war on secular humanism, which it blamed for, among other things, its godless socialism and interest in controlling the environment and energy.[33] Secular human-ism was a rebellion against the sovereignty of god and threatened the world in serious ways. One believer, Franky Schaeffer, wrote a book called *A Time for Anger: The Myth of Neutrality* (1982), warning the West against

> an electronic dark age, in which the new pagan hordes, with all the power of technology at their command, are on the verge of obliterating the last strongholds of civilized humanity. A vision of darkness lies before us. As we leave the shores of Christian western man behind, only a dark and turbu-lent sea of despair stretches endlessly ahead . . . unless we fight.[34]

Puritans were now seen as less interested in democracy than they were in the right church and faith. By the 1980s, a countdown to Armageddon had begun. "We need to get active," writes Hal Lindsey in *The 1980's: Countdown to Armageddon,* "electing officials who will not only reflect the Bible's morality in government, but will shape domestic and foreign policies to protect our country and our way of life."[35]

American and Middle Eastern fundamentalisms were beginning to mirror each other. In 1974, a group of Israelis who believed that "Judaism and Western culture were antithetical" formed the "bloc of the Faithful," or Gush Emunim, with the objective of redeeming Israel and the entire world.[36] The bloc helped elect Menachem Begin and the Likud party in 1977 (Ariel Sharon, head of the Israel Lands Commission in Begin's cabinet, immediately declared his intention to settle one million Jews in the West Bank within twenty years), but they were terribly disappointed when the prime minister they helped elect signed the Camp David treaty with Anwar Sadat later that year. Two years later, it launched the Tehiya party "to fight Camp David and prevent further territorial concessions." As one Gush rabbi explained:

> The Redemption is not only the Redemption of Israel, but the Redemption of the whole world. But the Redemption of the world depends upon the Redemption of Israel. From this derives our moral, spiritual, and cultural influence over the entire world. The blessing will come to all of humanity from the people of Israel living in the whole of its land.[37]

In Egypt, Anwar Sadat's Open Door economic policy (*infitah*) divided the country into two: a small section of privileged Egyptians and huge, disenfranchised masses. New, more radical organizations, such as the Muslim Society and the student organization *jamaat al-islamiyya* came to light. More women started wearing the scarf in an attempt to "return to self," and renowned speakers denounced the new culture as Pharaonic, that is to say, pagan. The influential Muslim scholar and mufti (acknowledged dispenser of *fatwas,* or religious edicts) Yusuf al-Qaradawi said:

> Egypt is Muslim, not pharaonic . . . the youth of the *jamaat islamiyyah* are the true representatives of Egypt, and not the Avenue of the Pyramids, the theatre performances, and the films. . . . Egypt is not naked women, but veiled women who adhere to the prescriptions of divine law. Egypt is young men who let their beards grow. . . . It is the land of al-Azhar.[38]

In Iran, the Islamic cause was mounting against a brutal regime that didn't hesitate to kill citizens. But the tide swelled and the regime gave up. Khomeini returned in 1979. His arrival, writes Armstrong, "was one of those symbolic events, like the storming of the Bastille, which seem to change the world forever."[39] It was a rapturous event, akin to the return of the Hidden Imam in the Shiite mythology.[40]

As Khomeini was toppling the shah of Iran (1978–79), Jerry Falwell founded the Moral Majority in 1979 and teamed up with right-wing conservatives to shape what would soon become the New Christian Right. They set out to ban objectionable authors, such as John Steinbeck, Joseph Conrad, and Mark Twain; form school curricula; and bring God back into the schools. In 1981, Mel and Norma Gabler said they objected to the "liberal slant" in the Texas school curriculum because of its

> open-ended questions that require students to draw their own conclusions; statements about religions other than Christianity; statements that they construe to reflect negatively on the free enterprise system; statements that they construe to reflect positive aspects of socialist or communist countries (e.g., that the Soviet Union is the largest producer in the world of certain grains); any aspect of sex education other than the promotion of abstinence; statements which emphasize contributions made by blacks, Native American Indians, Mexican-Americans, or feminists; statements which are sympathetic to American slaves or are unsympathetic to their masters; and statements in support of the theory of evolution, unless equal space is given to explain the theory of creation.[41]

Armstrong's breathtaking survey of five centuries of monotheistic responses to what the Qutbs described as the *jahiliyya* reminds us that the phenomenon of Islamic fundamentalism is part of a larger world history. As she explains in the afterword, "The desire to define doctrines, erect barriers, establish borders, and segregate the faithful in a sacred enclave where the law is stringently observed springs from that terror of extinction which has made all fundamentalists, at one time or another, believe that the secularists were about to wipe them out."[42] Although all fundamentalists are driven by a survival instinct,[43] one must still ask whether a more egalitarian economic structure could help people transition into a new faith without much anxiety. Also, Armstrong in her masterly treatment of fundamentalism in *The Battle for God* doesn't explore in as much depth as, say, Wafik Raouf, Richard Fletcher, or Bernard Lewis whether Islam's rigid fundamentalism is aggravated by Islam's historic rivalry with Christendom, the cultural entity that defined the new Axial Age (in her breakdown of historical epochs). American conservative Protestants may be appalled by secular humanism, but they at least are challenging a homegrown intellectual movement (in the sense that American and European cultures are part of a common tradition), not one imported or, even worse, as in the case of Islam, imposed from above by historic foes.

The interaction between Arabia and Europe, to be sure, dates from antiquity: there were Arab Roman emperors; Arabs were influenced by Aramaic and Hellenic traditions; Abraham, Mary, and baby Jesus were among the 360 idols of Ka'ba; the Prophet Mohammed participated in an extensive commercial traffic between Arabia and Byzantine Syria. But the rise of Islam may have indicated a desire for autonomy from neighboring religions, perhaps reflecting Arabia's cultural and economic maturity.[44] The Prophet Mohammed, who was born in a Roman-Semitic, not Hindu, environment, promptly reoriented Muslim prayers toward Mecca and away from Jewish Jerusalem in 624 in order to differentiate his faith from older Jewish and Christian ones.[45] So if Islamism is defined as a "movement of intransigence" (*courant de l'intransigence,* in the expression of Wafik Raouf),[46] then it may be fair to claim it appeared with Islam itself. For no sooner was the Muslim prophetic message embraced by Arabs than a process of Islamic expansionism began in the Byzantine empire, Russia, Mesopotamia (which was mostly Christian in the early seventh century), North Africa, and southern Europe.

This state of affairs was obviously upsetting to Christians, who had dominated much of the Mediterranean basin and the Near East for the previous two centuries and now saw Islam and its prophet as bloodthirsty, intolerable impostures, the parasitic and uncouth children of Ishmael, Isaac's second-class son. (In a fascinating footnote, the psychoanalyst Fethi Benslama theorizes that because the births of Isaac and Jesus could only be explained through God's direct intervention, but not that of Ishmael, born to a young and fertile woman, Islam categorically rejects the doctrine of God's fatherhood. It's as if Islam had been severed from God's genealogy till the birth of Mohammed.)[47] Even as Christian scholars denounced Islam in polemical treatises in the guise of disputations, Muslims kept moving into the heartlands of Christianity. Yet as the Muslim empire grew, the conquerors needed Christian know-how in administration. So the Muslims cantoned themselves in segregated garrisons (such as Basra, Fustat, and Kairaouan) and simply imposed a poll tax on the People of the Book.[48]

With the building of Baghdad in 762, Islam had come into its own, incorporating the customs of conquered civilizations and the knowledge of the Greeks, mostly translated from Syriac by Christian converts. (A similar process was taking place in Spain where Arabized Christian converts were called Mozarabs.) Yet Muslims evinced no interest whatsoever in Christian countries and peoples, except when they had to deal with them in war or business. Initially, this was explainable: the Abbasid empire, with its center in Baghdad, was far more advanced than anything in Christendom. (France, for Ibn Hawqal, was good only for its slaves, although the famous Abbasid caliph Harun ar-Rashid did send an elephant to Charlemagne when the latter was crowned Emperor in 800.) There was in fact regular contact and, during this period, much Muslim influence on European culture. "Christian and Muslim [simply] lived side by side in a state of mutual religious aversion," a tense sort of *convivencia* that has lasted to this day.[49]

The defeat of the Byzantine army at Manzikert in 1071 and Turkish control of parts of Asia Minor, however, prompted the defeated Byzantines to seek the help of the Latin Christian Pope Urban II, whose call for a crusade tapped on a psyche seething with loathing for Muslims, whose treachery was popularized in the eleventh-century epic poem "Chanson de Roland." So the Crusades were launched, leading to centuries of conflict, the establishment of Christian principalities, known as *Outremer,* and the defeat of Muslims in Sicily, Malta, and Spain between 1060 and 1212. The Crusades had an incalculable impact on Europe, but this impact barely registered in the Islamic world—a remarkable testament to Muslim indifference to Christian marauders. Even as Christians concocted the legend of Prester John, a mighty Christian ally in Asia who could team up with European Christians to defeat Muslims and recapture the Holy Land, and later sought to lure conquering Mongols into Christianity in a fatal alliance against Islam, this and other legends remained mere dreams—until, that is, the advent of the colonial period. This is not to say that loyalties were invariably fixed in one direction; people from both sides—the

Christian El Cid is a famous example—crossed back and forth between Islam and Christianity, without much damage to their social standing. By the fourteenth century, the parochialism of the Middle Ages was also giving way—through travel accounts like Marco Polo's—to the awareness of a wider world inhabited by all sorts of different people.[50]

Although the drive for crusades never vanished, by the late Middle Ages, Western Christendom was mired in its own internal political and military squabbles and wars, leaving it little time or energy to undertake the expeditions of its forerunners. Still, the Ottoman incursions were countered with the same zeal (Constantinople fell on May 29, 1453, to Sultan Mohammed II, who had grown up dreaming of replicating Alexander the Great's exploits). Most of Al-Andalus was in Christian hands, while Prince Henry the Navigator, who had captured the Moroccan town of Ceuta in 1415, saw himself as a crusader. But monks like the Provençal poet Honorat Bouvet (author of "Sarrasin") or the Majorcan Ramón Lull (1232–1315), the indefatigable intellectual who championed the study of Arabic and oriental cultures (and who was stoned to death in Tunisia for his proselytizing), John de Segovia (d. 1458; the teacher of Hernando de Talavera, the first archbishop of Granada), and the German Nicholas of Cusa (d. 1464) inaugurated a culture of dialogue and tolerance through learning and the questioning of certitudes. Yet Muslims, even towering fourteenth-century figures like Ibn Battuta and Ibn Khaldun, never cared much to find out about their neighbors to the north. Up until the seventeenth century, the East was the site of the Holy Land, the major pilgrimage center for Christians and a center of commerce and trade; the flow of traffic was often from West to East (the Crusades have been described by Jean Delumeau, professor at the Collège de France, as "armed pilgrimages"); but there were practically no Muslim tourists in Europe, as there were no holy sites in that continent for Muslims to visit, no permanent embassies, while travel in infidel land was discouraged by Muslim jurists.[51]

Given Islam and Christianity's encounters in jihads and anti-jihads, or Crusades and anti-Crusades,[52] it is not surprising that the Qur'an was first translated into Latin by an international team led by the Englishman Robert of Ketton and the German Hermann of Carinthia during the Crusades of the early twelfth century, not to be read for its own sake but for the purpose of refuting Islam.[53] Christian-Muslim clashes are not registered in literature alone; even popular staples of our diet today are the outgrowth of this enduring enmity. The failed takeover of Vienna by the Ottomans in 1683 inspired Viennese bakers to invent and eat the croissant, the symbol of their enemy. But what's a croissant without good coffee? As fate would have it, while rampaging through the Ottomans' abandoned camp, the same Austrians found bags with a grain that tasted too bitter, mixed the grain with milk and sugar, and soon baptized the new drink "cappuccino," in honor of a monk (capucin), Fra d'Aviano, the "indefatigable preacher for anti-Ottoman crusades, whose sermons strengthened the hearts and spirits in the certitude of the victory of the cross over the crescent [croissant]" (and who was beatified by John Paul II in 2002).[54] And, as if to add insult to injury, the coffee that Europeans imported from Middle Easterners would soon be grown outside Arab lands, in new European colonies, and sold back to them.[55]

The Muslim Ottomans' takeover of Constantinople in 1453 and their march on Vienna in 1683, however, constituted the last expansionist move before Muslims retreated into a defensive (but semantically confusing)[56] nationalism to resist Europe's colonial venture. Arab nationalism, whether liberal and secular or conservative and Islamist, is, in the end, held together by its anti-Western bias. In fact, the very term *West* (*gharb*) is part of an etymology whose variants include self-exile, or becoming a stranger to oneself (*taghrib, ightirab*).[57] This may explain why the West is targeted by Islamists more than any other culture;[58] in the Muslim imaginary, it stands for nothing less than the struggle for survival.

Fueled by its long rivalry with Christianity, its existential fear of annihilation in the ruthless swamps of modernity, and its dependency in a global capitalist economy, fundamentalism and extremism challenge Muslims and non-Muslims to find solutions without betraying their cultural traditions. In the case of contemporary Islam, the Qutb brothers offer one way out, while progressive Muslims and Islamists, whose views are best represented by the struggle of women to carve out spaces of autonomy in what has long been a patriarchal culture, are pointing toward a new consciousness that might mitigate the anxiety of annihilation without undermining the tenets of the faith. It is a very appealing and strategically useful position, one than can yield tremendous possibilities for positive change. Yet one must still ask whether the moderating influence of Islamic liberation theology still leaves intact the foundations that nurture extremism and promote tyranny. Is progressive Islam or Islamism (an approach now eagerly pursued by governments combating terrorism) the answer to the Muslims' debilitating cultural paralysis in the age of modernity? Or is it an intermediary phase in the quest for a broader, more robust culture of unshackled intellectual dynamism and freedom of belief and expression? While this question will be explored at more length in the remainder of the book, the rest of this chapter will show how Muslim women and their status in Muslim societies have been at the vanguard of cultural and political change, even as Western governments, after 9/11, have been trying to introduce more democracy and reform into the Middle East and the Muslim world in general.

On Friday, October 10, 2003, Shirin Ebadi, a fifty-six-year-old Iranian judge (one of the few women to occupy such a post in the country's history), lawyer, human rights activist, prolific author (eleven books at the time), and mother of two children was awarded the $1.32 million Nobel Peace Prize, beating 164 contenders, including Pope John Paul II, for her tireless work in protecting the rights of women in her conservative nation. Speaking with her hair uncovered in Paris, she immediately used the occasion to call on her government to respect the rights of women and children in Iran and remind the world audience that "there is no contradiction between Islam and human rights," and that "if a country abuses human rights in the name of Islam, then it is not the fault of Islam." She was also clear about opposing foreign intervention in the affairs of Iran because "the fight for human rights is conducted in Iran by the Iranian people." That the Nobel committee wanted to stress that Islam and women's rights are not incompatible (or, that is, that Islam is not monolithic) at a time when a spin on world events was conspiring to make it appear so was a welcome relief to many people who had argued that Islam could lend itself to progressive change if used imaginatively. Ebadi doesn't call herself feminist (she sees women and children's issues as part of larger social ones), nor does she call for a "secular" society; instead she sees her struggle against conservative religious power holders in Iran as a matter of interpretation. For this position, Ebadi, who had been jailed by the Iranian conservative regime, was labeled by Iranian exiles an apologist for political Islam.[59] (Iranian exiles weren't the only ones to disagree with the Nobel decision. Lech Walesa, who founded and led Poland's Solidarity trade union, confronted Communism, and won the 1983 Nobel prize, told a Polish TV station that the decision of conferring the prize to Ebadi was "a big mistake, a bad mistake, an unfortunate mistake" because the Nobel committee didn't grant the award to the Pope John Paul II. But out of deference to the pope, he said that he wasn't going to contest the nomination.)[60]

On the same day that the Nobel Peace Prize was awarded to a Muslim woman for the first time in history (and only the third Muslim ever, after President Anwar Sadat in 1978 and the PLO's Yasser Arafat in 1994, which he shared with Shimon Perez and Yitzhak Rabin), King Mohammed VI of Morocco opened his country's parliamentary season by urging male and female members of parliament, all covered equally, like the king himself, from head to toe in Morocco's traditional white garb, to scrap the country's family law, known as Mudawwana, which had discriminated against women and children, and to implement a new family code. The new code gives equal rights to women, raises the marriage age to eighteen, streamlines divorce procedures, defines the terms of custody and alimony (children would generally be retained by their mother until the age of fifteen, whereupon they are given the choice of which parent to live with), gives greater protection to children (including those born out of wedlock), and, without banning it (as "Commander of the Faithful," the king said he cannot make illicit what God has made licit), makes polygamy practically impossible. It was a historic event that brought Morocco's family laws closer to those of Tunisia, leaving way behind the archaic legislation in the rest of the Arab and most of the Muslim world.

As Commander of the Faithful, the modernizing monarch relied on an "intelligent rereading of religion," according to Nadia Yassine, arguably the monarchy's most outspoken critic and the most powerful Islamist in contemporary Morocco, a move that in her view goes back to the roots of Islam.[61] Later that month, in an interview with Morocco's official news agency, Maghreb Arabe Presse, the president of the Hassan II University in Casablanca, Rahma Bourkia (a member of the committee that had made the recommendations to the king) said that such changes to family law were in perfect harmony with Islam and the *sharia* since, in addition to asserting the dignity of women, the new law guarantees "justice and equality within the family."[62] To prove his point, the following month the Moroccan king invited Professor Naji Mekkaoui from Mohammed V University in Rabat to give a lecture on the family at the prestigious royal lectures series held during the holy month of Ramadan. Professor Mekkaoui's lecture was titled "The Universality of the Family Structure in a World of Multiple Particularities," reminding the assembly that the family is both a universal and particular system and that the family in Islam is primordial since it covers all members of the family.[63]

What struck me about this event was the somehow muted and marginal response by the Western media to what was arguably the most radical legislative act in the Muslim world after 9/11. It obviously far superseded Ebadi's well-deserved prize in significance, for millions of lives and the entire edifice of family life in a Muslim society were about to change. That such a radical change was not as newsworthy as the affairs of the Middle East shows that the latter has a stronger hold on the popular imagination than those of a peripheral, Atlantic Muslim nation. Because of its political continuity (despite the rupture of French and Spanish colonialism in the first half of the twentieth century), proximity to Europe, relatively peaceful coexistence of Islam and Judaism throughout history (although Judaism was never equal to Islam in status), deeply entrenched French culture, good historic ties with the United States (the first nation to officially recognize the fledgling republic), and good-will mediation in the Israeli-Palestinian dispute, Morocco is somehow considered a case apart in the Arab and Islamic worlds. One could certainly make the claim that the more-than-a-million-person march in Casablanca in the spring of 2003 to condemn the terrorist attacks against Jewish and Spanish sites, an event in which Jew, Berber, and Arab (the three main ethnic groups in the country) joined hands to proclaim loudly their attachment to their common Moroccan heritage, is unique in the post-9/11 world. It was in Morocco, too, in 1984, that Jo Ohana, the first Jew in any Muslim country, was elected to parliament.[64]

In any case, while such changes were unfolding in Morocco, in Aubervilles, not too far from Paris, where Ebadi was celebrating Nobel's recognition of her mission, Lila and Asma, two Muslim teenage sisters, were crying because they were expelled from the Lycée Henri-Wallon for wearing the veil, leading the younger of the two, Asma, to vow to become a lawyer. Reflecting on the fate of Muslim women across the Muslim world, the *Le Monde* chronicler wondered, in an ambiguous comment smacking of resilient Orientalist fantasies, whether women would choose to take off their veil if they were recognized and respected.[65]

What is one to make of the veil, then? Is it a token of women's oppression? A sign of their piety? There is no clear answer, precisely because much of the conflict pitting Muslim activists against the West and its secular allies in the Muslim world is played out in the domains of dress and demeanor, as if these were the unmistakable markers of identities. Anyone unfamiliar with Muslim societies shouldn't think for a moment that a covered woman is not sexy or seductive! Many men from Muslim societies could testify to that, but the anthropologist Fadwa El Guindi, in a comparative study of the veil across cultures, shows that one of the main functions of dress is concealment, which often enhances attraction.[66] Today, of course, the *hijab* (not synonymous with the veil) is no longer the marker of nobility that it had been in pre-Islamic civilizations, like the Assyrian or the Christian. The following passage in I Corinthians 11:3–7 shows how the head veil confers status on women, even as it turns them into second-class citizens in the religious polity to which they belong: "Any woman who prays with her head unveiled dishonors her head—it is the same as if her head were shaven. For if a woman will not veil herself, then she should cut off her hair, but it is disgraceful for a woman to be shorn or shaven, let her wear a veil. For a man ought not to cover his head, since he is the image and glory of God; but woman is the glory of man."[67] The veil, however, still offers portable *privacy* (an English word with no equivalent in Latin or Arabic) and the power to see without being seen.[68] El Guindi quotes Fra Mauro, a sixteenth-century monk cartographer to the Court of Venice, who wrote that "true meaning lies as if hidden behind a series of waxed seals . . . breaking one open only inspires the need to break open another. . . . each meaning crumbles under the pressure of knowing. . . . This is the principle of the veil well known to the Saracens."[69] Paradoxically, it was this culture of harems that fired Europe's Orientalist fantasies, often depicting lascivious naked women consumed by desire. It was mostly a fantasy, for we know the French, as Frantz Fanon reported ("The veil helped the Algerian woman to meet the new problems created by the struggle"),[70] waged a war on the veil in Algeria because it was an indomitable weapon for the resistance. These Orientalist depictions—baths, harems, and veils—were more a reflection of "a desexualized society" than that of Muslim life. Muslim culture does encourage "asexual 'solidarities'" full of affection and love, but nothing that resembles European portraits of it. As was the case in the Algeria of the 1950s, the veil now is the dress code for a committed, activist Muslim generation of women, as they move in and out of sacred spaces, an attribute once reserved only to the hajjis (title given to Muslims who have performed a pilgrimage to Mecca). They use it to counter work conditions and social spaces that are degrading to women, and to declare their beliefs publicly. We are back to the Algeria of the 1950s.[71]

El Guindi is an anthropologist, but Nadia Yassine begins her book, *Toutes voiles dehors* (All veils/sails outside) by announcing that she is lifting her veil to provoke through French; to open her mouth; to embark on a trip through culture and history; to give voice to those without words, the Sisyphuses of all nations, those who keep struggling for change without ever succeeding, on whom she calls to revolt, to shake up their orders; she lifts veils against winds and tides, against uniform thought.[72] The title suggests ultimate, adventurous sailing, all with the purpose to help re-enchant modernity and rescue Islam from bad Muslims.

Yassine surveys the vast scene of secular modernity, ranging from pop culture, literature, and the arts, to unveil abundant evidence for the total alienation of the moderns and their desperate quest for meaning and faith, even as they are beholden to the implacable dictates of their "secular Medusa." Everything, she finds in this first act of unveiling, is corrupted by the absence of religion. She records Pablo Picasso's confession that he produced absurdities to please an ignorant public (less illustrious artists have also known the value of snobbery) and thus never achieved the mastery of classical masters he had aspired to emulate. And although humans are more alienated and oppressed than ever, they talk about human rights as if such rights were achievable under present global conditions. She unveils Enlightenment philosophies, which, with their attachment to rationalism, bred and projected a tenebrous light on the South.

Having blamed Descartes for starting this destructive trend, she then turns on Darwin for having inaugurated a "liberation ideology," that is, liberation from religion, but an ideology that is itself a religion with its priesthood, rituals, and jargon. No one, particularly people in the South, has seen globalization coming; we no longer inhabit History; careful deliberate thought has been chased away by information; but the ultimate horror is economic. In such a milieu, democracy is a seductive concept deployed to enrich tyrants; globalization is a system of power relations, a project of domination, a tool for the West's cultural hegemony, a weapon in the U.S. arsenal, a system of pauperization. Communication, a natural vital need, becomes (dis)information, the real ephemeral, the natural immaterial.

Communication, the "villainous sorceress with evil powers," reduces every-thing to images. Wanting to know more, we know nothing. And as we overdose on information, cretinism runs rampant.

It is this Western-driven modernity that collides with Islam and its values. Islam helps people find equilibrium, the very thing lost under the auspices of modernity. It is utopian in the sense that it refuses despair and surrender. Yassine thus quotes Jacques Monod on utopia as not the unreal-izable but the not-yet-realized. For why would Muslims, wretched and poor, still provoke fear and anxiety? Why would a war of images be deployed against Islam?

Yassine reminds her readers that the West's anxiety over Islam has no end, even though Muslims, like most of the world's non-European peoples, live in European time (Greenwich) and are arranged in European space (Mercator projection). Europe, forged through the hatred of the Arab, is in fact the anti-Islam. Louis Triaud called it Europe's "Islamic unconscious," while Fernand Braudel used expressions such as the "Counter-West," the "other" Mediterranean. In short, Europe, to Yassine, is an anti-identity, but one that may nevertheless be useful to connect the two cultures.

I think Yassine raises an important issue that is often overlooked in the loud clash between the West and Islam, for if the West—that is to say, Western Europe's extensions in the modern world—exists as such only because it is that which is not Muslim, or perhaps what Edward Said might have said in his classic *Orientalism* (1978), "Oriental," then it would seem that blaming Islam for its inability to adapt to modernity, as we shall see in the next chapter, leaves out the contribution of the West to this seem-ingly insoluble dilemma of adaptation, since the West, as such, depends on the sharp dichotomy separating it from Islam, or the Orient. The prob-lem of Islam, read in this light, turns into a global ontological conundrum, since neither Islam nor the West could have existed, or perhaps exist, with-out the tensions and rivalries that divide and unite them at the same time. Islam and West turn into false categories, mere fictions, but indispensable nevertheless, since in the end most identities, in Benedict Anderson's famous statement, are imagined.[73]

But let's go back to Yassine. She doesn't spare despotic Muslim regimes, beginning with the bloodthirsty, scheming, tyrannical, undemocratic, elit-ist Umayyads. She thinks that the *fitna al-kubra* (Great Upheaval) is an axial moment in Islamic history. It led to the rise of extremisms, split Islam into two major trends (Shiism and Sunnism), instituted the cult of *fardiya* (individualism, one-man rule), and abrogated the recently acquired rights of women. These were all slidings (*glissements*) from the righteous caliphal culture that preceded the Umayyad reign, and so such a patriarchal culture deserves to be colonized, since it produces the worst possible women.

The time has come, then, to lift the veil on the purity of the Islamic message. After showing how the Bible is a patchwork of fictions, she unmasks European translations of the Qur'an (*translation* is betrayal: *traduir* and *trahir* share the same root in French, as *traduttore* and *traditore* do in Italian) to affirm the authenticity and miracle of the holy book. And after a typical tour of Islam's contribution to science, she reveals that in Islam knowledge and science are for humanist purposes (adoration/prayer), whereas in the secular West it works for power, violence, and domination/doubt. Finally, Yassine condemns corrupt Muslim powers and indicts Westernized postcolonial intellectuals as she works against an intense, dark, Cartesian, Darwinian modernist opaqueness, made worse by disinformation. And she does all this with her hair covered.

Though Yassine represents a progressive strain in the Islamic fundamentalist movement, she echoes much of the criticisms by fellow Muslims toward secular political and social arrangements, often the by-product of what has been variously referred to in this chapter as *jahiliyya,* a new Axial Age, or mere modernity. Well before October 10, 2003, when Morocco's king publicly declared his intention to give more rights to women (and children), the government had attempted to implement a series of laws to expand and protect women's rights, especially in the area of family law, still regulated by a strict Islamic doctrine.[74] But this well-intentioned and timely project encountered stiff resistance from Islamic groups, including women, who outnumbered their secular sisters in marches and public demonstrations (such as the one that took place on March 12, 2000).

The government's initiative (originally drafted in French and announced on March 19, 1999, as the *Plan d'action national pour l'intégration des femmes au développement*), which included new provisions on abortion, use of condoms, sexual preferences, was attacked as a Western ploy to introduce an un-Islamic morality to the country—never mind that these proposals were attempts to remedy real social situations. Raising the marriage age for women to eighteen and men to twenty, the Islamists argued, runs contrary to God's natural laws.[75] Moreover, de-Islamicizing family law would not make Morocco more competitive with the United States or other advanced Western economies, since such initiatives (including literacy programs for rural women) would have the effect of integrating more people into the capitalist economy and making them more dependent on the world's corporations.

Even the moderate minister of religious affairs at that time, Abdelkabir Alaoui M'daghri, author of *al-mara'tu bayna ahkam al-fiqhi wa a-da'wati ila a-taghyeer* (Women between religious law and the call for change), has strongly stated that there is "no freedom, dignity, or rights for Muslim women outside of Islam." In Islam, the minister has argued, certain laws are based on unambiguous textual truths that cannot be modified or altered without leading to *kufr* (disbelief), although the *fiqh* (jurisprudence) is open to rereading. On the issue of equality between men and women, M'daghri says that sex differences are affirmed in the Qur'an and that God's creation cannot be altered. Western women suffer because their societies do not extend to them the rights such as the ones prescribed in the Qur'an. By being forced to enter men's arenas and compete, Western women are being masculinized, even while Western men are being more feminized in the workplace. M'daghri opposes absolute gender equality since this concept leads to confusion and deforms the injustice it seeks to remedy— social chaos and family dysfunction being the prevailing state of affairs in secular societies. What are needed are justice, dignity, and fairness within the natural system of differences that Islam allows for. On the question of men's leadership (*qawwamun*) over women, M'daghri states that in Islam men are responsible for the dowry, maintenance, protection, and security of women. They are entrusted with this role because they are biologically stronger. The fact that women claim to have been oppressed in the past only proves this point, as 'Abbas Mahmoud al-'Aqad (the legendary Egyptian cultural critic) has pointed out, since both men and women shared the same social and natural conditions from which men emerged the dominant sex. Yet while affirming these natural differences, Islam deliberately disentangles them from the realm of arbitrary power. What women are opposing are exploitation and oppression, things that are rejected by Islam itself. The author is rather fuzzy on the difficult issue of inheritance. Moreover, like the Islamist critics of the government plan, M'daghri is opposed to raising the age of marriage, entrusting divorce decisions to courts (not husbands), giving custody of children to women who remarry, and he seems to be uncertain about a woman's dues in case of divorce. Even on the question of the veil, he sees no reason to challenge the conservative view: the veil allows women's bodies to be present/absent (*hadiran gha'iban fi nafsi al-waqt*) and is not an impediment to a productive life, as the case of Christian nuns continues to demonstrate.

Given this overwhelming response to the government's proposed reforms in 2000, I didn't expect substantial change in family law three years after the *Plan d'action national* had been scrapped. Had there been a popular plebiscite on women's rights in 2003, or had there been no determined royal will, I don't think the new family law would have seen the light of day. Even with the full power and authority of the king and government behind the new law, Moroccan men, I was told in a recent visit to Morocco, are conspiring with the '*udul* (family law judges) to circumvent its provisions.

Again, this is not an exclusively Muslim problem. We have seen in Armstrong's account of the new Axial Age of Reason, as Muslims are fighting out their future, non-Muslims are also wrestling with establishing secular laws derived from the European philosophical traditions. In Israel, for instance, religious edicts such as *shmita* ("the sabbatical when the land is supposed to lie fallow"), working and scheduling El Al flights on Saturdays, selling pork, or even establishing a constitution were still hotly contested issues by 2006. Orthodox Jews insist that constitutional law (even it were established) will never supersede religious law on matters of freedom of religion, marriage, and identity. Indeed, "it wasn't until 1992 that the subject of human rights was touched [in Israel]—and then incompletely," as the *New York Times* reported in 2000, "because of the controversy sparked by even the fundamental idea of making man, and not God, central."[76] Still, Orthodox Jewish women, like their Muslim peers, are now challenging the tenets of divinely sanctioned laws known as Halakha by organizing reading groups to read the Talmud, lead prayers, and even, with the complicity of sympathetic male teachers, be ordained as rabbis. (In 2005, two Muslim women, one an African American academic, the other a Moroccan immigrant in Italy, caused a major stir when they led or tried to lead prayers in mosques. For now, the most that can be granted to Muslim women is the role of *murshidat,* or counselors, as Morocco has started doing to tackle extremism.)[77] Such radical challenges to orthodoxy, however, are not necessarily driven by secular concerns as much as for the need to enhance awareness of Jewish law and give women a more central role in the Jewish tradition. In the United States, the modern Orthodox Joseph Lieberman's candidacy to the vice presidency in 2000 foregrounded the vexed issues of negotiating religious obligation with secular political principles. Lieberman's accommodations and Jewish women's demands for leadership involvement, however, are not shared by the uncompromisingly Orthodox, or, for that matter, Southern Baptists, one of whose intellectual leaders—R. Albert Mohler Jr., president of the Southern Baptist Theological Seminary—wrote to the *New York Times* affirming his community's attachment to biblical standards on gender and sexuality and the faithful's unambiguous rejection of modernity.[78]

There is another way in which Muslims and Jews, for instance, share common cultural experiences, and that is as minority religious communities in the classical lands of Christendom, mostly in Western Europe. Sander Gilman noted how Jews in the past and Muslims in the present have dealt not only with secularism but also with a barely disguised bias against both religions. "Scratch secular Europe today," writes Gilman, "and you will find long-held Christian presuppositions and attitudes toward Jews and Muslims present in subliminal or overt forms." The ongoing demonization of Muslims sounds so familiar that Gilman wonders whether the two communities should forge alliances.[79]

How, then, does one protect the rights of Muslim minorities in a Westernized world? One could argue that one must defend Judaism, Islam, Christianity, and other nonsecular traditions as vital cultures entitled to their own cosmologies in order to maintain a vibrant multicultural world that enhances diversity. But that leaves the question of modernity, or what the Qutb brothers called *jahiliyya,* a burning and unsettled issue. Making a case for religious rights is certainly indispensable, but that still doesn't answer the challenge posed to us by Sam Harris and Daniel Dennett about redefining the role of religion in a world far removed from and far more complex than the Middle Eastern milieus in which such religions first appeared. Progressive Islamists like Nadia Yassine do not seem to differ much with the conservatives and die-hard patriarchs they argue with, since both genuinely believe that Islam is the solution to modernity and the chaos it engenders in the world and in human hearts.

This consensus on basic fundamentals leads one to wonder whether Islam has become the unsurpassable horizon of people in Muslim societies, even those born to Muslim parents anywhere in the world. Are Muslim intellectuals forever banned from examining their traditions (*turath*) critically, relying on a rigorous rational examination of texts and cultures without conceding anything to revelation? Is modernity truly (perhaps fatally) incompatible with being Muslim? Can one be a Muslim without necessarily believing in the religion's myths of creation, or in its theology? Can one, in short, be Muslim without believing in Islam, or in prophecy, as Muslim heretics once did? How should Muslims define and deal with modernity? These are not new questions, and many answers have been given in the past. But they keep returning with the same urgency, as if decades, if not centuries, of discussion and debates are canceled by every new generation of Muslims, or by every new trend in scholarship. Even more important, can one be Muslim and modern without renouncing one's cultural singularity? Such a question begs more definitions, for merely to invoke the loaded term of *modernity* raises a host of issues, which in the case of Islam revolve around matters of authenticity and (abject) imitation. The solution of heresy, or *zandaqa* (explored at length in the final chapter of this book), may well be the best multidimensional solution to these nagging and unresolved questions. But for now we must examine the question of modernity in Islam and why outside solutions, including "regime change," are not the right answers.

chapter 3

Islam and Its Discontents

Books that cannot bear examination certainly ought not to be established as divine inspiration by penal laws.

—JOHN ADAMS

Texts have to be read as texts that were produced and live on in the historical realm in all sorts of what I have called worldly ways.

—EDWARD SAID, preface to the twenty-fifth anniversary edition of *Orientalism*

In the summer of 2005, a hard-hitting Moroccan weekly, *Le Journal Hebdomadaire,* reported on the case of a Moroccan state functionary in his forties, raised in a pure Muslim household, who was so overtaken by anxiety attacks that he couldn't go to work anymore and finally found his way to a psychiatrist's office in Casablanca. What drove this hapless man to this state was his growing doubt about the Qur'an as the word of God. The notion of apostasy (*ridda*) must have surely frightened him, for to change one's faith in a Muslim society (the number of Muslim-born converts to Christianity in Morocco has been a hotly disputed topic in recent years),[1] the magazine's dossier on the subject made clear, is something that cannot even be contemplated—it's *impensable* (in French); to proselytize on behalf of other religions is a crime punishable by a prison sentence ranging from six months to three years. People are still being tried and sent to jail for such offenses. Worse still, many religious scholars, such as the ubiquitous Dr. Yusuf al-Qaradawi, are clear about the punishment meted out to the apostate: death. All religious schools in the Muslim Sunni tradition agree on this. It was, therefore, not surprising to learn the following year about the genuine fright of a forty-nine-year-old Moroccan woman who speaks Hebrew fluently, had embraced Judaism, and was in the process of formally converting in Israel, where she had lived for ten years, when she had been threatened with deportation back to her native country for not being in the country legally. It was hard to imagine a worst case for a Muslim in the current global conditions.[2]

In *Le Journal Hebdomadaire,* a Moroccan university professor, Abdessamad Dialmy, noted that forcing Muslims to stay within the faith turns Islam into a biological fact (*fitra*) and forces them to be loyal subjects of the caliph (monarch, ruler), for the caliphal order takes precedence over notions of modern citizenship that form the basis of all world treaties designed to uphold civil rights. There is a Moroccan human rights organization actively engaged in defending the rights of citizens, in conformity with the Universal Declaration of Human Rights (UDHR) and the 1979 International Covenant on Civil and Political Rights, but few cases of this sort reach its desk, another telling indicator about social mores. Never mind, as Dialmy puts it: Moroccans are primarily "geographical and cultural Muslims" whose fear of social rejection keeps them away from the fundamental right of examining and choosing their own beliefs. If apostasy is still a punishable crime and social taboo in what is arguably the most liberal society in the Arab world, the burden on freethinkers is worse since Islamist groups have made it a point of their ideological agenda to identify apostates and make them targets of their furious piety.[3] Thus it would seem that a person born in a Muslim society has no right to think for him- or herself, a situation that is vital to unraveling the crisis besetting the Muslim world today. For as Dialmy puts it, "the struggle for religious freedom in today's Muslim societies is the main struggle, the key to the major problems of political power, the family, women, and sexuality."[4]

Given this environment, liberal publications such as *Le Journal* or *TelQuel,* another daring weekly (both weeklies are routinely sued), resort to the old tactic of medieval heretical writers, the *zanadiqa,* whose poetic license allowed them to express views that might otherwise be dangerously unpopular. Thus in its issue of May 14, 2005, *TelQuel* featured the great liberal (and libertine) traditions of Islam from around 740 to 1200 A.D., evoking the decadent nightlife of Baghdad in the late eighth century, with its literary salons, mixed company, and the free flowing of wine and verse. Writers and poets are highlighted in a special section: like the Arab Persian Abu Nuwwas (762–813), the "libertine of Baghdad" and "happy transgressor" (as Abdelwahab Medeb calls him), the spokesman for what his contemporaries called the Modernist School, the poet who preferred the pleasures of Baghdad to the solemnity of Mecca; the Sufi Al-Hallaj (857–922); the skeptic Abul ʿAlaʾ al-Maʿarri (973–1058); the famous twelfth-century Aristotelian philosopher and commentator Ibn Rushd (known in the West as Averroës), who, relying on ancient Greek philosophers (the *qudama* or *umam as-salifa,* as ancient Greeks were called then), affirmed the equality of men and women without negating real sex differences. But there are others, like the philosophers Al-Jahidh (d. 869) and Al-Farabi (d. 950), the theologian Ibn al-Rawandi, the disciple of the great philosopher Al-Kindi (d. 870); Al-Sarakhsi (d. around 899); the physician and thinker Abu Bakr Razi;[5] the poets Ibn Hazm (993–1064) and Omar al-Khayyam (1038–1124). All were *zanadiqa,* in one way or another, although some got away with their views because their poetry and language skills gave them safe passage.[6]

Are such uncensored publications stirrings of liberal change, one might ask? Maybe, but to stay with the example of Morocco in 2005, what is one to make of the case of Nadia Yassine, whose views I sketched out at some length in the previous chapter, the daughter of Sheikh Abdeslam Yassine, the leader of the outlawed Islamic organization *alʿadl wal ihssan* (Justice and Charity) and herself a grandmother and member of her father's organization. After a visit to the United States and a talk at Berkeley, she publicly stated her preference for a republican political system, thereby indicting Morocco's monarchical regime. A progressive Western-educated Muslim who champions women's rights, she has irked Westernized liberals and conservative Islamists alike, not least because she is perfectly fluent in French and Islamic cultures.[7] *Le Journal* and *TelQuel* may speak for a mostly secular (albeit still Muslim) constituency, while Nadia Yassine speaks for a particular Islamic ideology. Accepting the fact that state religion and Islamism are discredited everywhere, are these the best options available to Muslim reformers today? A nondescript secularism and a progressive Islam? For the most part, the answer is yes, not least because even some of the most ardent secularists generally stay within the broad parameters of the Islamic faith. Yet the attempt to break away from orthodoxy and shatter the prison house of the *impensable* has been going on for at least two centuries, so far without making a noticeable difference.

A scholar invited by *Le Journal Hebdomadaire* to give some perspective on apostasy in Islam is Rachid Benzine, one of the most sought-after commentators on the reform movement in Islam and the author of a book that seems to have had some impact on the Moroccan public scene. His *Les nouveaux penseurs de l'islam* (The new thinkers of Islam) is, in some ways, a testament to the long struggle to redefine Islam in at least the past two centuries, and the still uncertain outcome of such attempts. A significant number of scholars, preachers, and anticolonial activists have been preaching change, some going as far as to call for a reevaluation of Islam and the Qur'an. One can legitimately say that Islam has been—and still is—undergoing a process of radical rethinking, often fraught with tensions and perils, but one that nevertheless belies the notion of a monolithic, unchanging, and uncontested notion of the religion. This process of reform, initially dubbed *nahda,* meaning Awakening or Revival, was initiated by activist scholars like the tireless Persian speaker Jamal al-Din al-Afghani (1838–1897), known in the Arab world as the Sage of the East (*hakim al-sharq*), who left no written corpus, and his disciple, later Egypt's grand mufti, Mohammed Abdu (1849–1905), a scholar who espoused rational and progressive approaches. But Abdu's disciple, the Syrian Mohammed Rashid Rida (1865–1935), distorted his master's capacious, open, and pluralistic model in favor of a more traditionalist approach, one later espoused by the Wahhabis and Hassan al-Banna (1906–1949), the founder of the Muslim Brothers. (Benzine astutely reminds his readers that the weakening and fall of the long-decadent and conservative Ottoman Empire gave rise to the birth of the pro-Wahhabi Saudi regime and the state of Israel, both events with major consequences in the course of modern Muslim and Arab histories.)[8]

To be sure, the encounter of the West and Islam has caused serious "traumas"[9] from the very start, but the most recent cataclysmic shock to Islam is clearly the landing of Napoleon Bonaparte, on July 1, 1798, in Alexandria and the invasion of Egypt. It was a brief occupation (three years), but it did have a major impact on the rest of Arab and Muslim history, as Muslims awakened to their weakness in relation to a powerful and still-ascending Europe. To jump-start their development, Muslim scholars scrambled to reconcile Islam and the West, with Francophile figures like Sheikh Rifa a-Rifa al-Tahtawi (1801–1873) and the blind scholar Taha Hussein (1889–1973) taking the lead. Politically, the task of violently secularizing an Islamic political entity in the image of the French model would fall on the Turk Mustafa Kemal Atatürk (1880–1938).

Rare among these reformers were the radical, forward-looking, and progressive scholars like the Delhi-born Sayyid Ahmad Khan (1817–1889) (known as "Sir Sayyid") and the Egyptian Ali Abderraziq (1888–1966), who, in 1925, one year after the collapse of the Ottoman caliphate, refuted the legal view that religion and politics were indissociable in Islam, a view that incurred the wrath of the religious and political establishments but is still alive in the work of Mohammed Saïd al-Ashmawy. The literature of reform between, say, the mid–nineteenth century and 1940, is actually rich and varied; traditionalists were countered by preachers of syntheses (such as Taha Hussein), arguing that the larger Mediterranean sphere had long united Islam and Europe. It is also worth noting that admirers of the West often thought of France, not the still-distant United States, as the model.[10]

One noteworthy contemporary reformer is Abdul Karim Soroush (his real name is Hossein Dabbagh), a daring scholar who brings together his early scientific education, his self-taught knowledge of Western philosophy, and the writings of a variety of Muslim scholars to call for a new open theology dubbed *kalam jadid*. Religion, in this view, may be divine and celestial, but its interpretation is, in the words of Benzine, "human and terrestrial." Because the Muslim crisis unleashed by the confrontation with modernity resulted in the "ideologization of religion" through an overemphasis on the legalism of *fiqh* and *sharia* at the expense of ethics and spirituality, and the emergence of an Islam of identity, religion has turned into an authoritarian instrument, not a philosophy of dialogue and freedom, both of which are essential to democracy. Thus Soroush champions critical reason against the hermeneutic one, skepticism against absolutism, rights against obligations, and the love of God (the essence of Islam) against opportunistic religiosities.[11]

Mohammed Arkoun, the Kabyle (Berber) Algerian son of a grocer and himself at one point on track to be so, is now the world-renowned but controversial professor emeritus at the Sorbonne who spent much of his career uncovering the Arab humanist legacy of the tenth century (in figures such as Ibn Miskawayh) and challenging orthodox theologians and jurists, whose job is to "manage the sacred" and guide consciences. He values the cultural over the theological and wants to subject religion to an "interrogative reason" (*raison interrogative*). He also pays careful attention to the complex Qur'anic phenomenon: the Qur'an as the Word of God; the Qur'anic discourse, meaning the oral transmission of the Word of God to the Prophet during a limited period of time (610–32) and, through him, to his companions; and the gathering of the revelation in one volume, the *mus'haf* (a project that took place between 632 and 661, that is, in about thirty years).

Arkoun notes that the Qur'an undergoes a tremendous shift when it passes from its oral phase to the written one, since the oral phase was dialogical, self-correcting, palimpsest-like, whereas the written one immediately conferred a sacredness on the text and made textual negotiations almost impossible. God was addressing the human conscience in the oral phase, whereas the written one, a feature of the Islamic event (as opposed to the Qur'anic one), narrowed the scope of God's revelation.[12] By the tenth century, the forces of orthodoxy were busy establishing the parameters of what is intellectually permissible and impermissible in the domain of thought (*pensable* and *impensable*), explaining that the time has now come, through anthropological and genealogical readings (Michel Foucault is one of the influential figures on Arkoun) to bring the *impensable* out of the shadows. Thus, the Islamic imaginary, shaped by the advent of the *mus'haf,* needs to be deconstructed. Muslims, like most so-called People of the Book (mostly, in this case, the Abrahamic religions), need to revitalize their relationship to religion and the Qur'an through the lenses of linguistics, history, anthropology, hermeneutics, psychology, and other academic fields. Such an approach would allow Muslims a better examination of the "semantic foundation" (*couche sémantique*) of the Qur'an and thus break open the locks of "fossilized" tradition. For Arkoun, also influenced by the work of Fernand Braudel, the Islamic event is mostly a Mediterranean one, part of a wider circle of cultures and civilizations that appeared around this basin.[13]

Mohammed Abdu, Taha Hussein, and Sayyid Qutb applied the technique of literary analysis to the Qur'an, but it is the Egyptian Amin al-Khuli (1895–1966) and his graduate student Mohammed Khalafallah who are the precursors of this still embryonic movement. To look for literary tropes in the Qur'an would imply that the Revelation is similar to other human literary creations and thus would take away from its divinity, since the miracle of the Qur'an relies, for the most part, on its inimitability, or *i'jaz,* a fact that itself relies on the intellectual neutrality of the prophet, the empty vessel theory, the notion that the prophet is a mere conduit to God's message without any human imprint whatsoever. Yet of course the Qur'an is revealed in a human language—Arabic—one that was widely spoken in the region. Moreover, as some of these scholars would argue (beginning with Mohammed Abdu's commentary, *tafsir al-manar,* itself influenced by the work of the medieval philologist and literary critic Abdal-Qahir al-Jurjani [d. 1078] in his famous work *The Inimitability of the Glorious Qur'an*), the Qur'an is not a work of history but an ethical and spiritual guide. Taha Hussein, who studied under Émile Durkheim in France, got in trouble for dismissing the famous pre-Islamic odes against which the Qur'an was and still is measured for its miraculous prose and for claiming that the story of Abraham in the Qur'an was meant to facilitate coexistence among the three monotheistic faiths, even while it asserted the primacy of Islam. Even Sayyid Qutb, who began his career with a literary analysis of the Qur'an, as in his 1947 book, *mashahid al-qiyama fi al-qur'an,* dealing with the last day and the resurrection, was criticized by Hassan al-Banna, the founder of the Muslim Brothers.

But none proved more controversial than Amin al-Khuli and Muhammed Khalafallah, both erudite memorizers of the Qur'an at an early age. Al-Khuli, whom Benzine considers "the first modern Muslim scholar to have employed the literary method to analyze the Qur'an" and the "spiritual father" of this method, not only saw unity among all religions, but he also saw the Qur'an as the Arabs' most influential, most representative literary piece. He believed that the Qur'an doesn't have the same impact without a thorough knowledge of the Arabic language (a view that led him to work on a dictionary of the Qur'an) and the context of the Revelation. In other words, one has to have a good grasp of the dominant, local Arab spirit of the Prophet's time to appreciate the Qur'an; such knowledge is in fact indispensable. And like Abdu, Al-Khuli saw the Qur'an primarily as an ethical and religious document, not a record of history or cosmology.

Al-Khuli's influence would be carried on by his student and wife, Aisha Abdul Rahman, better known as Bint al-Shati'. Until her death in 1998, she worked to make her teacher and husband's work better known. But it is Mohammed Khalafallah (born before 1916 and died in 1998, the same year as Bint al-Shati') who provoked a major controversy with his 1947 polemical dissertation on the art of narration in the Qur'an. After breaking the narrative structure into historical, metaphorical (analogical), and legendary stories, he argued that the tales of Adam and Iblis (Satan), Noah, Abraham, Moses, and others were designed to give advice and provide comfort to the prophet Mohammed as he embarked on his trying prophetic mission; they were part of a divine pedagogy, part of a structure of warning (*'ibra*). When such ideas leaked out, his dissertation director, Al-Khuli, was fired and a *fatwa* declared him an apostate. (Khalafallah later changed the subject of his thesis but stuck to his mentor for a director.) His dissertation would be published in 1951 and reprinted two years later, and more recently in 1999.[14]

The case of Nasr Hamid Abu Zayd, the Egyptian scholar who "revived" Amin al-Khuli's call for a literary analysis of the Qur'an, and the pioneer of a new hermeneutics, is also telling. Another one who memorized the Qur'an early in life, he studied Arabic literature, delving into the works of such luminary literary critics as Taha Hussein, Mohammed Haykal, and Sayyid Qutb, and later mastered English through study at American University of Cairo, the University of Pennsylvania, and a four-year teaching stint at the University of Osaka in Japan. It was during this stay that he wrote two books on the textual analysis of the Qur'an (published in 1990 and 1992, respectively). In 1992, the year he married Dr. Ibtihal Yunis, a professor of French and comparative literature, his bid for full professorship was turned down and he was charged with apostasy. In 1995 and 1996, Egyptian courts found him guilty and nullified his marriage to Dr. Yunis on such grounds. The list of charges against him included the denial of the existence of angels and *jinns* (genies), the claim that certain descriptions of heaven and hell are "mythical," his presentation of the text of the Qur'an as a "human text," and his use of reason to discuss issues like inheritance, women, and minorities. Although the university reexamined his bid for tenure and granted it on May 31, 1995, he accepted an invitation from the University of Leiden in the Netherlands and left with his wife later that summer.

In his work, Abu Zayd has sought to renew the legacy of medieval scholars— Abu ʿUbayda (d. 825), Al-Jahidh, ʿAbd al-Jabbar (d. 1024), Abd al-Qahir al-Jurjani, and Al-Zamakhshari (d. 1144)—who thought it was natural to apply literary criticism to the text of the Qur'an. For Abu Zayd considers the Qur'an one of the world's great literary works, a text that has had an immense influence on the visual arts (calligraphy) and music (*tajweed*). Once freed from its intimidating stick-and-carrot structure, the text of the Qur'an (not the source or the transmission) opens up to analysis just like any other human text. The collected *mus'haf* certainly doesn't follow the chronological order of the Revelation (Medina verses do not follow Meccan ones), a fact that inevitably affects the context. Moreover, a scientific approach could help with abrogated passages. In short, the content of the Qur'an is a form of human communication—hasn't the Qur'an been revealed in Arabic to give Arabic-speaking people their own holy book?—and must thus respond to the basic rules of language and communication analysis.[15] Let's not forget that the Qur'an was first experienced as an oral event and its "canonization" into a written text could not help but modify its reception. Rearranging and transforming the Qur'an into a canonized document destroyed the historical context and naturally privileged the "semantic structure" over the original reality of the Revelation. The Qur'an that we read is in no way identical to the "eternal World of God."

Influenced by the work of the Russian semiotician Jurji M. Lotman (Abu Zayd translated two of Lotman's books), Abu Zayd, while affirming the fixity of the original historical context, sees interpretation (*ta'weel,* not the more superficial *tafseer*) as changing with contexts, since the context of reception is as important to the meaning of the Holy Book as the text itself. Abu Zayd's hermeneutics thus emphasizes the inevitable subjectivity of all forms of interpretation, leading to a "coloration" (*talween*) that can only be averted through an awareness of the reading process itself. Be that as it may, reading the Qur'an involves psychological, ontological, scientific, sociological, existential, phenomenological, and theological aspects, all of which determine meaning and the reading experience.

Another scholar who agrees with much of this thinking is Abdelmajid Charfi (b. 1942), one of a number of Tunisian intellectuals rethinking the meaning of Islam, following in the footsteps on Mohamed Talbi (b. 1921, whose recent reflections I will discuss below). Charfi thinks that reform could only come out of the mosque and privileges the Qur'an as the only guiding text for Muslims, while playing down the Sunna, for not being consistent with the Qur'anic message or for being based (as in the case of the *hadith*) on dubious transmission (*isnad*) grounds. A prolific author who writes exclusively in Arabic, Charfi points out that in the writing of the Qur'an and the limiting of the range of interpretations (as the fear of dissipation haunted members of an expanding empire), the dialogic nature of the Revelation (essential in an oral culture, one in which the Prophet brought his own subjectivity to the process) was lost in the "canonization" of the message. Though minimal in number (between 220 and 250 out of 6,200 verses), the juridical and legalistic verses somehow came to dominate the ethical and spiritual dimensions. The Qur'an didn't detail the five pillars of Islam, prescribe ablutions (an older, albeit different, Jewish practice) or prayer prostration techniques (a Syrian method); it doesn't talk about apostasy, nor is it as prescriptive about individual or social practices as is assumed today. (Bruno Étienne, in his book *Islam, les questions qui fachent,* adds that neither jihad nor circumcision is a canonical obligation [*fard*] in Islam; each is merely a custom.)[16] Thus literalistic readings and the institutionalization of Islam have in effect canceled the spirits of freedom and coexistence inherent in the Revelation. Not only that, but the notion of Mohammed as the seal of prophets imposes closure on human development and impedes people from drawing their own conclusions from the long legacy of monotheistic prophecy. What Charfi understands by the notion of sealed prophecy is that God affirmed that humans are henceforth capable of thinking for themselves and no longer need the procession of prophets who had punctuated human history until then; sealing prophecy announces the advent of mature, independent human beings, not their enclosure in an unchanging orthodoxy. For these reasons, Islam must be reclaimed from conservative tradition, since our reality is radically different from that of early Muslims. Moreover, such a process of liberation can only happen in a secular environment, one in which the individual is fully free to choose as he or she pleases.[17]

There are obviously others who have questioned Islamic dogmas, people like the South African activist/scholar Farid Esack, who preaches an Islamic liberation theology, one that addresses all forms of injustice, including those within Islam. Most of the authors in Benzine's book are at the vanguard of what the Moroccan philosopher Abdou Filali-Ansary calls a "new Islamic consciousness" based on a liberating hermeneutics. Again and again, we keep going back to the polysemic nature of the Qur'anic text—at once the Word of God, a literary masterpiece, a historical document in the sense that it sheds light on the Arabian culture of seventh- and eighth-century

Hijaz, a source of legends, a code of law, and so on; it's a text that is long overdue for the application of the most advanced theories in linguistics and literary analysis. There is no reading without reader (is there a God without humans?), just as every reading is in fact a rereading, or even a new reading (new creation? new revelation?), since the context of reading is never the same. In short, Muslims need to assume, in the words of Arkoun, a "plural, changing, and welcoming rationality" (*une rationalité plurielle, changeante, accueillante*).[18]

While in Morocco in the summer of 2005, I also picked up a small book published that year by the grandfather of what has been termed the Tunisian school of Islamic reformers, Mohamed Talbi. Titled *Réflexions d'un musulman contemporain* (Reflections of a contemporary Muslim) and prefaced by Abdou Filali-Ansary, the book, available for about $1.25, is a remarkable glimpse at the problems facing Muslims today.[19] Filali-Ansary gets right to the point by asking, "How can one be a Muslim today?" If one thinks about it, this is a remarkable question, one that would have made no sense before, since Islam provides the certitudes to avoid such questioning in the first place. Filali-Ansary notes that whether for the believing Muslim or the cultural one, the past, with its own mind-sets and social orders, is no longer a reliable reference. Islam needs to be rethought, and so Filali-Ansary opens the door to Talbi, the scholar who has been pondering such change in Islam for decades.

A practicing Muslim influenced by Freud, Talbi makes it clear that Muslims need to liberate themselves from the past by better understanding it.[20] He casts his wide-ranging commentary on the reading of the Qur'an, the concept of the *umma,* the necessity of *ijtihad*—he calls it "permanent quest"[21]—the importance of straightening out misleading semantic ambiguities and imprecisions (terms such *hurr* and *mulhid*), and the need for a secular democratic space that allows for all thoughts and convictions to coexist. Talbi is right to remind us that Islam is as powerful a mobilizing force against injustice today as it was against colonialism before, and that the secular language of orthodox Marxism has no sway over "masses . . . imprinted by a diffuse and omnipresent religiosity" (the same situation, I might add, has long obtained in the United States); but to kill apostates in the name of Islam is a horror that destroys the very possibility of pluralism and "peaceful cohabitation."[22] This form of terrorism is what has delayed the advancement of Muslim societies and kept them pitifully behind.

Sometimes this violence toward the Other begins, benignly enough, in acts of sincere piety, for if sincere belief is not grounded in a democratic structure, it can easily build up toward fanaticism. Atheists—he prefers the adjective *nufati* (denier [of God's existence]), from the Arabic *yanfi,* borrowed from the Levantine poet Abul ʿAlaʾ al-Maʿarri[23]—must have a place in the sociopolitical order and a right to their beliefs. In short, Talbi has no alternative model to the status quo (how could there be one when Saudi Arabia and Iran, for instance, each have a system they think is best?)—only the absolute necessity to free ourselves from fear, participate in a universal modernity, promote total freedom of thought and expression, and institute a secular democratic order.[24] He continues:

> The West has acceded to democracy by claiming its history. It situates itself in a process of continuity and discontinuity, diachronically and synchronically with it. This tension created modernity, which is neither rupture nor linear process. It is the stimulus created by this tension that has made the West powerful and ensures its creative intellectual powers. Modernity is a permanent creative force; it is the energy that propels forward; it is the spirit of conquest of knowledge that improves the sort of humans daily. It is the force of overcoming. Do we [Arab Muslims] realize that modernity is all this?[25]

Hichem Djaït's collection of articles on Islam, written over the span of twenty years before 9/11, and now collected in *La crise de la culture Islamique* (The crisis of Islamic culture), also makes a strong case for the absolute necessity to embrace modernity, here defined as the latest stage in human development.[26] For human history has known or undergone three main modernities: the emergence of homo sapiens; the advent of the Neolithic Age about ten thousand years ago, with its invention of agriculture, religion, sedentary life, its hydraulic cultures and great civilizations; and finally, the "third modernity" that emerged in eighteenth-century Europe, building on the past and creating a new outlook altogether. Muslims live in this age and are part of it; they just haven't gotten ready to catch up to its premises and absorb them, as have Japan, Korea, and China, for instance.[27]

To be sure, European narcissistic attitudes (their sense of their greatness and low view of others) are partly to blame, but Islamism reflects the Muslims' intellectual poverty. "For fifty years," writes Djaït, "our countries have been [mired] in a cultural desert, affecting all fields, including our heritage as well as the appropriation of Western culture, in books, painting, theater, music, in areas of science as well as literature."[28] Though rarely—and only briefly—colonized throughout much of their history (as during the Crusades and the Mongol invasions), Muslims have been caught unawares by the advent of the history-shattering event of modernity, by what is now a decidedly universal heritage, not one that is limited to the Euro-American sphere. Moreover, Islam came to a standstill around 1500, and the West had nothing to do with that. Djaït is aware of how difficult change is for Muslims: "It needs time, effort, and a change of values."[29] We are talking here about subjectivities, the need to work on oneself (*un travail de soi sur soi*). Also we must realize that Muslims, unlike the Japanese or the Chinese, don't have a centralized state to push change; the *umma* "is a spiritual nation, which is in itself enormous and very little at the same time,"[30] because it doesn't have state structures, and if one wants to be happy in this world, one has to work within its material systems (that is, the state).

The crisis that Djaït identifies is in fact an overblown illness, a sickness, in the provocative title of Abdelwahab Meddeb's *La maladie de l'islam*.[31] Since nations are imagined, Meddeb, who is "symbolically constituted in the Islamic faith"[32] but chooses to be part of France and its secular legacies without giving up his Muslim genealogy, diagnoses Islam with the *maladie* of fundamentalism (the inexact translation of the French *intégrisme*).[33] As he puts it, "If fanaticism was the illness of Catholicism and Nazism the illness of Germany, fundamentalism is the sickness of Islam."[34] To trace the genealogy of this *maladie,* Meddeb goes back to one of the founders of the four Sunni schools, the eighth- and ninth-century scholar Ahmed ibn Hanbal (780–855). Ibn Hanbal preached the return to the golden age, glossing over the fact that three out of the four righteous caliphs were assassinated and that "a great deal of Muslim history unfolded in violence and civil war."[35] Ibn Hanbal's radical disciple, the Syrian theologian Ibn Taymiyya (d. 1328), having lived through moments of great danger to Islam during the Mongol invasions while the memory of the Crusades was still alive, devoted his life to denouncing and purging accretions, such as Sufism, from the literal body of Islam, and made the idea of holy war, or jihad, a major tenet of the religion, in fact, elevating it over four other pillars of Islam. He didn't leave a strong impression on the inveterate Moroccan traveler from Tangier, Ibn Battuta, who thought the Syrian theologian a bit deranged.[36] Yet it was the voice of this bellicose and censoring man that would be privileged by Islamists of the modern era, beginning with Mohammed ibn ʿAbd al-Wahhab (1703–1792), the unoriginal scholar from Najd who led the destruction of saints' tombs, so that today one cannot find a single saint's tomb in the whole country.[37] ʿAbd al-Wahhab's mediocrity was denounced at the time by other Muslim scholars, and the Wahhabites were chased out from the Hijaz by the Egyptian forces of Mohammed Ali. But his ideology took hold, and with the takeover of his old allies the Saud clan became the official doctrine of the country in 1932. Such a fringe theology may not have amounted to much, but with their petrodollars and technology, the Saudis exported its tenets around the world and did great damage to Islam by weakening the religion's creative powers.[38]

It helps to remember that reformers like Al-Afghani and his disciple Abdu were fascinated by European culture with its Enlightenment legacy and invoked it to combat local despotism.[39] Yet by the early decades of the twentieth century, Islamic activism acquired an anti-Western stance, culminating in the dark world of Sayyid Qutb, a man for whom "everything is wrong in human history and in actual life, every thought, every representation is so lacking that it needs to be abolished; everything—except the word of God as revealed in the Quran—must disappear."[40] The conjunction of such views with Wahhabism produced the worst type of Islamism (exemplified, perhaps, in the *sahwa,* as we saw in the previous chapter). Saudi Arabia welcomed the semiliterate graduates of Al-Azhar seeking employment in the 1970s. These Red Sea crossings forged a partnership between these two world visions, later implanted in Pakistan (the birthplace of Mawdudi, who had inspired Qutb) and in Afghanistan—the Taliban and Al-Qaeda, which at the time of this writing is run by a Saudi and an Egyptian.[41]

Meddeb also blames the amorphous, ideologically defined West for its refusal to acknowledge Islam as a form of internal alterity, its ways of excluding Islam, the ways in which it forfeits its principles and (in the guise of the American) extends its hegemony and uses double standards against Arabs and Muslims.[42] In fact, Meddeb sees striking common cultural traits among Americans and Saudis. Reflecting on Connecticut's code of 1650, as reported by Tocqueville, he finds the same violence against difference (based on biblical doctrines) and wonders whether Wahhabi Arabia and Puritanical America were baptized from the same font.[43] The culture of Saudi Arabia shouldn't, in his view, be shocking to Americans; even Ibn

Hanbal is recorded to have said that becoming wealthy is a divine duty, a fortune that, according to Ibn Taymiyya, should be at the service of the religion. The Islamists' war against pleasure, sensuality, seduction, and the aesthetic in general, and their elevation of blandness and prudishness as virtues shouldn't be unfamiliar to American puritans.[44] As Timothy Marr has shown in *The Cultural Roots of American Islamicism,* the rise of the Wahhabi movement on the fringes of the Ottoman Empire was, in fact, viewed quite positively by a few American Protestant ministers dreaming of removing the anti-Christian force of Islam from the Holy Land. In this reading, Wahhabism was a reform movement that would pave the way for the fall of Islam and the rise of Christianity; it would, as one Edward Dorr Griffin preached in 1813, help "banish the religion of Mahomet from the world." Perhaps this attitude explains why such kinship between the two worldviews endured all the way to the present, or why, as Meddeb put it, the Muslim who wages war against beauty and difference "can adopt the American way of life and still hold on to his archaic ways."[45]

This relationship between the United States and Saudi Arabia cemented over oil interests would not be disturbed until the ultimate Wahhabi, "the Wahhabi of Wahhabis," Osama bin Laden, emerged to produce what Gilles Kepel called *fitna* in the world.[46] To those with short memories, Meddeb reiterates that the Taliban are the "pure product of local Islamist traditions (Mawdudi), confirmed by Wahhabism (whose propagation is officially financed by Saudi Arabia through a network of religious schools that spreads its tentacles anywhere it can)."[47] It would be these same half-educated iconoclastic Taliban who, ignoring a significant medieval literature on Buddhism, blew up the United Nations–protected giants of Bamiyan on March 9, 2001, while the world watched in horror. Meddeb then wonders why politicians couldn't see that the destruction of the Buddhas was the prelude to the destruction of the Twin Towers in New York City ("the Buddhas of Wall Street," as Arjun Appadurai called them) and the massacre of human beings; why is it that our "decision makers," consumed by technical reasoning, couldn't make the connection between the symbolic and the real? "Aren't [the Taliban], even in their archaism, the unconscious children of the Americanization of the world? Dare I affirm that, if we had exercised our right of intervention to save the Buddhas, we could have avoided the loss of the Twin Towers in New York? Aren't the two sequences of destruction part of the same drama?"[48]

In Meddeb's account, Islamic extremism and terrorism are features of the Americanization of the world, a simultaneous adaptation and reaction to it. While European culture has changed social behavior, ranging from dress to culture, in the Muslim world (see the discussion of Bernard Lewis below), by 2001, "we have passed from the deconstruction of myths to their restoration, from the unveiling of women to their re-veiling. In short, we have changed eras. The world in its westernization has passed from the European way to the American one." The 9/11 "terrorists are as much a product of their societies' own internal evolution, proper to Islam, as they are the children of their age and of a world metamorphosed by Americanization."[49]

Bruno Étienne's primer on Islam also concludes that the problem may well be the alliance of Saudi neofundamentalists and their American peers.[50] As I mentioned in the introduction, even Marc Anna, known as Alexandre Del Valle, a far-right expert on fear, warns against the collusion of fundamentalist Islam and WASP American Protestantism in his book *Islamisme et États-Unis: Une alliance contre l'Europe:* "The two civilizations, Islamic and Americo-Puritan, are both founded on the total eradication of millennial cultures [*cultures plurimillénaires*] that have preceded them." Muslim fundamentalists and WASP Puritans are both against Europe as they try to annihilate the cultural identity of Europeans. This new, anti-European order appeared so real that Jean-Pierre Péroncel-Hugoz, a reporter for the prestigious *Le Monde* and author of a 1983 book (*Le radeau de Mahomet*) warning against the rising threat of Islam to Europe, wrote an afterword to Del Valle's book, forging a new term to describe this alliance, *Islamerica*. For the Del Valle of before 9/11 (he has since been rehabilitated to fit into the new security expert doctrine, erasing the United States and its allies from his discourse, and reducing his apocalyptic warning to Islam alone), the United States, through its "McWorld civilization," is engineering a "cultural genocide," even as Muslims are bent on the theological and demographic conquest of Europe. Thus it behooves European defense experts to confront the enemy's new weapons of mass destruction, like "MTV, M6, Fun Radio, NRJ, McDonald's," and Hollywood.[51]

Such views, together with the books and authors mentioned above, show unambiguously that quite a few—though one must be careful not to exaggerate the trend—Arab and Muslim intellectuals are actively engaged in assessing their legacy and religious traditions in the age of modernity. The difference between their work, though, and, say, the sweeping commentaries of senior Orientalists like Bernard Lewis is that despite their criticism of Arab Muslim culture they also castigate the West for contributing to the Muslim predicament. When taken in isolation, Lewis's diagnosis of what went wrong with Islam is for the most part right; still, what Lewis leaves out is in the end as important as what he chooses to highlight.[52] The history of rivalry between Christianity and Islam does explain why members of others faiths—Hindus, Buddhists, or Confucians—had an easier time adopting European modernity and why Muslims failed to divine "the talisman of Western success" because they attributed their failure to religious or political causes.[53] However, this is not to say that Muslims are incapable of living up to the modern age. Although many Muslim scholars have repeatedly stated that Europe, and then the West, have had a long head start over Islam by virtue of being the birthplace of what Djaït calls the third modernity, Muslims do live in the modern age. To say, for instance, that the Muslims' propensity for tales, recitation, and chronicles or annals, as opposed to the West's interest in the novel, theater, and history, is a marker of the Muslims' democratic deficit is a stretch.[54] Muslims are doing quite well in the West's art forms, although one could agree with Lewis that just "as some Europeans managed to create a Christianity without compassion, so did some Middle Easterners create a democracy without freedom."[55]

Despite its social constraints, Islam was far more tolerant than and never as prosecutorial as Christendom in the precolonial period, but it has fallen way behind on the issue of human rights in the past two centuries.[56] Though women, slaves, and non-Muslims were canonized as communities set apart from free male Muslims, all three, up until the twentieth century, enjoyed human rights not always available to their peers elsewhere. Britain did much to curtail the slave trade, but Muslims also came to abhor the practice. The work of the Moroccan historian Ahmed Khalid al-Nasiri (1834–1897), the decree of the Bey of Tunis enfranchising black slaves in 1846, and Ottoman mid–nineteenth century reforms granting equal status to non-Muslims (all measures influenced, to some extent, by Europe) made many Muslims anxious. In the Hijaz, for instance, Sheikh Jamal, the Chief of the *ulema* of Mecca, issued a *fatwa* denouncing these reforms and thereby authorizing the killing and enslavement of infidel Turks.

Still, slaves and non-Muslims gradually gained more rights, but the journey was tougher for women, although women like the Persian Qurrat al-ʿAyn (1814–1852) and Princess Taj es-Saltana militated on behalf of women's rights and had an impact, including on the constitutional revolution of 1906–11.[57]

To Lewis, Muslims have been playing the "blame game"—depending on the time and season, accusing Mongols, Christians, imperialists, Jews, Americans, bad Muslims—without changing their condition.[58] Yet ironically what they blame others for is in fact not a cause but an index of their failure. For Lewis, adopting secularism and fully enfranchising women are the only hope that Islam has left in the near future to overcome its deadly impasse.[59] But this may not be easy to do. Because Mohammed was a prophet and statesman at once, there has never been a separation of state and church in Islam. No church imposing an orthodoxy ever came into being, either. Only the "Holy Law of God, promulgated by revelation," "amplified and interpreted by tradition and reasoning" counts. To change or alter rules, rulers simply resort to disguise (the sort of *hila* resorted to by the king of Morocco when he decreed the overhaul of family law by quoting selectively from Islamic texts).[60] While no Arabic expression seems to encompass the notion of secularism or the French *laïcité* (neither does English in the latter case), terms such as *ladini, almani,* and *ilmani* (as Talbi also pointed out) connote different meanings. This doesn't mean that Muslims have no experience in what is now called "civil society": the *waqfs* (religious and charitable endowments), Sufi fraternities, guilds, clans, and neighborhoods provided many protections to the individual and community, but there are no corporate legal persons in Islamic law (such as cities and colleges).[61] Finally, though secularism was initially devised as the solution to a very Christian problem, it may well be the answer to Muslim states and the only Jewish state in the Middle East.[62]

There we have it: no serious mention of the role of the West and its colonial policies toward the Middle East in general. To find out how the West has exacerbated the Muslim predicament is not necessarily to engage in the blame game, but to dissect the complex and multilayered forces that perpetuate the Muslim condition. Muslim or Islamically constituted thinkers, as I have shown above, also denounce the status quo in Muslim societies. Djaït, for instance, minces no words in describing the trivial social life in most Arab Muslim societies, noting that anyone who lives in them cannot avoid noticing that for many people happiness consists of perpetuating a monotonous status quo, taking care of family affairs, and engaging in gross, ostentatious displays of wealth and power, compensating—and this must be understood, since it is not mentioned explicitly in his book—for a widespread, perhaps even pathological, servility. There is no ingrained notion of human dignity, and the seemingly heightened preoccupation with cultural identity is rarely matched by the willingness to struggle for modernity—as Japan and China, for instance, have done.[63]

But Djaït, Meddeb, and others do not overlook the complicity of the West. Although Muslims have created their own weakness, so to speak, and therefore, as the Algerian scholar Malek Bennabi (d. 1973) put it, became colonizable (Bennabi's term is *colonisabilité,* or colonizability), the external reasons for such failure are nonetheless real.[64] Meddeb reproaches the West for deliberately keeping Arabs and Muslims at arms' length, relying on the fuzzy myth of the second-class status of Ishmael in biblical accounts to discriminate against them. The West needs to get rid of its conscious or unconscious Islamophobia and incorporate Islam's influence in literature, the arts, and the sciences, as Jacques Derrida and Jean-Luc Nancy have recommended.

Bruno Étienne has called into question the very notion of the West on which Bernard Lewis and Samuel Huntington, for instance, construct their binary views. If the West is, as Emmanuel Lévinas described it, "the Bible plus the Greeks," Islam must be Western, too. Both cultures have "common sources and their destinies are linked."[65] Karen Armstrong, meanwhile, has called on Western people to "become aware that it is in their interests too that Islam remains healthy and strong." The West may not be responsible for all of Islam's ills, but it "has certainly contributed to this development and, to assuage the fear and despair that lies at the root of all fundamentalist vision, should cultivate a more accurate appreciation of Islam in the third Christian millennium."[66]

By the same token, one must stop claiming that religion is the cause for war. The two World Wars in twentieth-century Europe cost more lives than all the religious wars of the previous two thousand years combined. And such a tally does not include the horrors of Stalinism, the Red Khmers, and China.[67] A just political order that ends the "diabolization" of the Palestinian, the Arab, and the Muslim could do more for peace than maintaining false essentialisms on both sides. (Interestingly, one of Meddeb's recommendations was intervention in Iraq to end Saddam's dictatorship, a fait that is now accompli!)[68]

Is criticizing the intellectual failure of Muslim societies in the past five hundred years and blaming the West for hardening Islamic orthodoxy enough to find a way out for Muslim cultures? Would implanting a dynamic tradition of *ijtihad,* the (re)opening of the long-shuttered doors of intellectual and scientific innovation, make a difference? Even if genuine political freedoms were inaugurated, would the Muslim world change substantially? I doubt that. For if one pays careful attention to the writings of Muslim reformers such as Talbi, one still finds the indispensable attempt to prove one's Muslim-ness while making a case for secularism. The argument seems to go like this: I am a good Muslim, I do my prayers, but I believe in a secular political and social model, since only such a model respects the right to difference and nurtures the pluralism that is so essential to democracy. This line of thinking goes beyond a progressively defined Islam, since it privatizes matters of faith and does away with the notion of a caliphal order. But there is something strangely American about this solution, for if political structures were to be made secular, without a radical change in social habits, secularism could very well maintain and probably intensify the religious experience, as Karl Marx noted in his "On the Jewish Question."

There are also those, like the Franco-Algerian sociologist Leïla Babès, who go beyond even the most Islamically progressive positions on women and the veil but still assume the divinity of the faith itself. In *Le voile démystifié* (The veil demystified), Babès doesn't lose any time stating that the veil has no real religious significance, even though it may be mentioned in the Qur'an.[69] The whole issue of veiling, therefore, is not about the veil but about men's mental health and their relationship to women's bodies. For to say that women veil so as not to provoke men is an argument that today appears "absurd, grotesque, and archaic";[70] it is to prove, however inadvertently, that Muslim men troubled by women' bodies are backward and cannot control their animal (perhaps violent?) instincts. It is, in fact, to assume the failure of Islam itself.[71] The frequency of the questions addressed to the *ulema* about which sexual practices are licit and which ones are not is a good index of this cultural pathology. For instance, the Egyptian sheikh Al-Qaradawi, who once detailed how women should be beaten, openly stated in a family program on the TV station Al-Jazeera that fellatio is allowed in a sexual relationship.[72] Yet because *fitna* implies both seduction (a strikingly beautiful woman is someone who causes *fitna*, too) and sedition, women are closely associated with social discord, and so the veil covers and contains this danger.[73]

Islam is certainly against exhibitionism, but it doesn't mandate covering up. The term *hijab* is broadly defined in the Qur'an; the only verse that uses the term in the sense of veil (33:53) is about the Prophet's wives, probably in response to his companion Omar's insistence that they do. (Apparently, Omar was embarrassed when he caught the Prophet's oldest wife, Sawda, trying to relieve herself in the open.) The verse, which was revealed in 627, fifteen years after Mohammed's prophecy began, shows how a scatological event turned into a divine order ensuring purity![74] The *hijab* was also a way to make people understand that the Prophet needed privacy with his wives. It is an "exclusive privilege," since the Prophet's wives, declared mothers of all Muslims, were forbidden to remarry.[75]

The veil is a modern issue, too. No scholar before the twentieth century insisted on the veil as a condition for piety,[76] for if the veil were required for piety, it would have been explicitly stated in the Qur'an, as is the case with other obligations.[77] During his travels, Ibn Battuta encountered pious but uncovered, even partly naked women in the Maldives. Wallada, the daughter of an eleventh-century caliph in Muslim Spain, was a poet who used to hold a literary salon, enjoyed an open relationship with the poet Ibn Zaydun, and didn't wear the veil.[78] On the contrary, the veil, as is well known, is an ancient pre-Islamic tradition that should have been canceled by Islam, since it is the practice of the *jahiliyya* (in the sense of the pre-Islamic period, not the Qutbs' concept), the symbol of bourgeois snobbery conveniently adopted by oppressive Muslim men.[79] Islamist men are so preoccupied with the ʿ*awra* (a term with a double meaning of that which is shameful and that which is revealed) that they have gradually turned the whole woman's body into one, including her voice, and confined her in the *niqab* (a term that doesn't exist in the Qur'an) to hide the last inch of her skin and institute a dreadful ideology of the antiaesthetic.[80] Even the less draconian measure of covering one's hair is a technique of containing women. Throughout history, the cutting of hair was associated with humiliation, defeat, and weakness (as in the Samson myth, for instance).[81]

For Babès, there is simply no excuse to justify this state of affairs—the best-educated women who veil suffer from Stockholm syndrome (when victims grow fond of their kidnappers).[82] By confounding religion with identity, these well-meaning women make Islam appear totalitarian, leaving no room for other forms of identity outside of the religious. They also reveal the extent of the "divinization of textile, [the] fetishization of the scarf [*fichu*]" in Muslim societies.[83]

Babès's approach is more daring than most, for it expands the notion of identity away from its religious confines, but it still relies on the textual recuperative project, which itself assumes the infallibility of the Qur'an as the Word of God. Of course, anyone who reads Babès's book comes away with the indelible impression that the author is brazenly secular and modern. Yet even such an author somehow contradicts her own project by both rescuing the Qur'an (and hence religion) from its bad interpreters as a tactic of liberation (she applauds the king of Morocco's success in granting more rights to women, a process, she thinks, that cannot be replicated elsewhere due to Morocco's exceptional historical circumstances) and reminding the veiled women suffering from Stockholm syndrome that human rights in the West were acquired outside of religion, not because of a better understanding of it.[84] What Babès or very few Muslims are willing to take on is the tyranny of the sacred, which ultimately structures human and social behaviors in the Arab Muslim world. Embracing a progressive interpretation of Islam may seem to be the best solution for Muslims in the present, mostly because Islam is a fact of life in Muslim societies and there seems no practical way of changing the situation. The problem with that approach, however, is that once one posits the Revelation as a nonnegotiable act, one is conceding, admittedly out of convenience, much of the ideological and cultural terrain to the *ulema* and the mostly conservative juridical corpus that underpins their theology. For it is the *ulema* who are the final arbiters in matters of faith in Muslim societies, and it is they who maintain the oppressive tautologies and cultural conformities that make independent thinking, at least in matters of religion, a near impossibility.

Earlier in this chapter, I outlined the views of several Muslim reformers who have made the case for a literary and theoretical analysis of the Qur'an, but they almost all did so without questioning the authenticity of the Revelation, making sure to separate the two in any meaningful discussion of the Holy Book. Whether such thinkers believe in the Revelation or not, there is practically no Muslim literature yet treating the Qur'an as a text *and nothing more.* For this kind of work, we have to rely on Western scholars, whose work is nevertheless openly available in bookstores, at least in Morocco. Alfred-Louis de Prémare's *Aux origines du Coran,* a book published in 2005 by the same press that issued the work of Djaït, in fact takes on the Qur'an as a human and historical text and urges approaching it from this perspective.[85] In Prémare's analysis, not only does the Qur'an not reveal much about its own history (there is no mention of companions by name, for instance), but much of the traditional exegesis was also informed by unreliable methods, such as using the dubious tradition of the *hadith* to read back the circumstances of the Revelation into the Qur'an. Prémare is not anxious to affirm the divine nature of the Qur'anic Revelation—whether it is the Book of God, *kitab allah,* or the Mother of All Holy Books—he is only interested in the history of the text as text. The definitive version of the Qur'an was compiled in 936, thereby proscribing the various contending versions. It was a sort of textual consensus vital to a deeply divided political community desperately in need of an ideology and mythology (three out of the four righteous caliphs had been assassinated; there was rapid expansion and confrontation with older civilizations; and so forth). The diffusion of the printed version started only in the eighteenth century, whereas today's standard version (based on the Kufa reading, one of seven traditional readings) was printed in Cairo in 1923.[86]

A literary reading would reveal that the assembled Qur'an (*jam' al-qur'an*) into a heterogeneous corpus of texts—and *suras* (chapters, originally a Syriac term) with astonishingly variable lengths, forms, and textures—doesn't seem to follow any discernible internal logic. *Sura* titles were added later; sometimes, they make no sense whatsoever, as in the case of the long *sura* misnamed Cow or Heifer (it contains only few verses related to that topic). What give coherence to the Qur'an are its frequent rhetorical refrains, rhyming, and recurrence of "doctrinal themes." A few *suras* (such as III, Al-Masad) do not make sense at all without later interpretations. Psalmodies, *saj'* (combining the cadences of oratory and poetry), and long prescriptive/legislative passages add up to the *qur'an,* meaning "communal recitation," as in the Syriac *qeryan,* from which *qur'an* is derived. The Qur'an thus has a liturgical function in Islam, although the corpus wasn't necessarily designed with that in mind.[87]

The context of the Revelation relies on the chronicles (*akhbar*) of the prophet and his times, a prevailing form of historiography in ancient Arabia. Whether dealing with secular (history) or religious matters (*hadith*), ninth-century *akhbar* relied on a carefully chosen, albeit necessarily subjective, chain of transmitters of events and sayings—the process is known as *isnad*—stretching all the way back to the prophet and his times. The *tabaqat* of Ibn Sa'd (d. 845) belong to the secular model, whereas the authentic *hadith* of Bukhari (d. 870) and Muslim (d. 875) belong to the religious one. (The *hadith*, like the Jewish Torah, began as an oral tradition that was written down over time.)[88]

The *akhbar* are an inadvertent testimony to the fact that several versions of the Qur'an existed and that the *mus'haf* (codex) that came down to us may not be the sole undertaking of the caliph 'Uthman, as is generally believed (*mus'haf 'Uthman*, or the codex of 'Uthman) but the result of a century-long process during which other codices appeared and were circulated, before they were proscribed by the caliph 'Abd al-Malik in a 695 address to the people of Medina. This was the time of the Great Upheaval, or *fitna al-kubra*, following the death of the prophet. The history of canonization is certainly important if we consider that it was only in the tenth century that the expert Ibn Mujahid made the codex of 'Uthman official with seven slight variations in reading.[89]

The Qur'an is a polemical book, too, in the sense that polemics—argumentations, refutations, responding to the accusations of unbelievers and detractors—is one of the "dominant discourses" in the text. The latter makes a point of countering those who accuse the prophet of being a poet (although the Qur'anic syntax doesn't approximate the well-known element of classical Arab poetry, *shi'r*, but is closer to the psalms and hymns and perhaps, in certain cases, to *saj'*, "cadenced and rhyming prose"), a seer or fortune teller, and a recorder of older stories (*asateer*, not the same as legends). The Qur'an's defense of its own authenticity is rather ad hominem, since the contesting parties are never identified in the text, although the *akhbar* make an effort to elucidate the context and people involved. Throughout the Qur'an one discerns an editor's hand, such as when God speaks in the first person and third person in the same breath, or when verses are discarded, replaced, abrogated, and forgotten, without notice. (Aisha once complained that one *sura*—The Factions—was substantially reduced in 'Uthman's version of the Qur'an.) The Qur'an also responded to those who claim that some foreigner was coaching Mohammed by saying that the Qur'an is revealed in Arabic, not in a foreign language. It is thus clear that an editing process was going on in at least the first century of Islam.[90] In short, often opaque (because of the archaic and difficult language used, even for ninth-century commentators), elliptical, and highly allusive, the Qur'an needs to be more thoroughly studied as a corpus of texts, a codex.[91] It certainly is far from being *mubeen* (clear). When the German scholar Gerd Rüdiger Puin examined the excavated Qur'anic parchments unearthed in the Great Mosque of Sanaʿa in 1972, the Qur'an appeared as a palimpsest, "a kind of cocktail of texts," some probably older than Islam by a century.[92] And then there is the other German philologist, Christoph Luxenburg, who discovered that approaching the Qur'an as an Arabic-Syriac text helps elucidate obscure or inconsistent passages, but confers a whole new meaning on the Revelation itself.[93] In any case, even if the meaning of the Qur'an is created by its Muslim interpreters, not the other way around, the "world's most ideologically influential text," in Toby Lester's definition, needs to be better understood, if only to allow for a better understanding of Islamic civilization.[94]

The publication and distribution of Prémare's book in Tunisia and Morocco herald, to me, the other, yet untrodden path in contemporary Muslim history. The questions that come out of such textual, semiotic, and historical analyses of the Qur'an are bound to unsettle believers, for faith in matters of religion is by definition absolutist, as Sam Harris notes in his book. Since a person cannot believe and not believe at the same time, this inability to be and not be puts people in front of the impossible choice of either choosing faith or opting to rely on their critical intellectual faculties. In fact, such a dilemma may also be what is haunting Muslims (and others who share a similar commitment to religion, as well) in the age of universal education and literacy. For regardless of the debates swirling around the contentious issue of modernity—whether it is of European or Western provenance, or a universally shared stage of human progress, a question that we will come back to in the final chapter—modern education and the commitment to a set of beliefs articulated in the distant past are bound to lead to a rather schizophrenic outlook, one that can only be overcome if the two faculties—faith and reason—are scrupulously kept away from each other. I will say more about this later, but for now I will posit that the trend toward extremism in matters of faith appears as a necessary compensation system, a survival mechanism, a form of over-coming what are otherwise two irreconcilable parts of the same individual. It is committing a form of violence against one part of oneself in order to prevent the total breakdown under the weight of these two radically different forms of experiencing reality.

Yet overcoming this duality is not as easy as one might imagine. Religious practices, whether in the form of collective prayer, chants, or recitation, induce a state of well-being that no other secular form of communal experience can possibly match, a fact that may very well explain the durability and persistence of archaic worldviews in the twenty-first century. Such views are woven around a set of rituals that the Enlightenment philosophies have not successfully matched in the political and social systems they inspired. It is perhaps our failure, as twenty-first-century humans, to devise new ways to reproduce the feelings that have historically emanated from religious experiences that gives monotheism, with its singular worldview, its redeeming and terrifying power. Violence against oneself erases doubt and confusion, enriches emotions, and is projected outward toward those who don't meet our standards of perfection.

Islamism, however, with its delusions, cannot endure in a world traversed by a consciousness shaped by a more accurate knowledge about the past, as the reliable critic of religious thought Sadik J. al-Azm put it recently; it is, in fact, already on its way out, a thing of the past, perhaps the gasp of a dying order. Impotent, resentful, and politically reckless, there is no going back for Islamism to a golden age or creating a functioning *umma,* the large, transcontinental community of Muslims that existed only as a form of subjectivity, never as a political reality. Napoleon's landing in Egypt was indeed an irreparable rupture in Islamic history, one that Muslims would be better off heeding right away:

> In fact, modern Europe's violent intrusion into the Islamic and Arab worlds created a final and decisive rupture with the past that I can only compare to the no less final and decisive rupture caused by the violent Arab-Muslim intervention in Sassanid Persia. And just as the history of post-conquest Persia stopped making sense without the Arabs and Islam, the post-Bonaparte history of the Arab world stopped making sense without Europe and modernity. In my view, there is no running away from this reality no matter how many times we reiterate the partial truth that modern Europe got it all from

us anyway: Averroes, Andalusian high culture and civilization, science, mathematics, philosophy, and all the rest. Without finally coming to terms, seriously and in depth, with these painful realities and their so far paralyzing contradictions, we truly will abdicate our place in today's world.[95]

No wonder Al-Azm, the former chair of the department of philosophy at the University of Damascus, is supporting a fellow Syrian citizen's attempt to translate and publish cheap editions of major works in the modern Western philosophical and literary canon in Arabic, all in a belated attempt to educate the public about civil society and democracy.[96]

In 1935, seventy years before the Moroccan man in Casablanca (whose case opens this chapter) sought psychological help for his doubt about religion, Taha Hussein, the blind and legendary Egyptian man of letters, published a story about Adeeb, a man of letters who is barely thirty and has grown to reject his country's conservative Islamic heritage.[97] (Hussein dedicated the story to those who had stood by and supported him during his trials and good times, including when he was unjustly expelled from the university and when he was later reinstated.) While his friend and protégé, the narrator of the story, an Al-Azhar student (or Azhari), aspires to be a reformer in the tradition of Mohammed Abdu, Adeeb opts for a secular education in France. To do so, he coldly repudiates his wife, Hamida, and declares to his interlocutor that he is ready for a life of pleasure and sin in Europe:

> I know a great deal about Europe. I have read many of the novels sent to us and have heard much of the narratives of those who travel to it and who live there. All this causes me to anticipate that I shall fail to resist the European lifestyle and its temptations which one such as I, faithful to his wife, should be capable of resisting. I am quite confident, sir, that I shall sin and that I shall drown in vices alone. . . . I shall be immersed in adultery up to my ears.[98]

This act of callous disregard for Allah and human feelings offends his Azhari friend greatly, but then he, too, immediately collapses in a soul-searching binge, remembering Mohammed Abdu, who once said, "Whoever goes to France is an atheist or, at the very least, an infidel."[99] The narrator quickly gets embarrassed—self-conscious, perhaps—and feels as if his Azhari dress (turban, *gilbab*) rests on nothing but thin air.

On the British ship taking him to France, Adeeb writes to the narrator about the remorse that is destroying him inside, although he manages to rescue himself by reading the power of such remorse as an index of his own humanity and high moral values. Thereafter, he confesses to yet another episode in his relationship with his now ex-wife, Hamida: the upper-class and better-looking woman had chosen to marry him after he had been turned down by Fahima, a childhood promise, because of his ugliness and rather grotesque features. Yet it is this woman he cruelly divorces, and now that she is no longer his, he is once again face to face with his ugliness.

As soon as he settles in his comfortable bed with its soft sheets and pillows at the Hotel Genève in Marseilles, he becomes so overwhelmed by Fernande, the maid who serves breakfast and seems to walk on air, that he decides to lie and stay one week in Marseilles before heading up to Paris. Finding strength in Al-Akhtal, the seventh-to-eighth-century Christian Arab poet and womanizer who refused water as the drink of donkeys, he orders beer in his room but is disappointed when the drink is served by a "pale man," not his muse.[100] While waiting to see Fernande, he writes and grows more infatuated, mesmerized, and intoxicated; he asks himself, "Is it not possible that there should exist an invisible, scheming force which drove me beyond the sea to encounter this strange land as a contrived trap and conspiracy, so that I may fall prey to the devils of sin, seduction, and corruption?"[101] He wonders whether he is going mad as his self-hatred intensifies.

While the narrator prepares for his Al-Azhar exams (which he later fails) and his university exam (which he later passes), Adeeb excels in his studies, achieving in one year what it takes years for others to do. Just as he has with Fernande, Adeeb falls in love with Paris, insisting to his friend back in Egypt that it must be experienced and lived in to be known, that no one can describe it and do it justice. He compares the French metropolis to the "light, open air" one experiences after emerging from the suffocating, tenebrous vaults of the Great Pyramid in Egypt. "Learn, then," Adeeb writes, "that life in Egypt is life in the depths of the pyramid and that life in Paris is life after you escape these depths."[102] Such love forces him to stay in Paris during the Great War, somberly dreading the annihilation of the city, which in his eyes would mean the end of all civilization:

I stand alone before these things and I ponder about a people marching toward them, wishing them harm, not averse, perhaps even desiring to annihilate savagely and totally crush them so that they may erase Paris, so that they may erase France, not caring that if they will have erased all civilization and will have declared in the dawn of Christian history, that the century, which has reached its twentieth year—that the era of civilization, science, philosophy, thought, and art—is on the brink of collapse, that it is time for humanity to rest from its intense, fertile endeavors and to fall back on this barren repose fraught with debasement, sterility, and degradation.[103]

He therefore ties his fate to the city's—and a new girlfriend, Aline, pushing aside Fernande, with whom he has had an affair.

It's now the narrator's turn to go to France's Montpellier University, with an obligatory stop at Hotel Genève in Marseilles, leading Adeeb to wonder whether he is looking for Fernande, practically the embodiment of French womanhood. Adeeb now sees himself as hopelessly impure, a hard-working and equally hard-playing man, "a toy thrown back and forth between the institutes of knowledge and the houses of pleasure."[104] He believes that he still possesses "a measure of willpower," but he obviously cannot break away from this pattern, which has made his study of Latin erratic and spotty. He begins to blame his irregular and unpredictable upbringing in Egypt:

I have come to feel that it is my upbringing in Egypt which virtually drove me to all this and imposed it on me. For I was not brought up with regularity. My upbringing and education did not follow well-defined and consistent methods. My whole life was greatly agitated, driving me right and pushing me left, sometimes trapping me between the two. Had I remained in Egypt, I would have spent the rest of my life as I had started it—in a state of constant agitation, disorganization, and aimlessness. But I traversed the sea to a society where irregularity has no place, where our feeble and disoriented souls are unprepared to function.

I was not successful in facing this new life and bearing its burdens.[105]

Only "destiny" can now sort out his fate; its will, he suggests, will be done. The pattern of studious reclusion and total abandon in pleasure leads him to see but not fear the approaching ghost of madness. "Rather, I advance toward it like an audacious lover. For how can I shun madness when it assumed the form of Aline?" he asks in a letter. After spending two weeks in Aline's company and indulging in a life of hedonism, he takes the Latin exam, returns the test unanswered, and fails, although, it turns out, he could have easily passed.

Some time later, after a three-month stay in Egypt, the narrator returns to France and goes to Paris, only to find Adeeb as he had described himself in the letters, alternately immersing himself in study and alcohol, talking mostly about Aline. The intense intellectual conversations that brought them together in Cairo are now gone. Within months, Adeeb grows afflicted by the thought that he has become the target of the ungrateful French whom he once vowed to defend with his life. He now thinks of himself as the embodiment of Germany, France's archenemy. He writes to his professors and to politicians about his condition and suspects a plot to exile him to the Far East. Paris, like Aline and all women, turned out to be treacherous. Paris "was the faithful embodiment of this disloyal girl called Aline, who had disregarded his rights, forgotten his friendship, and utterly repulsed his love. Aline had begun to plot against him with the conspirators and to deceive him along with the plotters."[106] He suspects her of telling on him because he had revealed to her his marriage proposal to one of his professors' daughters. Now, once again, Adeeb pleads with his friend, the Azhari narrator, not to let him be exiled to the Far East and to help him return to Egypt instead. The irony cannot be more telling.

At the end of the novel, the narrator receives a "huge suitcase" from the concierge and a letter from a mutual friend (Aline?), telling him about a room in her house that has been locked for a year and that contains "many books and objects of no value." Decades later, the narrator opens the suitcase and beholds a "magnificent, melancholic, frank literature, unknown to our language and its contemporary writers." He decides to publish the contents someday and write a book about his friend, but then he wonders whether "the conditions of Egyptian literary life [could] someday permit the publication of these masterpieces."[107]

The narrator's tantalizing question clearly remonstrates Arab and Muslim cultures for having so utterly failed, after more than seventy years, to engage modernity in a creative way and make way for the kind of free-thinking, or *zandaqa,* that had energized Islamic intellectual life in its early centuries. Ten years after the publication of Taha Hussein's novel, the great twentieth-century Arab philosopher Abdel Rahman Badawi (1917–2002) published a book on the history of atheism in Islam, arguing that early Muslim freethinkers not only have secured a preeminent place in the history of world atheism, but thinkers and writers like Ibn al-Muqaffaʿ, Ibn al-Rawandi, Razi, Jaber ibn Hayyan, Abu al-ʿAtahiyya, the musician Ibn Zakariya Razi, poets like Abu Nuwwas, as well as the Ismailis represent an Enlightenment trend (*nazʿat a-tanweer*) and a philosophy of progress that ran against Sunni orthodoxy. Razi's denial of prophecy (the salient expression of Muslim atheism), for instance, foreshadows the Enlightenment philosophies of the eighteenth century, which makes him a "first-rate intellectual, one of the rare free minds in history, and one of the most daring thinkers known to humanity."[108] Almost fifty years later, in 1993, Badawi's book was reissued "as one of the most important books published in Arabic in the 20th century," perhaps the first of its kind ever to shed light on one of "the darkest periods in our Islamic history" and to discuss the phenomenon of atheism in Islam. The book operates in a forbidden minefield, wrote the publisher in a stirring foreword, and acts as a "counter history" within the vast ocean of histories of faith (*iman*), representing Islam's other voice, so to speak. Even more remarkable is the fact that Badawi's book was originally published as part of a series on Islamic studies, thereby implicitly attesting to the fact that atheism (which Badawi considers to be a necessary philosophy in any civilization) is part of the Islamic legacy. These were some of the reasons that made the reissuing of the book necessary, particularly at "this dangerous juncture in our modern history" (*tarikhuna al-muʿasseer*).[109] (Badawi eventually gave up on his native culture and spent the rest of his life in self-imposed exile in France.)

Doling out death sentences for apostates, threatening women for uncovering their hair, assassinating writers for blasphemy (as Muslim extremists tried to do by stabbing the eighty-two-year-old Egyptian novelist and Nobel laureate Naguib Mahfouz, in 1994), suffering various forms of political tyranny, chafing under a stifling cultural conformism that severely punishes difference as betrayal, trapped in a false duality that divides the world into the decadent West and a martyred Islam, and living in societies where businessmen are more interested in ostentatious displays of wealth and power than in books and art, Muslims are still as confused as Adeeb in Taha Hussein's heart-wrenching tale of loss, still trying to work their way out of Islam's centuries-long crisis. The swamps of cultural and intellectual depredation reach such intolerable levels—as they did in Taliban-ruled Afghanistan and Baathist Iraq—that one could easily make, as did Meddeb, a case for outside intervention to unshackle the tentacles of oppression. These two nations, where all opposition and dissent were summarily wiped out with ruthless expedition, needed to be jolted out of their self-destructive ways, if only to rescue a long-suffering and innocent people from the blood-thirsty regimes of fanatics and despots. It was left to the U.S. government, against vociferous domestic and international opposition, to undertake this Herculean mission.

We all know that the United States is the indisputable military power in the world, unmatched in all of history, but was it the right nation to sponsor the *cultural* transformation of Muslim societies? Isn't the United States itself fast descending into the same quicksand of decline from which the Arabs and Muslims have been unable to extricate themselves? By the time the United States intervened in Iraq, the great republic founded by thoughtful and pragmatic deists, that first experiment in history to remove kings and their gods from government, was in the throes of a massive cultural, political, and economic transformation. One couldn't find a better expression to describe its conflict with Muslims than the Arnoldian image of armies clashing by night. The U.S. government sallied forth on the wings of optimism, but American society was beset with problems so numerous and intractable that it became hard to connect the ambitions of a state abroad with the dire conditions of its people at home. The clash of two fundamentalisms in the desert of the Middle East was so dramatic, nearly biblical in scope, so utterly wrapped in the fog of self-deception that one could be excused for thinking about the long history of Crusades and anti-Crusades. The sorrows of the past had appeared in new armor, dashing any hope we may have harbored to learn from humanity's never-ending list of follies.

chapter 4

Regime Change

If there is anything David Hume and John Adams understood, it is that you cannot sustain liberal democracy without cultivating liberal habits of mind among religious believers. That remains true today, both in Baghdad and in Baton Rouge.

—MARK LILLA, "Church Meets State"

The protection of the rights of nonbelievers is one of the unfinished tasks of the United Nations.

—ROBERT F. DRINAN, S.J., *Can God and Caesar Coexist? Balancing Religious Freedom and International Law*

Anyone interested in finding out about how Islam is, in some ways, the mirror image of the Calvinist American soul, the potential manifestation of the promises that could not be kept, the vows canceled by the republicanism of the Enlightenment, had only to pay attention to the unfolding news in the Middle East, the ancient, biblical lands that are the target of the earth-shattering efforts of the United States to promote freedom in the first decade of the twenty-first century. One almost got the impression that this was a strange new crusade, not to defeat Islam but to enshrine it and give it a user-friendly look without diluting, in any way, its powers to control and contain cultural and intellectual difference. Perhaps America's relationship with its repressed theological foundations was being acted out in the infernal terrains of Afghanistan and Iraq, the places it was actively changing in a glimmer of its image. *Regime change,* sure, if by that one means new governments and new political processes; but if one was expecting new cultural foundations of freedom to emerge out of the war, we would have had to wait for a long time. The Islamic Republic of Afghanistan and the Republic of Iraq have been created in the image not of the United States—although a passing look would certainly give that impression—but of the *ante*–United States, the time before the United States, the colonial period, with its pilgrims undertaking their own *hijras* to the West, its Mayflower Compacts, its visions of a "city upon a hill" (without, of course, its necessary doctrine of brotherly love), the fire-and-brimstone warnings against defiling the faith. All of this, the legacy that was irretrievably transformed by the Enlightenment legacies of republicanism, was being, haphazardly, unconsciously reproduced in enemy territory, in the lands of Islam. President George W. Bush was chastised for using the term *crusade,* but that objection was an impulsive reaction, a political move without much thought, since the slightest consideration of the U.S. venture would reveal that his was no typical medieval crusade. If anything, it was a crusade against America's secular legacy, the attempt to bring back the Puritan repressed in Muslim lands. It was, in case this is becoming too circular and allusive, the zealous attempt to make Afghanistan and Iraq more properly *religious* (meaning Islamic), not less. The Taliban, those freedom fighters of old, proved to be too incompetent, and the Baath Party too murderously secular. In short, what was happening in Afghanistan and Iraq after 9/11 was the alliance of rival religions against the liberal legacies that constrain evangelical movements at home. Afghanistan and Iraq are not being made more secular; they were just given new political processes. Both emerging democracies make it clear that the inviolable litmus test of all legislation and public freedoms is the supremacy of Islam, even though Iraq is a multireligious state, housing different religious practices (both Afghanistan and Iraq are multiethnic).

The preamble of the new constitution of the Islamic Republic of Afghanistan (in force since January 4, 2004) opens with the customary prayer verse, "In the name of God, the Merciful, the Compassionate" and quickly asserts the country's belief in "the sacred religion of Islam," which means that although others have the right to their own beliefs, "no law can be contrary to the beliefs and provisions of the sacred religion of Islam." Because of this mandate, the country's official calendar is Islamic, but its business one is solar. The flag contains the insignia of a *mihrab,* the niche inside the mosque where the imam leads prayers facing Mecca, and, as the Constitution states, "the sacred phrase of 'There is no God but Allah and

Mohammad is his prophet, and Allah is Great.'" The national anthem will mention "Allahu Akbar." No political parties that espouse views that are contrary to Islam will be allowed; the state undertakes to protect its people from un-Islamic traditions; all members of the government and presidents must be Muslim and "swear to obey and safeguard the provisions of the sacred religion of Islam"; family law must obey the Hanafi school of jurisprudence, while the Shiites could be ruled by their own doctrines; and, finally, an article ensures that such Islamic provisions cannot be amended. The constitution of Iraq, on the other hand, simply states that "Islam is the official religion of the State and it is a fundamental source of legislation," and that "no law that contradicts the established provisions of Islam may be established."[1]

Having affirmed Islam as a nonnegotiable fact of life, both constitutions go on to talk about liberty; democracy; the rights of citizens to education; health care; the protection of rights and property, both private and public; due process—in short, all the good laws one might find in a secular, capitalist regime. Both legal documents are clearly inspired by American law, but what is missing (the reader must have guessed it by now) is what is abundantly present—that is, the overwhelming presence of Islam as a source of legislation and legitimacy. There is no God in the American Constitution (shall we call it the mother of all constitutions?), no religious requirements to hold office—Muslims, even in that distant past, would have been eligible to become presidents—while the two regimes supposedly changed by the United States to promote democracy foreclose the possibility of a Christian, let alone a Jew, or even worse, an atheist, ever having that opportunity. We kept hearing that the Bush administration respected the cultures of the countries it wanted to change, but why change them if freedom of thought was going to be constrained by such draconian requirements, provisos, and exclusions? Was regime change the crusade of the equal-opportunity religious against the secular and the freethinker, acted out in the cradle of civilizations and its rugged environments? The common agenda of the U.S. religious right and traditional Islam was, in fact, explicitly articulated by Dinesh D'Souza, the conservative author and commentator. More than three years after the U.S. invasion of Iraq, he wrote that "instead of trying to unify America and the West, the right should highlight the division between red America and blue America, and also between traditional Islam and decadent Europe. By resisting the depravity of the left and the Europeans, conservatives can win friends among Muslims and other traditional people around the world."[2] Such a strategy would redefine the "left as the enemy at home," the unwitting accomplices of Osama bin Laden.

Few, if any, conservative intellectuals have expressed the affinities between traditional Islam and American conservatism as D'Souza has in his understandably controversial but rather stunning book, if only for lifting the lid on the repressed element in American culture I alluded to earlier. The Indian-born author accuses the secular left—which, in the U.S. context, means liberals—of fostering "a decadent American culture that angers and repulses traditional societies, especially in those in the Islamic world." In fact, he goes further and says that had American liberals not tried "to undermine the traditional patriarchal family and promote secular values in non-Western cultures," "Osama bin Laden would have never launched the 9/11 attacks," for Islam doesn't hate the West because the West is modern, but because mainstream Western culture is decadent. Muslims don't hate freedom, but "the kind of freedom associated with drug legalization and homosexual marriage." He quotes Ayman al-Zawahiri, Osama bin Laden's partner, saying, "The freedom we want is not the freedom to use women as a commodity to gain clients, win deals, or attract tourists; it is not the freedom of AIDS and an industry of obscenities and homosexual marriages; it is not the freedom of Guantanamo and Abu Ghraib." Thus, Muslims reject the social sickness of the West, "the demented societies that destroy religious belief, undermine traditional morality, dissolve the patriarchal family, and corrupt the innocence of children." Because American popular culture is "producing a blowback of Muslim rage," conservatives ought to dissociate themselves from liberal America and explain to traditional Muslims that they, too, are horrified by liberal depredations. There is, in D'Souza's view, no clash of civilizations in the Huntingtonian sense, but a clash within civilizations, "a clash between liberal and conservative values within America" and "a clash between traditional Islam and radical Islam" in the Muslim world. In this clash, one ought to recall that most of the world in Africa, Asia, Latin America, and, of course, the Muslim societies, is conservative, and so U.S. conservatives are part of the global majority, so to speak. Moreover, there is no comparison between European fascism and Islamic extremism, for the latter is based on religious piety, while the former is inspired by atheism. From his own experience growing up in Mumbai and renting an apartment to a Muslim family, the author knows firsthand how piety dictates moral behavior among Muslims.[3]

Muslim leaders like Khomeini, Ali Shariati, Mawdudi, Sheikh Mohammed Husayn Fadhlallah, Hussan Turabi, not to mention Sayyid Qutb, "have developed a critique of America and the West that is far more sophisticated and comprehensive than anything produced by the Marxists and the communists." Even the late Sunni terrorist Abu Musab al-Zarqawi is quoted saying that "America came [to Iraq] to spread obscenity and vice and establish its decadence and obscene culture in the name of freedom." The condemnation of what the Iranian woman lawmaker Masoumeh Ebtekar, "the first woman to serve as vice president of Iran," called the "Hollywood lifestyle" seems to be widely shared. One Islamic radical, a former resident of California, for instance, described the United States as a "collection of casinos, supermarkets, and whorehouses linked together by endless highways passing through nowhere." Islam, for fundamentalists, is therefore "the last bastion of monotheism in a pagan world," the last hope before the whole world turns into "Planet America."[4]

Are Muslim fundamentalists right? Well, D'Souza's mother shares some of their repulsion for American TV programs and even thinks that Americans on these shows "seem very weird and abnormal." In Hollywood's view of life, "children are usually wiser than their parents and teachers, who are often portrayed as fools and bunglers. Homosexuals are typically presented as good-looking and charming, and unappealing features of the gay lifestyle are either ignored or presented in an amusing light. . . . nobody goes to church. . . . [People] have premarital sex, but very rarely does anyone contract a sexually transmitted disease." Adultery, too, is glamorized in this "increasingly pornographic" culture. "Where, then, are the moral standards in American popular culture? It seems that there are none, just as Muslims allege." America's "new liberal morality," the mainstreaming of what were once bohemian values, "has contributed to making American culture more trivial, debased, and degenerate. Now this gross underside of American culture is being exported to the world," and Muslims are, understandably, resisting it.[5]

Patriarchy is not necessarily against women, as D'Souza knows from his experience growing in India: "I am not a Muslim, and I grew up in India in a society like this. I can testify from personal experience that traditional systems of this sort do not breed passive, submissive women. My two grandmothers were both tyrants who ruled over their husbands. Patriarchy doesn't make women less powerful—it merely diverts their power to the domain of the household." Liberal views of women's roles are therefore bad, and Muslims are right to keep them away. But attacking family values is not part of the Enlightenment's classical liberalism. Today's liberal views allow men to enjoy women without being responsible, a deal that is better for men than polygamy, a situation that is only now becoming recognized.[6]

It's time, therefore, for American conservatives to realize they have little in common with the American left or with liberal Europeans, and to ally themselves with traditional Muslims instead of trying to unify America and the West. They must "stop attacking Islam" and let them forge their identity, not impose some "ridiculous" Kemalist model on them. It's "a two-front war," which means that "in order to crush the Islamic radicals abroad, we must defeat the enemy at home."[7]

Dismissed by many reviewers on both sides of the political spectrum and described as a "mullah" whose goal is to globalize "theoconservatism" in order to better withstand, and perhaps roll back, the pervasive influence of secularism, D'Souza's zeal, like the zeal of all fundamentalists, emerges out of a culture that is already predisposed to such beliefs.[8]

Anyone watching the American cultural scene in the years after 9/11 has noted this confluence of interests since regime change in Afghanistan and Iraq has coincided with the rise of religious zeal and an ever-dogged determination to contain liberal secularism in the regime changer's home turf. After all, while the United States was busy changing Afghanistan and Iraq in 2004, one of the most significant cultural events taking place in the United States was the reaction to, and wild success of, *The Passion of the Christ,* a controversial film in Aramaic (a dead language extant only in a remote part of Syria) by Mel Gibson about Jesus's last hours. People were so profoundly moved by the graphic suffering of Jesus that some viewers were inspired to repent their sins. In Texas, a man surrendered to the police after watching the film and confessed to the murder of a pregnant woman who had been suspected of hanging herself. Another man was jailed after stalking Mel Gibson and demanding that the actor and filmmaker pray with him.[9] So powerful was Gibson's movie that *New York Times* cultural commentator Frank Rich labeled 2004 the Year of *The Passion:* "As we close the books on 2004, and not a moment too soon, it's clear that, as far as the culture goes, this year belonged to Mel Gibson's mammoth hit."[10]

In the previous year, the big news was from the southern state of Alabama, where Chief Justice Roy Moore had defied a federal ruling to remove a "5,280-pound monument of the Ten Commandments that he secretly installed one night in the lobby of the State Supreme Court." Known to his supporters as the "Moses of Alabama," with his monument called "Roy's Rock," he had gathered quite a following of people who turned the courthouse into a pilgrimage site. This is how the *New York Times* described the scene on the hour he was ordered to remove the monument:

> As the clock struck 12, the crowd assembled in front of the courthouse burst into "God Bless America." The muggy plaza was clogged with dozens of little girls wearing Jesus T-shirts, bearded men with thick arms and Confederate flags on their backs, black people, white people, the young, the old, the in between, a man who walked from Texas dressed in a monk's frock and another who drove from San Diego in a red truck with a sign that said "Shame on America."

Many were happily arrested during the episode, reading the whole drama as a trial for their besieged faith.[11] The "Ten Commandments judge," as he got to be known, was charged with ethics violations and suspended from his office pending a judicial court hearing later that year. But when the hearings got under way in November, Chief Justice Moore was unrepentant and insisted that God was the basis of the country's law. Once again, his supporters rallied to his support:

> Shortly after sunrise Wednesday, several dozen of Chief Justice Moore's supporters bowed their heads and held a prayer circle on the courthouse steps. Young men blew curled rams' horns as a call to arms. Two women wore black veils, "to mourn the death of America," they said. One burly man named Matt strutted up the courthouse steps dressed in a green army helmet and flak jacket "to wage war for God."
>
> Whether or not Chief Justice Moore emerges with his job, his popularity seems to be only growing.
>
> On Wednesday, as the proceedings began inside the same courtroom where Chief Justice Moore used to bang the gavel, a long gold bus circled

downtown Montgomery with a banner on the side: "Alabama Save the Commandments Tour."

When the court reviewing his case ousted him, Mr. Moore announced that "the battle to acknowledge God is about to rage across the country."[12] By the end of 2004, the Associated Press reported that the ousted judge was praying about whether to run for governor of Alabama.[13]

Episodes like these show that devout Christians in the United States (much like their Muslim counterparts in Islamic societies) have come to see their country taken over by an irreligious liberal dogma and a cult of political correctness that trivializes their faith and the cultural foundations of their nation. Abortion remains a deeply divisive issue, turning court appointments into tense political battles. The study of evolution as a scientific fact is questioned in several states. The president of the country, who had once declared his favorite political philosopher to be Jesus Christ, is reported to start his days reading from the homilies of Oswald Chambers, a Protestant minister, and begin his cabinet meetings with prayers.[14] Not long after the shock of 9/11, the country was galvanized by a court ruling that upheld the suit of an atheist parent in California to remove the phrase *under God* from the Pledge of Allegiance that his daughter was forced to recite, ushering the country into heated debate over the merit of such phrases in several public documents or ceremonial traditions, sending the issue all the way to the Supreme Court. Instead of sorting out the thorny issue of religion and politics in public life, the Court simply decided that the aggrieved parent didn't have the legal right to sue on behalf of his daughter. And as 2004 was coming to a close, a movement had emerged to save Christmas from liberals who, through their "political correctness," had turned the major Christian celebration into one holiday among others.[15]

Many liberals seem to assume that only evangelical Christians, mostly from the South, are to blame for such fundamentalist tendencies, but one finds traces of this form of godliness in the most unexpected liberal circles. Former President Bill Clinton sought religious counsel after his affair with intern Monica Lewinsky was exposed, and it is not uncommon for pop artists and film stars to embrace a religious cause. The respect Americans have for religion—all religion, as we shall see later, although Christianity tops the hierarchy—was forced to my attention when, during the all-star concert celebrating pop singer Bob Dylan's thirtieth musical anniversary held on October 16, 1992, the popular and rebellious Irish singer Sinead O'Connor was booed off the stage by Dylan fans. Before that fateful moment in Dylan's musical gala, she had appeared as a musical guest on NBC's *Saturday Night Live* and in the midst of her performance tore up a photograph of Pope John Paul II as she charged the pontiff with being a child abuser. The European singer had no idea what trouble she was getting into. According to one account,

> the NBC switchboard was immediately inundated by complaints (supposedly 4,484 in all) called in by outraged viewers. Denunciations of Sinead's "blasphemy" poured forth from all kinds of religious figures and celebrities, including Frank Sinatra, who was quoted as saying he wanted to "punch" the singer "right in the mouth." NBC was eventually fined $2.5 million by the Federal Communications Commission (FCC), which had never before fined the network for content aired on *Saturday Night Live*.[16]

And so at the Dylan event, for that mortal sin, rock music fans in New York City refused to let her sing.

If religion has such an effect on Dylan and *Saturday Night Live* fans—the very type of people considered to be decadent, even satanic, by die-hard Christians in other parts of the country—then one must take religion seriously in America. As Alexis de Tocqueville wrote in the 1830s:

> On my arrival in the United States, it was the religious aspect of the country that first struck my eye. As I prolonged my stay, I perceived the great political consequences that flowed from these new facts. Among us, I had seen the spirit of religion and the spirit of freedom almost always move in contrary directions. Here I found them united intimately with one another: they reigned together on the same soil.[17]

Interestingly, though, Tocqueville was never able to gauge how much of that outward devotion was a sincere expression of inner faith or part of an implicit social contract: "I do not know if all Americans have faith in their religion—for who can read to the bottom of hearts?—but I am sure that they believe it necessary to the maintenance of republican institutions. This opinion does not belong only to one class of citizens or to one party, but to the entire nation; one finds it in all ranks."[18]

To me, it is impossible to understand the United States without a sense of its religious beginnings and the enduring impact of these religious traditions on American culture and politics. Actually, if one were to read the founding documents of American culture, one is struck not simply by the fundamentalism of the British settlers who, through their literacy, created the foundational myths and moral edifice of what later became the United States, but also by how utopian and egalitarian their vision was. America's first leaders, such as William Bradford (1590–1657) and John Winthrop (1588–1649), forfeited good lives in England and undertook perilous journeys to the New World because they felt oppressed by the Church of England, much as many Muslim purists find the state version of Islam in most Arab and Muslim nations intolerable. Like biblical tales of the prophets and the prophet Mohammed's *hijra* (migration) from Mecca to Medina fleeing persecution, the course of American history was shaped by Pilgrims seeking to establish a new order away from corrupt and fallen regimes.

The hapless but determined "Saints" who boarded the *Mayflower* in 1620 (non-Separatists were "strangers," a designation that interestingly had also been applied to visitors of the British parliament from 1575 until it was scrapped in 2004 and replaced by "members of the public")[19] and survived the arduous Atlantic crossing (half of the initial 102 passengers who boarded in Plymouth, England, on September 6, 1620, died within a year) had a working document, an oath, a Covenant to guide them in a cold, forbidding wilderness, isolated, as they had come to lament, ironically, by the "mighty ocean" from "all the civil parts of the world." But twenty-four years after the Pilgrims had landed in America to form a perfect Christian community, many simply broke away for better prospects. As William Bradford lamented,

> And thus was this poor church left, like an ancient mother grown old and forsaken of her children, though not in their affections yet in regard of their bodily presence and personal helpfulness; her ancient members being most of them worn away by death, and these of later time being like children translated into other families, and she like a widow left only to trust in God. Thus, she that had made many rich became herself poor.[20]

Not long after the Separatists established themselves in New England, John Winthrop, a Cambridge-educated Puritan, delivered a sermon to immigrants aboard the *Arbella,* acknowledging the existence of social classes (rich and poor), a fact ordained by God Himself. But he spent the first—and major—part of the sermon exhorting his community to embrace justice and mercy, finding numerous examples in the Bible that require self-sacrifice to help those in need, never expecting anything in return, certainly not a payback if the recipient of a loan cannot afford it. To Winthrop, God has designed the world in such a manner so that

> every man might have need of other, and from hence they might be all knit more nearly together in the Bond of brotherly affeccion: from hence it appears plainely that noe man is made more honourable than another or more wealthy etc., out of any perticuler and singuler respect to himselfe but for the glory of his Creator and the Common good of the Creature, Man; Therefore God still reserves the propperty of these guifts to himselfe as Ezek: 16.17. he there calls wealthe his gold and his silver, etc. Prov: 3.9. he claimes theire service as his due honour the Lord with thy riches, etc. All men being thus (by divine providence) ranked into two sortes, riche and poore; under the first, are comprehended all such as are able to live comfortably by theire owne meanes duely improved; and all others are poore according to the former distribution. There are two rules whereby wee are to walke one towards another: JUSTICE and MERCY.

The Bible in the hands of this extraordinary governor looks like a liberation theology treatise, a form of Christian communism, complete with a Jubilee year that cancels all debts and spares the land. Winthrop told his sea-borne congregation about the early members of the Church who had disdained private interests and viewed common possession as the only godly path. He thus recommended love, not a legal doctrine, as the foundation for mercy, for love solidifies communal life and makes mercy easier to practice. For him, a Christian community is one that is bonded through unconditional love, for "love among Christians is a reall thing not Imaginarie."

In the brief second part of the sermon, Winthrop told his fellow travelers that such a community could only come together "under a due forme of Goverment both civill and ecclesiasticall. In such cases as this the care of the publique must oversway all private respects, by which, not onely conscience, but meare Civill pollicy doth binde us; for it is a true rule that perticuler estates cannot subsist in the ruine of the publique." The community, this "Citty upon a Hill," had to be anchored in brotherly love as it enters into a "Covenant" with God and undertakes His commission.[21]

I can't think of a more inspiring beginning than the vision of the new world order embedded in the Mayflower Compact and in Winthrop's sermon aboard the *Arbella*. It's as if the Christian world were being made anew, as if God, by forging another covenant with the wandering Pilgrims (Saints, Separatists, or reformers), were giving Christianity another chance. And, of course, in the minds of these early settlers, Christianity, if cleansed from the corrupting influence of Catholicism or the authoritarianism of popery, was the only acceptable universal order. The faithful were to organize themselves in a civil government and run their affairs through elections; yet this was not for the purpose of freedom but for the greater glory of God. When, on July 3, 1645, Winthrop addressed the General Court on the qualities, qualifications, and responsibilities of the magistrate and on the meaning of liberty, he divided the latter term into natural (which allows people to slide toward mischief and evil) and "civil and federal," or "moral, in reference to the covenant between God and man in moral law." In the latter definition, which was the only one acceptable from a Puritanical point of view, people simply surrender to established authority—as a wife does to her husband, or the faithful to the Church—in order to reap the benefits of freedom. Winthrop had simply replaced the pope with a more abstract sovereignty, one upheld by Calvinist doctrines.[22]

It's hard to put a modern label on such an order—one might call it a Christian democracy or democratic theocracy, one that is closer in spirit to modern-day Iran than to the contemporary United States of America.[23] American presidents do occasionally allude to their nation as a "city upon a hill," but they don't seem to have Winthrop's ideals in mind. Ironically, the Puritans' ideals are easier found in a Middle Eastern country like Iran, or the emerging democracies in Afghanistan and Iraq, where Muslims are still in the throes of a maddening crisis trying to reconcile the sacred and the secular, figuring out how to be Muslims without forcing one's neighbors to do the same, and, basically, trying to be free in God, not away from Him. For too many Muslims today, God in fact is very much the God of early America—all sovereign, powerful, vengeful to the extreme, but also merciful if one adheres to the letter of the faith. It is a god that usually appears in times of trouble, as when Jonathan Edwards delivered his famous sermon "Sinners in the Hands of an Angry God" to his congregation at Enfield, Connecticut, on July 8, 1741, and prefaced it with a soul-shaking and awe-inspiring passage about God's powers of vengeance and recompense from Deuteronomy ("Their Foot shall slide in due Time"). The preacher—like a modern-day extremist imam—lashed out at the faithful, threatening the unconverted, the unregenerate, and the un–born-again among them with an eternity of bloody torture in hell, their bodies crushed by an angry God who cares nothing about their late supplications for mercy:

> If you cry to God to pity you, he will be so far from pitying you in your doleful Case, or shewing you the least Regard or Favour, that instead of that he'll only tread you under Foot. And tho' he will know that you can't bear the Weight of Omnipotence treading upon you, yet He won't regard that, but he will crush you under his Feet without Mercy; he'll crush out your Blood, and make it fly, and it shall be sprinkled on his Garments, so as to stain all his Raiment. He will not only hate you, but he will have you in the utmost Contempt: no Place shall be thought fit for you, but under his Feet to be trodden down as the Mire of the Streets.

Christians are always one step away from death and a bottomless pit of hell, Edwards told his congregation over and over again. There is no security in health, prosperity, or just plain religiosity. The unborn "have no Refuge," the "World of Misery, that Lake of burning Brimstone" is extended under them, and were it not for the mysterious pleasure of the sovereign God, the earth would not hold them for a second. But Edwards was howling in the wind, looking back in time to the plantation that Bradford and his two dozen or so fellow travelers had established after much endurance and suffering, only to see it wither away under the pressure of rigid doctrine and the pursuit of material well-being.[24]

This is the sort of language that Muslim extremists hear today, the kind of discourse that inflames their passion and leads them to embrace futile causes. It may be Islamism's last gasp, as Sadik J. al-Azm postulated, but it is powerful enough to unsettle the world.

Despite the heroic stand he took, Jonathan Edwards was losing control over the destiny and interpretation of Christianity in America, his case providing an interesting lesson to die-hard Muslim fundamentalists whose goal is to freeze the faith in a timeless capsule. Edwards couldn't push back the course of history—and no, there is not, ever, any going back in time. Protestant evangelicalism, Mark Noll tells us in his magisterial study *America's God,* was becoming as different from early Protestant theology—including colonial theology as late as the mid–eighteenth-century Great Awakening—as was the Protestant Reformation of the early colonial settlers from Roman Catholicism. This transformation was part of "a general shift within Western religious life," as new ideas and economies were replacing older ones. Key words such as *freedom* and *justice* no longer denoted the same things. Though Americans were more religious than their European counterparts, they had grown to believe in the antiauthoritarian and antielitist doctrines of "commonsense" (translated as making up one's own mind) and free-market principles, both of which were vigorously denounced by the reformers of the Great Awakening. In short, "after the 1780s, republicanism (wherever found along a continuum from classical to liberal) had come to prevail in America; very soon thereafter, commonsense principles (whether defined in elite or populist terms) were almost as widely spread; and in the same post-Revolutionary period, Protestant evangelicalism (however divided into contending sects) became the dominant American religion." By the 1830s and 1840s, the synthesis of all three currents—which only happened in America—had become "not only the most powerful value system in the nation, but also the most powerful system *defining* the nation." Even the Civil War was religious in a way that the Revolution never was.[25]

Quite a few prominent figures of the American Revolution believed that a Christian foundation was indispensable to the success of the new republic. In 1800, Benjamin Rush (1745–1813), one of the most forceful exponents of this synthesis, wrote to Thomas Jefferson:

> I have always considered Christianity as the strong ground of republicanism. The spirit is opposed, not only to the splendor, but even to the very forms of monarchy, and many of its precepts have for their objects republican liberty and equality as well as simplicity, integrity, and economy in government. It is only necessary for republicanism to ally itself to the Christian religion to overturn all the corrupted political and religious institutions of the world.[26]

Five years earlier, William Smith, provost of the College of Philadelphia, though still a loyalist, expressed the same sentiments in a sermon:

> Illiberal or mistaken plans of policy may distress us for a while, and perhaps sorely check our growth; but if we maintain our virtue; if we cultivate the spirit of Liberty among our children; if we guard against the snares of luxury, vanity and corruption; the Genius of America will still rise triumphant, and that with a power at last too might[y] for opposition. This country *will be free*—nay for ages to come, a chosen seat of *Freedom, Arts,* and *heavenly Knowledge:* which are now either dropping or dead in most countries of the world.[27]

As the philosopher Charles Taylor noted, "for all the well-documented tensions between Christianity and the republican tradition, the United States starts its career by linking the two closely together."[28] Samuel Miller, an influential Presbyterian, while denouncing atheism, materialism, and social breakdown, spoke of republican government as a divine system that checks abuses.[29] Another New Jersey Presbyterian, Jacob Green, did the same in 1780. Vice is bad, he wrote, because "it provokes God to withhold his protection, and punish a sinning people by permitting usurpers and tyrants to seize on their natural rights, and reduce them to a state of bondage. . . . Vice has a *natural* tendency to the loss of freedom. . . . Vice enfeebles the mind, unmans human creatures, and [in] many ways puts them into the power of those who watch for an opportunity to subjugate them."[30]

Such statements show that the second half of the eighteenth century was marked by the turn to moral philosophy and republicanism,[31] concepts that would have been utterly offensive to earlier Protestants. For Cotton Mather, education meant the pursuit of piety (exactly as stipulated in the Qur'an), while Aristotelian moral philosophy was a "sham," a "vile Peece of Paganism."[32] (It's interesting to note, as we will later, that liberal Muslim philosophers such as Mohammed 'Abed al-Jabri are now trying to counter Islamic fundamentalism through the use of Averroës, the Arab Aristotelian philosopher.) Yet by the early nineteenth century, "statements uniting Christian and republican values had become so routine" that the visitor Alexis de Tocqueville remarked that only in America do the two belief systems—so much at odds in other countries—coexist in a seamless whole.[33]

Although some of the most influential Founding Fathers were either deists or men quiet about their beliefs, and although the "language of the nation's founding documents—the Declaration of Independence, the Articles of Confederation, and the Constitution—while respectful of the deity in general, was hardly evangelical in any specific sense," as Noll explains, "the central religious reality for the period from the Revolution to the Civil War was the unprecedented expansion of evangelical Protestant Christianity. No other period of American history ever witnessed such a dramatic rise in religious adherence and corresponding religious influence on the broader national culture."[34]

One explanation for such an odd outcome (given the Founding Fathers' general outlook) was provided by the historian Paul Johnson. To him, "Evangelicalism was a middle class solution to problems of class, legitimacy, and order generated in the early stages of manufacturing."[35] The Revolution had appealed to an older Christian messianic temper and was now unleashing a torrent of fevered religiosity that reflected the democratic spirit of the new nation. American congregations had no common faith, but they all insisted on the centrality of the Bible, through which they could seek Jesus and God's grace. Though wildly successful, by the 1830s, evangelicals had still not "transformed the United States into the kingdom of Christ." They had assumed that through a steady process of conversion their polity would come to reflect the general population's faith, but that didn't happen, which again led to the same frustration experienced by the Pilgrims.[36] Indeed, many saw religion as the only element that bound the country together. In 1852, Henry Clay worried that the "sundering of the religious ties which have hitherto bound our people together" would be the greatest danger facing the United States.[37]

There was much substance in this belief, despite the Founding Fathers' views; as Noll puts it, the "moral calculus of republicanism was—indeed, to some extent, remains—an extraordinarily significant assumption for many Americans, religious and nonreligious alike. As expressed in the first century of the United States, this calculus held that religion could and should contribute to the morality that was necessary for virtuous citizens, without which a republic could not survive."[38] One only has to recall George Washington's Farewell Address of 1796 to get a sense of this compromise:

> Of all the dispositions and habits which lead to political prosperity, Religion and morality are indispensable supports. In vain would that man claim the

tribute of Patriotism, who should labour to subvert these great Pillars of human happiness, these firmest props of the duties of Men and citizens. The mere Politician, equally with the pious man ought to respect and cherish them. A volume could not trace all their connections with private and public felicity. Let it simply be asked where is the security for property, for reputation, for life, if the sense of religious obligation *desert* the oaths, which are the instruments of investigation in Courts of Justice? And let us with caution indulge the supposition that morality can be maintained without religion. Whatever may be conceded to the influence of refined education on minds of peculiar structure, reason and experience both forbid us to expect that National morality can prevail in exclusion of religious principle.

'Tis substantially true that virtue or morality is a necessary spring of popular government. The rule indeed extends with more or less force to every species of free Government. Who that is a sincere friend of it, can look with indifference upon attempts to shake the foundation of the fabric?[39]

Even Jefferson viewed a Christianity cleansed from its excesses as the "most friendly to liberty, science, and the freest expression of the human mind."[40] Supreme Court Justice Joseph Story echoed this view in his *Commentaries on the Constitution* (1833): "Indeed, in a republic, there would seem to be a peculiar propriety in viewing the Christian religion, as the great basis, on which it must rest for its support and permanence, if it be, what it has ever been deemed by its truest friends to be, the religion of liberty."[41] Alexis de Tocqueville noted that "one cannot say that in the United States religion exerts an influence on the laws or the details of public opinions, but it directs mores, and it is in regulating the family that it works to regulate the state."[42] This explains why "by the early nineteenth century, evangelicalism was the unofficially established religion in a nation that had foresworn religious establishments."[43]

Americans now relied on the "Bible alone" or "sola scriptura" (predominantly the Protestant King James version) for the meaning of their faith. The Bible was the vehicle through which to contest traditional authorities and was sometimes seen as an essential document for the success of the new republic. As early as 1791, Benjamin Rush made a plea to include the Bible in school curricula: "We profess to be republicans, and yet we neglect the only means of establishing and perpetuating our republican form of government, that is, the universal education of our youth in the principles of Christianity, by means of the Bible: for this Divine book above all others, favours that equality among mankind, that respect for just laws, and all those sober and frugal virtues, which constitute the soul of republicanism."[44] Yet by the 1850s, Southerners were justifying slavery through literal readings of the Bible, arguing that slavery was acknowledged as a fact of life, while the abolitionists were also relying on the Bible to justify their cause. This "Reformed, liberal hermeneutic" was capacious enough to include readings that sounded like Karl Marx's *Communist Manifesto.* In an 1863 outline for a sermon, Charles Finney wrote:

> Christianity is radically reformatory. Satan has usurped the government of this world. . . . Christ has undertaken the work of counter-revolution. . . . to create all things new in the moral order of things . . . to reform or destroy, all governments that don't obey God. . . . It follows that conservatism is its great antagonist. . . . Conservatism is a disposition to preserve the established order. . . . Its law is custom—Precedent—Established usages. . . . It looks back for all that is excellent & counts progress insanity. . . . It is every where & evermore antichrist.[45]

The abolitionist Sarah Grimké relied on the Bible to emancipate women from male interpretations, but such views kept clashing against a strict literalism justifying "black chattel slavery." Not to accept slavery, pro-slavery Bible readers said, is not to accept God. Even rabbis entered the fray in defense of slavery. The country came to a theological impasse. By the time of the Civil War, "two cultures," Noll writes, "purporting to read the Bible the same way, were at each other's throats";[46] two major Christian nationalisms (much like the varieties of Islam today) were clashing. This peculiarly American form of biblicism had led to a crisis that the pages of the Bible simply couldn't resolve.

Ironically, it took a leader like Abraham Lincoln, a Northerner who reached out to both sides of the divide, but also a man who, unlike most of his contemporaries, doubted (but never entirely dismissed) whether the United States "had enjoyed, and would continue to enjoy, a unique destiny as a divinely chosen people,"[47] to settle the issue, not only with words but also with guns. Lincoln's qualified universalism was championed by the literary figure Ralph Waldo Emerson, who in eulogizing the slain president on April 19, 1865, said:

There is a serene Providence which rules the fate of nations, which makes little account of time, little of one generation or race, makes no account of disasters, conquers alike by what is called defeat or what is called victory, thrusts aside enemy and obstruction, crushes everything immoral as inhuman, and obtains the ultimate triumph of the best race by the sacrifice of everything which resists the moral laws of the world.[48]

This view, however, was in the minority. American "evangelical juggernaut" ensured that America's God would be the only God.[49]

The mixing of secular and sacred ideals within the political culture of the United States has given American culture a tone all its own. In a way, this cultural compromise mirrors the checks and balances in the political system, keeping Americans permanently caught in a battle of good against evil, conservatism versus liberalism, and Republicans versus Democrats. This national moral dichotomy hasn't been replicated in the economic sphere with the same fervor, however. Enlightenment philosophies and republicanism democratized the Christian faith and propelled it into new theological grounds, but they didn't bring back Winthrop's egalitarian ethos. The country's religious awakenings have more to do with matters of belief—evolution, abortion, homosexuality, existential angst, guilt—than with implementing Winthrop's model of "Christian Charity." The lack of programmatic concern for the poor and the absence of brotherly love to sustain it are often assumed to be legacies of America's puritanical past, but the doctrines of towering figures such as Bradford, Winthrop, and Edwards don't seem to suggest so. America's religious revivals, like all revivals, are selective and tend to reflect the crises of the present more so than they do the intent of the forefathers. It is the same with Muslims. Islamic fundamentalism is the symptom of a serious cultural crisis in the Islamic world more so than it is an attempt to resurrect the so-called glorious past of the early caliphs.

No wonder Muslim Americans who immigrated from Iran and Pakistan are worrying about the mounting influence of religion on public affairs in their adopted country. Upon the election of George W. Bush by millions of voters who had cast their ballots based on faith, an immigrant from Pakistan wrote to a columnist with the *San Francisco Chronicle* to express his fears because "if the nation has taught itself to think like religious fanatics, that damage will take years to repair."[50] Also, in response to a journalist's article about the lack of freedom of thought and speech in the Islamic Republic of Iran,[51] a writer from Reseda, California, wrote to the editor of the *New York Times* about his experience of reading Voltaire and Thomas Paine in Iran and how "disgusted" he had grown with Iran's "democratic theocracy": "I wanted desperately to read a [banned] book that was critical of the prophet, fundamentalist Islam and the ayatollahs." He did manage to read the book, but that experience stayed with him to "remind me of the utter importance of the separation of church and state, which, ironically," he added, "the current administration of my adopted country is determined to weaken."[52] While highlighting the significant differences between Asian and Arab (mostly Wahhabi) Islam (one tolerant, the other not), the Indonesian lawyer and author Karim Raslan also noted that the United States "with its crowded churches and Sunday preachers who fill sports stadiums . . . is actually more like my world than Europe is."[53] Though it can be a replenishing sentiment, nostalgia is often the ideology of the confused and disoriented.

Given America's hybrid ideology, blending the sacred and the secular in a tense compromise, one would expect that the U.S. government and political establishment would recommend such a formula to Muslims. But that hasn't happened, perhaps out of the concern that to say that religion is not compatible with democracy or freedom is to exhibit a Western bias and impose a totalitarian secularism on an otherwise deeply religious people. Scholars like Ian Buruma and Noah Feldman argue vigorously that an "Islamic democracy" is not in any way a contradiction. Perhaps Buruma was reacting to the neoconservative preference for the Turkish model, the call for a Kemal Ataturk or Chiang Kai-shek to impose a secular regime on Iraq. For Buruma, to present the options for Iraq as a choice between Ataturk and Khomeini is not really productive. As the case of the early history of the United States abundantly shows, one could argue, with "Enlightenment thinkers, like John Locke[,] . . . that a political system based on enlightened self-interest could not survive without a strong basis in religious morality." In fact, modern history has shown that

> anti-clericalism, much more than a history of religious zeal, formed the
> basis for many of the Middle East's bloodiest political failures: Nasserism in
> Egypt, Baathism in Syria and Iraq, the shah in Iran. These regimes were led
> by secular elites who saw religion as something that held their countries back

or in a state of colonial dependence. The fact that a number of iron-fisted reformers, like Nasser himself, were routinely the objects of assassination attempts by religious zealots showed the gap between the secular "progressive" elites and the people they ruled. When organized religion is destroyed, something worse often takes its place, usually a quasi religion or personality cult exploited by dictators. When it is marginalized, as happened in Egypt and other parts of the Middle East, it provokes a religious rebellion.

Because "the separation [of church and state] has never been absolute" in the West, there is no historical reason not to trust the process to work, particularly in a region of the world where the two spheres had never been successfully separate.[54]

Buruma relies, to some extent, on the constitutional expertise of Noah Feldman, who wrote a book delineating why there is no alternative to an Islamic democracy in Muslim societies. In *After Jihad* Feldman shrugs his shoulders at the nitpicking over the separation of powers or realms and simply asks, "What else is on offer in the Muslim world?"[55] The elected Islamists of Turkey have proven to be good democrats and have assuaged apprehensions. Still, Feldman does assume here—although elsewhere in the book he doesn't, or at least nuances this picture—a certain fundamental uniformity of people within Islamic cultures and is not quite sure how and whether Islamic constitutions will affect individual rights.[56]

The trouble with Islam, in Feldman's view, is the stranglehold of autocratic regimes, supported by Western powers, on ordinary Muslims' yearning for democracy. Such a democracy doesn't necessarily mean adopting "secularism of the Western variety," but a sort of blending between Islam and democracy, both "mobile" but flexible ideas that may clash and adapt. For Islam, contrary to prevailing assumptions, is capable of great flexibility, and no one is more adept at employing the latest technologies than the Islamists (an ironic rejoinder to Bernard Lewis). Not only that, but here Feldman joins scholars like Sadik J. al-Azm to say that violent Islamism (jihadism) is quite possibly in retreat, since 9/11 and other attacks may well be a "desperate gasp of a tendency to violence that has lost most of its popular support."[57]

If the Islamist threat continues to haunt the world's imagination, it is partly because autocratic regimes in the Middle East and the Islamic world have decimated all secular opposition and left enough of an Islamist presence to use as a bargaining chip with Western powers to maintain their hold, however despicable, on power. Yet for Feldman, not just Islamic but even Islamist democracy, as a short- or medium-term solution, is better for the West than secular autocracies. Islamism's strength, anyway, derives—as it always has—from its opposition to conditions of oppression and injustice. Given this dire situation, a "provisional synthesis between Islam and democracy," both admittedly "mobile ideas" because of their "universality, flexibility, and simplicity," is therefore the only solution. Feldman seems to assume that although minorities will be seriously disadvantaged, they will be all right, their status not too different from other minorities in other well-established democracies. All governments assume a certain religious or moral consensus, and many laws in the West are based on biblical precepts. Let us not forget, too, that democracy in the West "grew up among pious Christians," and God is still supreme in the United States.[58]

Neither the unequal status of women nor that of non-Muslims within Islam is an "insurmountable" hurdle to democracy, for if that were so, the Jewish state of Israel would not be democratic and atheists (a consistently maligned group) would not receive equal treatment in the United States. Perhaps, but don't these examples highlight the dangers of blending faith and politics in any nation-state? In a true democracy, atheism or the rights of minority ethnic or religious groups should not be an issue, for religion would have no influence whatsoever on legislative and legal affairs. Although Israel's Jewish identity and the rights of Arabs were still hotly contested issues in 2006, when the Parliament was attempting to draft a constitution, there is consensus among Israelis that an "American-style separation of church and state" in "a country founded as a Jewish state with a Jewish ethos and majority" is not a real option.[59] Even the highly sensationalized *hudud* punishments, which are rarely meted out anyway because of a standard of proof "that is extraordinarily difficult to reach,"[60] are not enough of a reason for Feldman not to try. Other laws, such as those covering the family, reflect social mores, as they do in the West, for democratic practice is often colored by local customs. Thus, Islam's radical egalitarianism, upheld by the leveling effect of the absolute sovereignty of God and the absence of a creed of chosenness, is a great asset in the synthesis of Islam and democracy.

Take Iran, for instance. This country presents the fascinating case of an Islamic state ruling over "the most important homegrown democratic movement in the Muslim world," a movement that if successful can have as profound an effect on the rest of the Islamic world as did the 1979 Islamic revolution. For despite its authoritarian, clerical rule, Iran still has one of the most vibrant democracies in the Islamic world, let alone the sclerotic Arab one. As *New York Times* reporter Michael Slackman wrote when Iran was once again turning into an international pariah due to the outbursts of its president and its pursuit of suspicious nuclear technology:

> Paradoxically, civil society here appears vibrant. It has not been crushed, the way it has by the authoritarian leaders in the Arab world. There is, on many levels, real politics here—often with the outcome unknown—and on the most important issues, leaders must draw consensus from the different levels of power. And so people in many spheres—arts, sports, politics, business—find themselves pressing against the limitations of what is deemed permissible.[61]

Elsewhere, modern Turkey's unprecedented wholesale repudiation of its heritage and its reinvention in the West's image—albeit without the democratic component—has not succeeded in burying the Islamic impulse. In fact, Turkey's Kemalism (the secular revolutionary ideology instituted by the founding father of modern Turkey, Mustafa Kemal Atatürk) has given rise nowadays to what Noah Feldman has called "suit-and-tie Islamists" who have proven to be some of the best democrats in a country in which ultimate power resides with the military, much as it does with the Supreme Leader in Iran. There is no getting rid of Islam in Turkey, for "the more truly democratic Turkey becomes, the more Islamic it is likely to be."[62] In any case, Kemalism is certainly not recommended for anyone aspiring to establish democracy in the Muslim world. There are also various democratic possibilities in South and Southeast Asia, in countries like Malaysia, Bangladesh (what used to be East Pakistan), and Indonesia. The future of democracy in semifeudal, poor, politically volatile, and nuclear-armed Pakistan, whose made-up name amounts to the "land of the pure," is also of great import to the world.

The Arabs, meanwhile, collectively offer the worse prospects for democracy, except, possibly, in oil-less monarchies like Jordan and Morocco. Oil-rich monarchies have no "fiscal connection" to the people they govern and are opposed by democrats and Islamists for different reasons;

in Egypt, "in many ways the archetypal Arab nation,"[63] Islamism is the only democratic alternative; and finally, only "external intervention" can bring about change in oil dictatorships that are not monarchies. That's why Iraq is now the testing ground of whether the mobile ideas of Islam and democracy can benefit the long-suffering people of that nation, and offer a usable model to their fellow Muslims in other nations. Islamic democracy, too, is the only contemplated solution for tribal, multiethnic Afghanistan. It was Islam that brought the country together to resist the Soviet invasion; it was Islam (albeit in its extreme form) that helped the Taliban control much of the country; and it is now Islam that is helping build a new democratic nation.

The gradual democratization of Muslim societies, with the assistance of the United States and the West in general, is the only way to avoid violent revolutions, reduce anti-Americanism, temper hostilities toward Israel, and improve the living conditions of Muslims. As Feldman sees it, because "the West is partly responsible" for the Muslim tragedy, it should help. Many Muslims admire American democracy and power; so if the United States encouraged meaningful self-government, it could make allies of the 1.2 billion Muslims worldwide. While America has a moral duty to help Muslim societies democratize—through a wide spectrum of options, ranging from economic incentives and trade to military intervention to facilitate "democracy building"[64] but not nation building—one should not equate democratization with Americanization (democratic models could be quite varied) or assume that democracy is a Western concept. Rather, it is a mobile idea, just as Islam or any universalist ideology is. (It is helpful to remember that India has a vibrant democracy.) The involvement of Islamists in civil societies in much of the Islamic world makes them uniquely prepared for the synthesis of Islam and democracy in a new political culture. In short, the promise and challenge of the post-jihad phase is to establish a workable combination of Islam and democracy.

Feldman's book is remarkably well informed, balanced, and culturally fair, but he still assumes, as did the Bush administration, in contrast to a neoconservative trend that wanted to impose a Kemalist doctrine on Iraq, that the solution to Muslims is an open political process, not a challenge to deeply entrenched cultural habits. One could live in a relatively liberal political state—as in contemporary Morocco—but still come across strongly delineated limits for the freedom of speech and thought, as I discovered on a visit during 2004 to the only private, American-style university in the country. Before I lectured to students in a class on comparative religion, the Western professor complained about the trouble he was having engaging the students. It didn't surprise me at all: the vast majority of Muslims want to think of themselves as educated and knowledgeable about other ideas and faiths, but very few are willing to adopt what Fethi Benslama calls a "suppositional atheism" (*athéisme suppositionnel*), that is to say, to suspend their convictions in order to unshackle their thought processes.[65] Such jealously held notions of self and identity make it rather perilous for scholars or thinkers to venture outside culturally sanctioned bounds. Feldman himself provides an interesting example in *After Jihad*. In 1985, when General Mohammed Zia ul-Haq added the supremacy of Islam in all legislative matters to the Constitution, he opened the door "for harsh blasphemy laws and the imposition of severe *hudud* punishments; and Islamists who sought to change other laws now had a powerful symbolic constitutional basis on which to rest their arguments." The *hudud* laws were particularly injurious to rape victims who were prosecuted for adultery if they couldn't produce four male witness to support their charges.[66]

A poignant example of *hudud* laws is the case of the forty-one-year-old Abdul Rahman Jawed, a severely mentally ill Afghani convert to Christianity accustomed to mistreating his father, wife, and children, whose case came to light in March 2006. After "wandering aimlessly through the world for years" and being denied political asylum in Germany in 2000, Abdul Rahman returned to his family, which instantly turned him in to the authorities to stand trial and possible execution for his apostasy under his country's new constitution and in full view of American administrators. The accused had converted sixteen years earlier, but that he could still be tried under the new U.S.-sponsored regime shows that the old tension between freedom of thought and belief and the supremacy of Islam had not been resolved by the U.S. intervention. Even when much of the world protested this barbaric treatment and backed the hapless Christian, Afghan Supreme Court Judge Ansarullah Mawlavizada said that if the apostate (who had converted abroad) "doesn't revert back to Islam, he's going to receive the death penalty, according to the law."[67] Later that year, Womankind Worldwide, a U.K.-based women's rights organization, published a report showing that five years after the U.S.-led regime change in Afghanistan, Afghani women were still being sold off as brides before the age of

sixteen, exchanged to settle debts and disputes, subjected to honor kill-
ings and high levels of violence, and were setting themselves on fire—all
in areas *not* controlled by the Taliban.[68]

Such attitudes should not have been surprising: in 1997, special rappor-
teurs for the UN Commission on Human Rights "found that there was
severe oppression in countries with an official state religion."[69] Even in a
modern and open society like Malaysia, whose population is about 60 percent Muslim, a Malay cannot renounce Islam and convert to another religion because, according to that country's constitution, to be ethnically
Malay is to be Muslim. To publicly convert could lead to incarceration in
a barbed, wire-ringed religious rehabilitation camp, not to mention the
usual social persecution meted out to apostates. Lawyers defending the
rights of apostates also receive death threats and seek police protection as
the country slides toward the increasing Islamization of public life. "It's
only a matter of time before Malaysia becomes another Taliban state,"
commented the director of Women's Aid Organization in August 2006.
Even in Thailand, the government is making concessions to Muslim insurgents in the far southern part of the country to allow the implementa-
tion of the *sharia* law in that region.[70]

To be sure, whether a state should establish an official faith for the country is a question that has yet to be fully addressed by the United Nations.
Along with most Muslim nations, the constitutions of the Republic of Ire-
land, Greece, and Malta explicitly or implicitly affirm a state religion;[71]
yet as Robert F. Drinan points out, how is one to reconcile such limits
with Article 18 of the Universal Declaration of Human Rights (UDHR),
which states, "Everyone has the right to freedom of thought, conscience,
and religion or belief, and freedom, either alone or in community with
others and in public and in private, to manifest his religion or belief in
teaching, practice, worship and observance." This principle is actually
quite universal; it is repeated in Article 18 of the International Covenant on
Cultural and Political Rights (ICCPR), Article 9 of the European Convention on Human Rights (ECHR), Article 12 of the American Convention
on Human Rights (AmCHR), somewhat acknowledged in Article 8 of the
Organization of African Unity's African Charter on Human and People's
Rights (AfrCHR), Article 14 of the 1989 Covenant on the Rights of the
Child (CRC) (the latter accepted by every nation except the United States).
It was, in fact, Article 18 of the UDHR that led the only six Muslim nations

present at the drafting of that document in 1948 to abstain from the vote.[72] One might agree with Feldman that Muslims are resistant to change, but this doesn't mean that pressure should not be placed on governments to simultaneously respect their citizens' traditions while de-Islamizing their constitutions. As Drinan thoughtfully puts it:

> One basic truth in the interaction of government and religion is that a government should not seek to create the values of the society that it manages. The government should reflect preexisting values on the fundamental issues confronting a society, such as the structure of the family and the nature and hierarchy of crimes. No government may invent its own morality; to do so would not be ruling with the consent of the governed. At the same time, no government can simply accept unilaterally a code of values inherited from the religious traditions of previous generations. Nevertheless, a nation should be slow to abandon laws, practices, and customs rooted in a consensus that derives ultimately from a religious framework.[73]

Drinan recognizes, perhaps like Feldman, that it may take time to separate the two realms of God and Caesar in Muslim societies, but there has been no hint of a trend in this direction among such states. The Catholic Church, as obstinate as it may appear to be at times, is in fact way ahead on the issue of separating state and church. The Vatican accepted the principle of Article 18 in the UDHR in 1965, when the Second Vatican Council adopted the Catholic Church's Declaration on Religious Freedom, known as *Dignitatis Humanae,* signed by Archbishop Karol Wojtyla, who later became Pope John Paul II, forcefully stating that governments should have no say in, reward, punish, or treat differently an individual's belief or lack thereof, thereby reflecting most human rights principles. Pope Benedict XVI, in an encyclical delivered in the first year of his pontificate (2005), repeated the same view when affirming that "the State may not impose religion" although "it must guarantee religious freedom and harmony between the followers of different religions."[74]

To say that we need to find a working formula for freedom in Muslim societies does necessarily mean encoding this modus vivendi in the language of a constitution, for to describe constitutions as Islamic or Christian, for instance, would be to exclude non-Muslims and non-Christians from equal status in the body politic and to coerce citizens into adapting to the state religion. Fundamentalists in Muslim societies thrive on the pretense that they are closer to the spirit of Islam than those who are busy studying, say, French literature or German philosophy. Time being what it is, the advantage in states with formally established religions is always toward the religious, which then narrows and limits political and social contestations to the interpretation of scripture, not the exploration of other non-Islamic traditions. Regular mosque attendance, daily recitations of the Qur'an, a major in Islamic Studies all may preclude a broader knowledge of the infinitely rich traditions of the world, but they do confer legitimacy and strengthen the hands of fundamentalists who, by virtue of their education, feel authorized to define what is and is not acceptable in an Islamic state.

The tyranny of majorities, as Alexis de Tocqueville noted, is ever a threat to the lofty outcomes of any democracy. While duly noting the Anglo-American exception of successfully blending "the *spirit of religion* and the *spirit of freedom*," because in some important way in the United States "religion is considered as the guardian of mores, and mores are regarded as the guarantee of the laws and pledge for the maintenance of freedom itself,"[75] he expressed real apprehension about the tyranny of the majority in such democracies, a feature that he found "most repulsive."[76] Where there is a strong cultural consensus, even if not legalized by the Constitution, as is the case in the United States, there is no relief mechanism for a person seeking leniency or justice if the majority rules that such a person is guilty or to be ostracized:

> When a man or a party suffers an injustice in the United States, to whom can he turn? To public opinion? That is what forms the majority. To the legislative body? It represents the majority and obeys it blindly. To the executive power? It is appointed by the majority and serves as its passive instrument. To the police? They are nothing but the majority under arms. A jury? The jury is the majority vested with the right to pronounce judgment; even the judges in certain states are elected by the majority. So, however iniquitous or unreasonable the measure which hurts you, you must submit.[77]

The unfettered and total power of the majority stifles independent thought, censors speech, and dampens creativity. "I know no country," Tocqueville stated, "in which, speaking generally, there is less independence of mind and true freedom of discussion than in America."[78] If someone transgresses the bounds of acceptable norms, he or she will face all sorts of exclusions and will be abandoned by friends, while those who share the writer's opinion will retreat into silence. The rule of the majority is, in effect, the perfect form of "despotism," since "literary genius cannot exist without freedom of the spirit, and there is no freedom of the spirit in America."[79] Although education is widespread, "genius becomes rarer,"[80] while right appearances and hypocrisy assume a vital role.[81] Under these conditions, and since Americans are constantly on the move making money, improving their careers, seeking profit, or, in any case, avoiding the appearance of idleness, "the majority in the United States takes over the business of supplying the individual with a quantity of ready-made opinions and so relieves him of the necessity of forming his own."[82] No wonder numbers count more than ideas. "It is the theory of equality applied to brains," Tocqueville noted rather ruefully.[83]

The specter of America's mediocrity and homogeneity "saddens and chills him," but Tocqueville didn't give up on the spread of democracy, which is inevitable anyway, provided it leads to the conditions of equality without the pitfalls of the American condition. "The nations of our day cannot prevent conditions of equality from spreading in their midst. But it depends upon themselves whether equality is to lead to servitude or freedom, knowledge or barbarism, prosperity or wretchedness," he concluded.[84]

It is important to remember that Tocqueville did not intend to write a "panegyric," as he put it, because, for one thing, he wasn't sure that American democracy was good for other nations. Like most people watching America today, he saw in "America more than America itself; it was the shape of democracy itself which I sought, its inclinations, character, prejudices, and passions; I understand it so as at least to know what we have to fear or hope therefrom."[85] To be sure, he did note that because of their accomplishments and successful democratic institutions Americans "have an immensely high opinion of themselves and are not far from believing that they form a species apart from the rest of the human race,"[86] a national idiosyncrasy that was also noted by the British writer Anthony Trollope's mother, Fanny Trollope, in her 1832 book *Domestic Manners of the Americans:*

> A single word indicative of doubt, that any thing, or every thing, in that
> country is not the very best in the world, produces an effect which must be

seen and felt to be understood. If the citizens of the United States were indeed the devoted patriots they call themselves, they would surely not thus encrust themselves in the hard, dry, stubborn persuasion, that they are the first and best of the human race, that nothing is to be learnt, but what they are able to teach, and that nothing is worth having, which they do not possess.[87]

Apart from noting Americans' sense of exceptionalism, Tocqueville also knew that the American political model cannot be reproduced elsewhere because

the Americans are in an exceptional situation, and [it] is unlikely that any other democratic people will be similarly placed. Their strictly Puritan origin; their exclusively commercial habits; even the country they inhabit, which seems to divert their minds from the study of science, literature, and the arts; the accessibility of Europe, which allows them to neglect these things without relapsing into barbarism—a thousand causes, of which I have indicated only the most important, have singularly concurred to fix the mind of the American on purely practical objects. His desires, needs, education, and circumstances all seem united to draw the American's mind earthward. Only religion from time to time makes him turn a transient and distracted glance toward heaven.[88]

The most important thing, as he wrote in the preface to the twelfth edition in 1848, is to "not turn to America in order slavishly to copy the institutions she has fashioned for herself, but in order that we may better understand what suits us," to "look there for instruction rather than models," and "adopt the principles rather than the details of her laws."[89] Tocqueville, in idiosyncratic prophetic manner, even pronounced the American model unsuitable to Muslim societies because, whereas American democracy and republicanism have always rested on a bedrock of Christian mores, such a combination would not work in the Muslim world partly because Christianity and Islam produce different effects and place different demands on their faithful.

In the United States, it would seem that Caesar's and Jesus's spheres have blended into a republican ideology that is balanced in a sustainable tension, as Noll has noted, but the situation in Islamic countries is radically different. The Qur'an is not like the Gospels; it is a different document, one that is far more prescriptive and legalistic. It operates, in fact, as a miniconstitution, since it reaches far deeper into the regulation of behavior and society than does the New Testament:

> Muhammad brought down from heaven and put into the Koran not religious doctrines only, but political maxims, criminal and civil laws, and scientific theories. The Gospels, on the other hand, deal only with the general relations between man and God and between man and man. Beyond that, they teach nothing and do not oblige people to believe anything. That alone, among a thousand reasons, is enough to show that Islam will not be able to hold its power long in ages of enlightenment and democracy, while Christianity is destined to reign in such ages, as in all others.[90]

One could say that what stands between the actually tyranny of the majority and the freedom of minorities in the United States is, in fact, the constitutional legacy of forcing the separation between private belief and public freedom. But it is a separation fraught with tensions and recriminations, particularly now as evangelical Christian movements and secularists are back in the ideological trenches, somewhat overcome, of the late eighteenth century. As I mentioned at the beginning of this chapter, it would seem that the United States is going back to its prerevolutionary cultural norms, or at least undergoing a major religious awakening that risks to tilt the balance in the direction of the theological, which is why it is even more urgent to heed Tocqueville's warning against the rule of the majority.

That the United States has become the ironic mirror image of the Islamic world is best illustrated by Noah Feldman's subsequent treatise on the "church-state problem" in his home country. Influenced by the synthesis in his own personal life—modern Orthodox Jew and American—and his work on Islam and constitutional democracy, he sets out to make sense of a country "divided by God" (the title of his book) and to figure out "what to do about it."[91] He clearly wants to strike the middle ground between what he calls "values evangelicals" and "legal secularists," by tempering the secularists' zeal and insisting that James Madison and Thomas Jefferson, both advocates of separating state and church, were not *secularists* in the modern sense of the word. Feldman then struggles to show that the constitution grew out of an implicit Protestant consensus; that Madison's preference was not to have a Bill of Rights; that the First Amendment was not intended to apply to the states; that the main goal was to protect conscience by opposing coerced taxation, even if presumably to benefit one's own cult. Even if the framers would not have cared about religious symbols in public buildings (such as the case of the Moses of Alabama mentioned earlier in this chapter), Feldman's critique of the legal secularists' logic remains unconvincing. Why not assume framers like Benjamin Franklin and Jefferson to have been social hypocrites *because of* the Protestant consensus?[92] Tom Paine, the man who inspired American troops to sever ties with tyrannical Britain, and who expediently used the symbolism of Christianity to advance the cause of the revolution, was certainly not a believer.

As rapid urbanization led to calls for public education to inculcate moral values and provide basic skills for the good functioning of republican government, a new theology of "nonsectarian" Christianity, with its canonical Protestant King James Bible—opposed though it was by orthodox Protestants and Catholics, for whom the King James Bible was unacceptable—became the unofficial religion of the United States, a fact that explains why the U.S. government forced Mormons to give up their right to polygamy and so interfered with liberty of conscience protected by the First Amendment.[93] Thus, the state-imposed "nonsectarian Christianity" proved that "religion used in the service of national identity need not be religion deeply felt."[94] It's an interesting proposition—one, however, that is unlikely to work in the long term, for religion, even if lightly felt, has the potential to intensify into the most extreme forms of piety if and when the faithful succumb to intolerable socioeconomic and political pressures.

It was therefore the rise of liberal trends in Christian theology (inspired by new scientific discoveries), the elite theories of "strong secularism" (such as evolution), and the pretenses of a highbrow culture that went with it that fueled the rise of Christian fundamentalism.[95] By introducing the notion of minorities and secularism for the first time to the American court system in the 1930s and 1940s, the Supreme Court empowered both legal secularists and their opponents.[96] As the Jewish and Christian heritages, together with the Protestant–Catholic divide, were collapsed into an indistinguishable Judeo-Christian culture, the new consensus of "evangelical fundamentalism" arose to defend the rights of (Christian) "minorities" under the sway of a legal secularist ideology. Questions of morality—such as abortion—united Protestants and Catholics for the first time in American history.

Liberals have been winning symbolic culture wars (against such causes as government-funded public displays of religion), while conservatives "have been winning the war over institutions and economics," which, as Feldman wryly implies, might be just fine for the liberal elites.[97] Part of the blame for this stalemate over the nature of America's national identity rests, according to Feldman, with the legal secularists who dismiss the majority consensus and treat religion as a "conversation stopper." Feldman rightly argues that one can engage values evangelicals in conversation, although he doesn't reflect on the limits of such conversations. Even if one were to approach values evangelicalism as "a type of multiculturalist pluralism,"[98] this latter-day attempt at nonsectarianism doesn't really resolve the foundational differences among the diverse faiths in the nation. Neither approach, then, seems satisfactory.

In the end, Feldman eschews the extremes of France's *laïcité* (the strict distancing of the state from all religious matters) and the constitutional arrangements he recommends for Muslims by acknowledging "the centrality of religion to many citizens' values while keeping religion and government in some important sense distinct."[99] This doesn't sound very different from the U.S. historical compromise, for while Feldman would allow public religious displays and speech (as part of a national conversation), he is opposed to funding particular religious agendas. The difference between symbolism and funding is crucial: "Speech and symbols, in other words, are not the same as funding. Talk can always be reinterpreted, and more talk can always be added, so religious speech and symbols need not exclude. Cold cash, by contrast, is concrete and finite, and thus subject to divisive competition of a different order."[100] This might allow minority religions (and there is nothing inherently wrong with being a minority) to lobby for more inclusion over time and secularists to define their own values in the national conversation.

In *After Jihad,* Feldman concludes with this rather enigmatic statement: "If there is to be a jihad of the peaceful sort, it will have to be one waged by Muslim democrats and America in tandem."[101] Here is another form of alliance between Islam and America, an alternative version to the one advocated by Dinesh D'Souza against leftists, his country's public enemy number one. But which America does Feldman have in mind? I have already argued that the America that made the case for and eventually set in motion a process of "regime change" in Afghanistan and Iraq seems to be more interested in establishing a democratic political process, not in facilitating the birth of truly democratic and pluralist traditions, ones that can encompass radically different views and belief systems without succumbing to endless strife. This is why I think Afghanistan, Iraq, and the Middle East in general, if not the world as a whole, are the places where the United States works out its own domestic tensions. (A fascinating illustration of this is the U.S. government's support for an antigay bill introduced by Iran at the United Nations at a time when the current administration was actively seeking to punish Iran for pursuing a nuclear energy program.)[102] Regime change, *à l'americaine,* is therefore unlikely to temper the drive toward fundamentalism that fuels extremist and violent tendencies, since religious fundamentalism hardens into systems that promise much and deliver little. One could think of fundamentalism as a form of nativism, since its main goal is to protect a nation's or people's identity from the threat of contamination, impurity, or even extinction. But it is also the outcome of precarious economic conditions, the sigh of the helpless and oppressed (to echo Karl Marx) in the cold world of cash interests, the reassertion of human dignity in the face of cruel depredations and countless forms of alienation.

There is no doubt that the struggle for survival in a world of plenty narrows the scope of tolerance by barricading the mind behind the fortresses of imagined identities and rock-solid religious truths. A people so preoccupied are unlikely to coexist with differences or genuinely believe in pluralism, nor can they be of much help to other nations. While it's not impossible to assume that the United States was motivated by reasonable intentions when it undertook regime change in Afghanistan and Iraq, the prospects for a vibrant tradition of social and intellectual freedoms in those countries, or in much of the Islamic world, are still not on the horizon, mostly because the United States has not insisted on its own revolutionary standards. What's worse, and sadly ironic, is that America itself is now so far removed from its own democratic principles that it, too, needs to actively reclaim its eighteenth-century heritage—its most precious legacy to humanity.

chapter 5

America and Its Discontents

No novelty in the United States struck me more vividly during my stay there than the equality of conditions.

—ALEXIS DE TOCQUEVILLE, *Democracy in America*

You can have wealth concentrated in the hands of a few, or democracy, but you cannot have both.

—LOUIS BRANDEIS

Two years or so after the events of 9/11, and not long after the United States invaded Iraq to liberate its people and spread freedom around the Middle East, some of my friends and colleagues became so disenchanted with President George W. Bush's policies that they seriously contemplated moving to Canada. Their sense of helplessness in not being able to stop the war in the Middle East and their fear of losing their civil liberties were part of such a generalized feeling among Americans with progressive and liberal views that *Harper's* magazine published a reader's guide to expatriating if the Republican Party won the presidential election on November 2, 2004. Bryant Urstadt, the author of this brief guide, began by outlining how difficult it is to renounce U.S. citizenship and explained that, despite being members of NAFTA, Mexico and Canada's immigration requirements have complicated the expatriation process; that France requires a rigorous assimilation process culminating in the publication of one's name in the *Journal officiel de la République Française;* that U.S. allies like Pakistan and Uzbekistan also have long waiting periods; that although citizenship in tropical Caribbean islands is still for sale, open slots are going fast; that Indian reservations within the United States are not much help since one retains dual citizenship and is therefore expected to vote; that residing on the high seas (that is, on some ship, whether a floating apartment house or a tanker) still doesn't clear you from membership in a nation, since both vessel and occupants are still citizens of land-based nations; that starting one's own nation is also not easy; and, finally, that obtaining world citizenship from the Internet-based World Service Authority may subject one to arrest at the borders of other nations who don't recognize the outfit. It turns out that "renunciants," as people who want to drop their U.S. citizenship are called, cannot sever ties with their country that easily. That may not be a bad thing, after all. The day after the outcome of the 2004 presidential elections, Sarah Anderson, a fellow at the Institute for Policy Studies, hastily listed ten reasons why American liberals and progressives should "stay in the belly of the beast" and not "buy a one-way ticket north," while the government of Canada (still attracting tens of thousands of Americans every year) promptly warned unhappy liberals that, unless they claimed refugee status, it would take anywhere from four months to a year to get their immigration documents in order.[1]

My friends' threats to leave the country were mostly an expression of strong partisan political views, but I couldn't help thinking about the irony of people in the freest country in the world, one that was in the process of liberating Afghanis and Iraqis from despotic regimes, seeking freedom in next-door, quiet Canada. Without the earth-shattering Declaration of Independence or the landmark U.S. Constitution, Canada has, in fact, long been the asylum for hounded slaves (particularly after the infamous Fugitive Act of 1850 that made it easy to recapture escaped slaves), conscientious objectors, draft dodgers, and many Americans who, for one reason or another, try to evade or leave the United States to remake their lives. The estimated one hundred thousand American opponents to the Vietnam War—half of whom were draft-age resisters—who fled to Canada in the 1960s and early 1970s constituted "the largest politically motivated exodus from the United States since the country's beginning." And more than half chose to stay, too, despite President Jimmy Carter's partial pardon (certainly not an amnesty) of draft resisters and army deserters in 1977. The reelection of George W. Bush in 2004 and the war in Iraq also prompted a motley group of Americans, ranging from middle-aged college professors and financial planners to draft dodgers, war deserters, young decorated soldiers, and Vietnam War veterans to register their dissent and seek freedom north of the border.[2]

How could one make sense of Americans seeking freedom away from their homeland, except as the failure of the present generation to build on and consolidate the legacy of the Revolution? Although the United States is already in its third century as a nation, whose creation was a landmark event in human history, unleashing hitherto unimaginable possibilities for human beings everywhere, it has yet to articulate a vision that would gather its citizens in meaningful rituals of social solidarity. The single-minded pursuit of riches and might has proven to be singularly injurious to the welfare of individuals and communities alike, since the obsession with personal advancement enervates the psyche and impoverishes the cultural traditions that might otherwise enrich lives and make them more meaningful. As this chapter shows, the evidence is now overwhelming that the republican experiment, painstakingly elaborated by the Founding Fathers, is being steadily undone by the takeover of a new corporate mind-set, which, according to Richard Sennett in *The Culture of the New Capitalism,* is condemning most American workers to a state of permanent angst.[3] A nation wrestling with such demons is hardly in a position to rescue fallen ones.

That America is a place of both hope and disillusionment has long been noted by observers of the country. This sense of simultaneous triumph and loss, self-affirmation and self-doubt, freedom and fear was noted by the Frenchman J. Hector St. John de Crèvecoeur (1735–1813) in *Letters from an American Farmer* (1782) and *Sketches of Eighteenth-Century America* (first published by Yale University Press in 1925). As with many writers and preachers in the American tradition before him, in the hands of Crèvecoeur America appears as a land of promise and the burial ground for shattered dreams, a paradise regained only to be lost again.[4] James, Crèvecoeur's American farmer who finds nothing more exalting that the ownership of his 317-acre farm, defines America as a middle-class nation of cultivators where "the rich and the poor are not so far removed from each other as they are in Europe."[5] It is an egalitarian republic: "We have no princes for whom to toil, starve, and bleed," he writes to Abbé Raynal, a controversial writer and champion of liberty; "we are the most perfect society now existing in the world."[6] This "great American asylum" is home to a "promiscuous breed" of mostly poor, hard-working, and industrious "English, Scotch, Irish, French, Germans, and Swedes,"[7] who no sooner set foot in America than they melt "into a new race of men, whose labours and posterity will one day cause great changes in the world." Leaving the old behind, the new American is reinvented in his or her new natural, political, and economic environment, becoming litigious in the process, since a free and property-loving people are bound to quarrel. The law inspects Americans' actions, while "our thoughts are left to God."[8]

There are no strangers in America, either, since everyone is essentially one, and the country is big enough to make room for everybody. Indeed, "this great continent must in time absorb the poorest part of Europe; and this will happen in proportion as it becomes better known and as war, taxation, oppression, and misery increase there."[9] As the European foreigner is naturalized, America will welcome her thus:

> Welcome to my shores, distressed European; bless the hour in which thou didst see my verdant fields, my fair navigable rivers, and my green mountains! If thou wilt work, I have bread for thee; if thou wilt be honest, sober, and industrious, I have greater rewards to confer on thee—ease and independence. I will give thee fields to feed and clothe thee, a comfortable fireside to sit by and tell thy children by what means thou hast prospered, and a decent bed to repose on. I shall endow thee beside with the immunities of a freeman. If thou wilt carefully educate thy children, teach them gratitude to God and reverence to that government, that philanthropic government, which has collected here so many men and made them happy, I will also provide for thy progeny; and to every good man this ought to be the most holy, the most powerful, the most earnest wish he can possibly form, as well as the most consolatory prospect when he dies. Go thou and work and till; thou shalt prosper, provided thou be just, grateful, and industrious.[10]

Religious without being zealots or even passionate about their convictions, Americans take property very seriously, writes Crèvecoeur:

> From earliest infancy we are accustomed to a greater exchange of things, a greater transfer of property than the people of the same class in Europe. Whether it is occasioned by that perpetual and necessary emigrating genius

which constantly sends the exuberancy of full societies to replenish new tracts; whether it proceeds from our being richer; whether it is that we are fonder of trade, which [is] but an exchange—I cannot ascertain.[11]

The typical American is a land merchant willing to settle, sell, and reset-tle again, braving uncertainty and danger in the process. He will likely have several occupations in a lifetime and be a "universal fabricator like Crusoe."[12] Always a stranger, the self-reliant, self-made, but essentially solitary American doesn't tolerate failure or weakness in others, brings the severity of the law to bear on the fallen, and, unless detected by the law himself, arms himself with deception to counter his deceptive partners:

> The law, therefore, and its plain meaning are the only forcible standards which strike and guide their senses and become their rule of action. 'Tis to them an armour serving as well for attack as for defence; 'tis all that seems useful and pervading. Its penalties and benefits are the only thing feared and remembered, and this fearful remembrance is what we might call in the closet a reverence for the law.
>
> With such principles of conduct as these, follow him in all these situa-tions which link men in society, in that vast variety of bargains, exchanges, barters, sales, etc., and adduce the effects which must follow. If it is not *bellum omnium contra omneas* 'tis a general mass of keenness and sagacious acting against another mass of equal sagacity; 'tis caution against caution. Happy, when it does not degenerate into fraud against fraud! The law, which cannot pervade and direct every action, here leaves her children to themselves and abandons those peccadilloes (which convulse not though they may [dim] some of the most beautiful colours of society) to the more invisible efficacy of religion.[13]

The new American has no option but to hustle and learn how to become more cunning.[14]

The country that promises so much to poor Europeans also inflicts in-humane cruelties on African slaves. Southern plantation owners do not want to hear even their own salaried clergymen preach leniency. Uphold-ers of the slave system invoke human nature and history to make their case, which leads James to wonder whether the "history of the earth" pre-sents "anything but crimes of the most heinous nature, committed from one end of the world to the other? We observe avarice, rapine, and murder, equally prevailing in all parts."[15] His view of the world begins to dim: "We certainly are not that class of beings which we vainly think ourselves to be; man, an animal of prey, seems to have rapine and the love of bloodshed implanted in his heart, nay, to hold it the most honourable occupation in society; we never speak of a hero of mathematics, a hero of knowledge or humanity, no, this illustrious appellation is reserved for the most successful butchers of the world."[16] The world now appears as "rather a place of punishment than of delight."[17] He wonders at how people suffer in well-endowed parts of the world because of tyranny and sees violence pervading all societies, be they republics or monarchies. Slowly, the farmer's exuberance and optimism give way to gloomy introspection, as the brutality, cruelty, and inhumanity of slavery awaken him to the dismal failure of all societies to ascend to a more humane world order.

Thus, after nineteen years of hard work on his farm, James comes to the bitter realization that the world has encroached too fast on his American Eden.[18] Imperial England has thrown his idyllic world into chaos. "Must those who are masters of two thirds of the trade of the world, who have in their hands the power which almighty gold can give, who possess a species of wealth that increases with their desires—must they establish their conquest with our insignificant, innocent blood?" he asks plaintively, eerily echoing what many Muslims, Latin Americans, and other people would say two and a half centuries later about the United States.[19] Despairing of the future, he resolves to free his slaves, give up on the American dream and its Christian underpinnings, and join the noble and peaceful Indians, the people Bradford and other Puritan settlers had branded as "savages." The farmer and his children would still be industrious and worship the Supreme Being, the universal god, but he would not let his children marry among the natives, for this would be "disagreeable" to "Nature's intentions, which have strongly divided us by so many indelible characters."[20]

This sense of high optimism in the revolutionary potential of the United States, coupled with the sobering realization that America's promise is forever receding into an unattainable future, has also been captured in Pulitzer Prize–winning historian Walter McDougall's *Freedom Just around the Corner* (not a reference to Canada, but an expression borrowed from Bob Dylan). McDougall concludes the first installment in a projected three-volume history about America's exceptional trajectory in modern history, forged by a breed of super hustlers, with the same note of disappointment.[21] After fleshing out many of the features already noted in Crèvecoeur's literary masterpiece and noting the genius of devising a system of "popular elections and divided sovereignties" that, along with other state and democratic prerogatives, guards against tyranny,[22] McDougall quotes David Tappan who, seven years after independence was declared and enthusiasm reigned over the country, wondered:

> Is human nature essentially different in this new world, from what it ever has been and still is in the old? Or are we more strongly fortified against the insinuating, bewitching charms of a prosperous condition? Are we a people of more established virtue than all others that have lived before us? Alas, Sirs, such self-flattering ideas are equally false and vain—our national character . . . is perhaps as degenerate as that of any people in the world?[23]

Not only this, but McDougall seems to have no illusions about the ultimate fate of human utopias and restless hustlers. He ends his book by referring to "The Crater" (1847), a story by James Fenimore Cooper, the author who had championed Americanism in his early career, about an island nation that starts out as a utopia and, over the course of history, disintegrates into all sorts of social strife before the whole nation is swallowed up in an earthquake.[24] It leaves the reader wondering whether the American experiment is another utopian dream gone awry.

The freedom that inspired but eluded pilgrims, revolutionaries, slave owners, capitalists, and imperialists has always defined and given meaning to American identity. In many ways, one cannot write the history of the United States without writing about its people's constant quest for freedom. As another award-winning historian, Eric Foner, showed in his epic study *The Story of American Freedom,* Americans have held on to the concept whenever they felt that their beliefs were not being translated into law or policy.[25] Yet the constant refrain of freedom may well indicate that freedom remains, as with all states of perfection, here or in the hereafter, a dream "just around the corner," to use McDougall's title again, never fully within reach. This could in fact be a problem for the American republic, since it predisposes citizens to constantly invoke a utopian ideal to settle even the most mundane of arguments. Americans have appealed to freedom to pray and engage in love, to liberate human beings from the shackles of slavery and protect the rights of slave owners and corporations from regulation, to fight communism and promote markets, to defend America from foreign threats and impose America's views on the world. Freedom, in fact, operates like an almighty deity available to whoever bothers to invoke it. Appealing to freedom in the United States is akin to involving God every time people disagreed. God becomes an equal-opportunity ally, joining opposite causes at once, turning, as often happens with freedom, into an all-purpose but empty ideal. It is certainly a "protean concept," as Foner states at the outset of his treatise.[26]

The lack of rhetorical consensus on the meaning of freedom could be traced to the two different views that arose from Enlightenment thought and that laid the basis of the American republic. Freedom entailed "republicanism" (participation in public affairs) and "liberalism" (freedom from political authority). Prior to the Revolution, economic dependents were not considered free and therefore were not fit citizens. One had to have a stake in society to be able to participate in it, a condition that excluded slaves, most women, and other disenfranchised groups. It never occurred to the Founding Fathers that the freedom of white men rested on the dependence of others. To white men, slavery simply meant taxation without representation. Among the fifty-five men who gathered in Philadelphia to write the Constitution, many were slave owners. Thomas Jefferson owned more than a hundred slaves by the time he wrote the Declaration of Independence, proving that freedom is not possible without the leisure derived from the slave system. The Constitution did include a sunset clause on the slave trade, allowing a transitional period of twenty years for slave owners to adjust, a provision that ironically resulted in the rush to import even more slaves to beat the deadline of January 1, 1808.[27]

Yet in this new "producer's republic," the U.S. Constitution erected a "wall of separation" between state and church and made it possible, as some complained then, for "a papist, a Mahometan, a deist, yea an atheist" to become president of the United States. For James Madison, the separation of state and church was crucial for the protection of liberties, including religious practices, which may explain why "more than one thousand three hundred religions are practiced in the United States" today.[28]

The Constitution created a race-conscious "American people." Blacks and Native Americans were not included, while the Naturalization Act of 1790 allowed only "free white persons" (no white aristocrats) to become citizens; blacks would only be added in 1870, nonwhites (Asians) in the 1940s. The Alien and Sedition Acts of 1798 (expiring in 1801) cracked down on both immigrants and dissidents, causing a public outrage that helped Jefferson get elected in 1800.[29] Thus was born Jefferson's "Empire of Liberty," with Americans constantly expanding their borders and annexing adjoining territories whenever they could. Foreigners were as dazzled by the free spirit that reigned in America then as they are now. A German immigrant in California wrote home to say that in America "there aren't any masters, here everyone is a free agent, [and] if you don't like one place you can go to another for we're all equal here,"[30] while one Norwegian immigrant exalted in his new status: "I am very proud of belonging to a mighty nation, whose institutions must in time come to dominate the entire civilized world."[31] It was free America's "manifest destiny" (an expression first used by John L. O'Sullivan, a journalist from New York in 1845) to grow into a superpower, as Tocqueville predicted.[32]

Even as Whigs and Democrats argued over the merits of a strong or weak government (republicanism or liberalism), "technological innovations in transportation and communication—the steamboat, canal, railroad, telegraph—linked farmers to national and international markets and, at least in the North, made them major consumers of manufactured goods." Banking and industry further fueled the spirit of entrepreneurship. The outcome was a new "market revolution" that redefined the meaning of freedom by reducing it to a question of personal, private choices, combined with the doctrine of self-reliance, but away from the prying reach of government and authorities:

> The opportunity for personal growth offered a new definition of Jefferson's pursuit of happiness, one well suited to a world in which democracy, territorial expansion, and the market revolution were shattering traditional spatial and social boundaries and making moving from place to place and status to status ubiquitous features of American life. Freedom suggested an unending process of self-realization by which individuals could remake themselves and their own lives.[33]

The new market revolution, underpinned by industrialization, relied on contractual labor or wage slavery, seen as a more insidious form of despotism, particularly in the South, where slavery was deemed the basis of freedom. Slavery had been part of the equation during the American Revolution, but wage slavery was not truly American. To counter such claims, the North defended "free labor," an ideology championed by the Republican Party, which by the mid-1850s had become the majority party in the North. Moreover, the nascent labor movement wanted to universalize private property, not abolish it,[34] as Karl Marx, for example, advocated in Europe.

It may be useful to note that Jefferson and Madison based their revolution on the economic model of an agrarian democracy. James Madison imagined a nation of small farmers protected by legislation that maintains the equality of conditions as the "workshop of liberty to the Civilized World";[35] yet the labor-intensive, plantation-style, and slave-dependent cotton economy preempted that notion. With the annexation of Texas in 1845, the inclusion of Mexicans, and a new wave of immigrants into the American population, the United States hardened its racist ideology. "In a country whose economic growth and territorial expansion required appropriating the land of one non-white group (Native Americans), and annexing much of a nation defined as non-white (Mexico)," writes Foner, "it was inevitable that nationhood and freedom would acquire powerful racial dimensions." As Catholic Mexicans and the Irish were being absorbed through annexation or immigration, "the idea that American freedom was linked to the innate liberty-loving qualities of Anglo-Saxon Protestants was widely popularized in the press and popular magazines. . . . The result was to reinvigorate long-standing hostility to 'Popery' and further reinforce the identification of liberty with the nation's putative Anglo-Saxon heritage." Even Abraham Lincoln, the Great Emancipator who didn't think of blacks as equal to whites, agreed that American liberty was not racially exclusive.[36]

The period after the Civil War, known as Reconstruction, gave birth to a new era of freedom for African Americans. The Thirteenth Amendment (abolishing slavery) was ratified in 1865; the Civil Rights Act (extending equal rights to all U.S. citizens, regardless of color) came in 1886; the Fourteenth Amendment (protecting the rights of all citizens), approved by Congress in 1866, was ratified in 1868; and the Fifteenth Amendment (equal voting rights) followed ten years later. Reconstruction did more than fulfill the promises of the Constitution; it was, according to Foner, "a radical repudiation of the nation's actual practice for the previous seven decades. Indeed, it was precisely for this reason that the era's laws and constitutional amendments aroused such bitter opposition."[37]

By the end of the nineteenth century, particularly in the decade of the 1890s, the country was afflicted with the worst recession of the century, huge disparities in wealth and income, and no more frontiers to conquer, a fact soberly announced by the Census Bureau in 1890 and popularized by Frederick Jackson Turner's famous frontier thesis three years later. Caught in the grips of laissez-faire conservatism and social Darwinism, American workers, whose ranks were swelling with 3.5 million new immigrants, had no option but to organize themselves (the American Federation of Labor, better known by its acronym, the AFL, was founded in 1895). Still, the progressive legacies of Reconstruction were nullified as race consciousness led to even stricter immigrations laws.[38]

The emergence of the "consumer" at the beginning of the twentieth century indicated a significant shift in Americans' consciousness. By 1928, André Siegfried, a Frenchman well acquainted with the United States, remarked that in this "new society," Americans' "standard of living" had become a "sacred acquisition, which they will defend at any price."[39] The Great Depression of the 1930s, however, brought to the front the dangers of unbridled capitalism and widely disproportionate distribution of wealth in the country, allowing Franklin Delano Roosevelt to launch the Second New Deal in 1935 and the Social Security Act as an "alternative to socialism and unregulated capitalism." (The Congress of Industrial Organizations [CIO] was established the same year, as was the Popular Front, an alliance of progressive and radical movements and parties.) These measures brought relief to the poor and blacks, who now abandoned the party of Lincoln and flocked to FDR's Democratic Party. Because freedom was now equated with home ownership, the government made it easier for blacks and the poor to get loans and built public housing, although, by 1938, the conservatives were making a comeback.[40]

The United States emerged from World War II as the torchbearer of freedom. The first human rights organization, Freedom House, founded by Eleanor Roosevelt, among others, was born in 1941. On January 6, 1941, FDR announced to Congress his Four Freedoms doctrine, one that embodies the "rights of men of every creed and every race, wherever they live."[41] He supported the call for an Economic Bill of Rights, a notion widely popular among workers and the middle class in wartime America (but which was watered down to the G.I. Bill of Rights in Congress). Racism was now viewed as un-American, by both blacks and liberal whites. In 1944, the Swedish scholar Gunnar Myrdal published *An American Dilemma,* commissioned by the Carnegie Foundation, concluding that racism had no place in "the American Creed." Ethnic Americans were included as equals. For the first time in U.S. immigration history, the Chinese were given an annual quota of 105 immigrants because of their alliance with the United States against the Japanese. Yet no one—not even the most liberal civil rights organizations—spoke against the internment of Japanese Americans in the United States, and blacks were still being lynched. In short, "full employment and fair employment became the watchwords of the progressive coalition that formed during the war," although businessmen were not thrilled. The latter emphasized "freedom of choice" as the most vital freedom of all, while their supporters in Congress introduced a bill to add "Freedom of Private Enterprise" as a "Fifth Freedom."[42]

Whether or not it was inspired by the Lenin Train of 1918, the conservative American Heritage Foundation, headed by Winthrop W. Aldrich, chairman of Chase Manhattan Bank, sponsored a Freedom Train in 1947, a traveling exhibition of America's major documents to "re-sell America to Americans." The exhibition didn't include the Thirteenth and Fourteenth Amendments or the Four Freedoms speech. It was the same year that the United States officially entered the Cold War, when President Harry Truman enunciated his Truman Doctrine, designed, as he put it, to "scare [the] hell" out of the American people, convincing them that Communism is a threat to their liberties. This fear would henceforth guide foreign policy while the government cracked down on dissent at home, instituted loyalty oaths, and fought unions. Anticommunism was used to roll back the New Deal, a tactical move that stymied Democrats (as it would in the 1990s with the stigmatizing of the word *liberal*). Some blacks wondered how Communism (supplanting racism) had become the new un-American entity.

Freedom was now associated with "suburbia utopia" and "consumer capitalism," with 82 percent of Americans, according to a 1958 poll, believing that "our freedom depends on the free enterprise system." The American Medical Association warned about the dangers of "socialized medicine" in its efforts to help defeat President Truman's plan for a national health insurance. M. C. Patterson, the vice president of the Chrysler Corporation, denounced "economic Spartanism" (the self-sufficiency that Ralph Waldo Emerson and Henry David Thoreau had advocated in the nineteenth century, and all major religions had preached throughout history) as socialism and a threat to "our free enterprise system." To show the strength of this system, another vice president, Richard Nixon, boasted to his rival, Soviet premier Nikita Khrushchev, in the famous 1959 "kitchen debate" in Moscow that American technology had managed to get rid of housework, liberating women from deadening chores, to which Khrushchev replied, echoing a great scene from Charles Chaplin's 1936 film *Modern Times,* "Don't you have a machine that puts food in the mouth and pushes it down?" Nevertheless, the Soviet Union bought into the U.S. ideology of measuring consumer products as an index of national freedom and strength. Interestingly, consumerism produced a monochrome blandness that led to more interfaith tolerance (America emerged as a Judeo-Christian society, as noted in the previous chapter), although by the late 1950s, sociologists began to detect a more insidious form of totalitarianism (the very thing the United States was fighting abroad) in the new culture of uniformity, orchestrated by powerful advertisement and public relations agencies.[43]

The time had come to revolt against the oppressive culture of the 1950s. Martin Luther King Jr. and Malcolm X emerged as spokesmen for two strands in the African American battle for justice, one reaching out to all Americans, the other preaching a more separatist ideology of black empowerment (although Malcolm X changed his stance after he broke with the Nation of Islam and traveled in Muslim lands). Because of this struggle, racism was outlawed as official national policy, leading the way to the immigration reforms of the 1965 Hart–Cellar Act that abandoned the national origins quota system. The gates were now open to massive immigration from Latin America and Asia. By 1976, the American public viewed America as a nation of all races and nationalities.

If the 1930s and 1940s were the decades of the New Deal, the 1960s was the decade of President Johnson's Great Society programs, one of the most progressive eras in American history. Johnson brought back FDR's lost "freedom from want" and signed a number of measures to fight poverty and discrimination. In 1964, Martin Luther King Jr. called for a "Bill of Rights for the Disadvantaged," and in 1966, his allies A. Philip Randolph and Bayard Rustin called for a "Freedom Budget."

Black struggles joined with young middle-class college students disenchanted with the status quo in a New Left movement opposed to the war in Vietnam and patriarchal authoritarianism. After the 1962 publication of Betty Friedan's *The Feminine Mystique,* dubbed the women's "Emancipation Proclamation," the kitchen, Nixon's emblem of American freedom in the Moscow debate, turned into a "comfortable concentration camp." The family was now the "the essential locus of women's lack of freedom." The Black Power movement inspired Chicanos, Native Americans, and homosexuals to do the same and demand more freedoms. Meanwhile, the Supreme Court strengthened freedom of speech and protected civil rights, emboldening all sorts of social groups to voice their grievances and seek remedies in court. With the rise of the New Left and the Sixties culture, America had come light years away from John Winthrop's universe. "Here was John Winthrop's nightmare of three centuries earlier made flesh," writes Foner, "a massive redefinition of freedom as a rejection of all authority." But the Sixties culture would prove to be enduring: many of its tenets have now become standard mainstream practices and expectations.[44]

Even as the New Left and the Civil Rights movement were leaving their imprints on American culture for generations to come, the conservative movement was getting ready to counterattack. The year Michael Harrington published his influential *The Other America* (1962) about the invisible poor in the United States, Milton Friedman published *Capitalism and Freedom,* calling for total laissez-faire capitalism. Meanwhile, the Republican Party nominated a very conservative candidate to run for president. In accepting his nomination in 1964, Barry Goldwater, author of *The Conscience of a Conservative* (1960), declared that "extremism in the defense of liberty is no vice" and that God had appointed the United States to lead a crusade for freedom across the world. In 1968, Republican Richard Nixon was elected president and reelected in 1972. In December 1974, General Motors sponsored yet another American Freedom Train to celebrate the bicentennial of American independence. This time, the exhibit didn't include original documents, only replicas, and was expanded to include artifacts of the consumer culture as the new token of freedom. By the 1970s, a neoconservative movement had risen and religious evangelicals, such as Jerry Falwell, were preaching that the Bible justifies "capitalism and free enterprise." No president had used the word *freedom* more extensively and deliberately than Ronald Reagan, who mixed economic laissez-faire and conservative values into a new public ideology in the 1980s. Anyone who was fighting a Soviet-style regime was considered a "freedom fighter" (a category that included the Taliban in Afghanistan). In fact, Reagan even claimed that the Russian language has no word for *freedom*. In 1986, Falwell changed his Moral Majority to the Liberty Foundation to reflect the mood of the age. Multiculturalism and identity politics, the outgrowth of the 1960s culture, came under attack, while books like *The Bell Curve* by Richard J. Herrnstein and Charles Murray (1994) and Peter Brimelow's *Alien Nation* (1995) got widespread attention. "By the 1990s, virtually no politician would admit to being a liberal," writes Foner. In 1996, President Clinton agreed to abolish the New Deal program of Aid to Dependent Children, known as "welfare."[45]

After 9/11, President George W. Bush launched Operation Enduring Freedom to punish the Taliban in Afghanistan and later Operation Iraqi Freedom to topple the regime of Saddam Hussein. When the French government refused to agree to a war in Iraq, most things French were discredited, including French fries, which Congress tried to rename "freedom fries." (The main sponsor of the bill, which never passed in the Senate, was Representative Bob Ney of Ohio, who later pleaded guilty in the Jack Abramoff corruption scandal in 2006. By that time, fries were quietly listed on the menu as French again. A lost cause, indeed!)[46] And part of this all-front freedom campaign was an attack on liberals who appeared ill suited to defend their nation, with their vaguely un-American, or, rather, French intellectual ways. In the 2004 presidential campaign, Senator John Kerry was often dismissed by his opponent as someone from Massachusetts, as if that state, founded by the Pilgrims, was not truly part of mainstream America. By the time the presidential race was coming to a close, evangelical Christians, Orthodox Jews, and Catholics were talking about an America that is enmeshed in a culture war and more divided than it had been before the Civil War. One evangelical organization, Focus on the Family, was telling its members that "the Bible teaches lessons about proper government, including not only opposition to abortion and same-sex marriage but also pre-emptive military action against suspected terrorists and looser environment regulations."[47]

In the face of this vociferous religious condemnation (some U.S. Catholics even wanted Kerry excommunicated for supporting abortion, although the Vatican didn't think he was a heretic),[48] Senator Kerry started quoting Scripture to highlight the Bible's emphasis on human solidarity and care of the weak.[49] After George W. Bush was reelected, Bob Jones III, the president of the fundamentalist Bob Jones University, wrote Bush a letter urging him to carry out his Christian-based policies to save liberal America from paganism. The founder and chairman of Focus on the Family, meanwhile, warned the Republicans who now controlled both the White House and Congress that they would pay a political price if they didn't deliver on their conservative promise.[50]

Eric Foner's history of *freedom* in America leaves the reader with the distinct impression that Americans have been negotiating the contradictory meanings of the word since the American Revolution, wavering between the republican ideals of strong government control dispensing justice and arbitrating among contending interests, and the more liberal definition of severing the individual from the oversight of the state and all regulation, an ideal that has been embraced by business interests, even though they benefit from the government's largesse in the form of contracts and other indirect costs and cause incalculable damage to the commons. As a free-market economy has come to be seen as the foundation of the country's political freedom, the claims of humans under social duress have been tougher to remedy. It may be that the hope fired by the American Revolution, as Foner wrote in a subsequent article decrying President Bush's appropriation of this "contested concept,"[51] is not extinguished and makes oppression harder to justify or maintain over time, but conditions are so radically different now that it may well be that both the America of the Pilgrims and that of the Revolution are in the process of being transformed beyond recognition.

Foner's version of this history, of which I have given a rather extended account, shows that the edifice of civil liberties rests on rather fragile foundations, dependent as it is on a precarious compromise, carefully etched in a constitutional language that has stayed the hand of absolutists throughout much of modern American history. But since the tendency in America, as in all utopian projects, is toward disillusionment and even tragedy, as Crèvecoeur's classic and McDougall's history, for instance, make clear, I wonder whether freedom will survive the ongoing Christian fundamentalist surge and the onslaught of commercial forces. We are already so far removed from the republican virtues that animated Jefferson and the generation that followed that the concept now is often confined to shopping choices (and we are practically all shoppers in what Guy Debord called the "society of the spectacle"), voting for prepackaged candidates in a plethora of elections, and maintaining the fiction of our private, secure space in a world lurking with all sorts of ghosts. The ingenious model combining Jesus Christ and John Locke, decidedly the most influential figure on the Founding Fathers, as Brooke Allen states in *Moral Minority,* is now faltering under the crusading spirit of a new fundamentalism, described by its adherents as "maximalism," which means the fundamentalists' "ambition to conform every aspect of society to God."[52] Although these new Christians claim to believe in American scripture, one that includes, in addition to the Declaration of Independence and the Constitution, the obscure Northwest Ordinance of 1787, which explicitly states the role of religion in "good government" (a fact that, as we saw in the previous chapter, was widely shared), their worldview is darkly medieval, despite the light that Jesus is supposed to bring to our troubled world. "These are days of the sword, literally," wrote Jeff Sharlet in a report on the movement in December 2006, as "affluent members of the movement gift one another with real blades crafted to medieval standards, a fad inspired by a best-selling book called *Wild at Heart.*" Like the Qutb brothers, these "maximalists" sound as alternatively oppressed victims and determined revolutionaries, believing in the nurturing fold of the "mother church," but knowing that the time now is for the "father Church," with its Old Testament creed of discipline and jihads.[53]

Whatever such fundamentalists, whose leaders sometimes confuse George Orwell with Orson Welles, say about their equal devotion to the foundations of the American republic, they are clearly worlds apart from the culture that made Benjamin Franklin, George Washington, John Adams, Thomas Jefferson, James Madison, and Alexander Hamilton, the main figures examined in Brooke Allen's religious portrait of these men. Like many of his comrades, John Adams was all too aware of the insidious power religion could have on unsuspecting minds. "There is a germ of religion in human nature so strong," he observed, "that whenever an order of men can persuade the people by flattery or terror that they have salvation at their disposal, there can be no end to fraud, violence, or usurpation." That Adams had little in common with the maximalists is clear from what he wrote in 1812: "Montesquieu had sense enough to say in Jest, that all our Knowledge might be comprehended in twelve Pages in

Duodecimo: and, I believe him, in earnest. I could express my Faith in shorter terms." Thomas Jefferson, who once summed up his views as epicurean, was even more straightforward. Sounding more like Sam Harris in *The End of Faith* than the fundamentalists who are trying to reclaim him as a misquoted Christian, he looked forward to the day "when the mystical generation of Jesus, by the Supreme Being as his father, in the womb will be classed with the fable of the generation of Minerva in the brain of Jupiter." He considered the notion of the Trinity absurd, "the hocus-pocus of a God like another Cerberus, with one body and three heads, [which] had its birth and growth in the blood of thousands and thousands of martyrs. . . . In fact, the Athanasian paradox that one is three, and three but one, is so incomprehensible to the human mind, that no candid man can say he has any idea of it, and how can he believe what present[s] no idea?"[54]

It is therefore not surprising that those who wanted to flee the country after the reelection of George W. Bush in 2004 were afraid that America's constitutional legacy was threatened by the ascendancy of powerful evangelical movements opposed to gay marriages, abortion and contraception,[55] evolution, racial integration, and peace. But few seemed to worry as much about whether the problems in the United States stem from the pursuit of a ruinous economic model. To be sure, the ideals of the early Pilgrims and the Founding Fathers have mostly vanished from popular sight, but it is the failure to ground the political and cultural on a solid, democratic, and humane economic base that is the cause, as we shall see in the rest of this chapter, of America's and, increasingly, the world's woes.

"As I see it," Alistair Cooke once wrote, "in this country—a land of the most persistent idealism and the blandest cynicism—the race is on between its decadence and its vitality."[56] In a way, America's legendary British observer was repeating what the first Pilgrim leaders had realized (and tried to prevent) early on in the process of establishing a new nation: that America would be torn between its saintly and worldly natures; its desire for righteousness and its pursuit of wealth and power; its shining beacon of hope and justice for the world's dispossessed and its constant intervention in world affairs; its attraction for hard-working, risk-taking, and entrepreneurial immigrants and its endemic fear of foreigners and alien influences; its striking openness and hospitality and its sometimes unforgiving, punitive impulse. These traits were discernible in the early colonial days and in the early decades of the new republic, but the greatest novelty today, and one that seriously risks undermining America's majestic political experiment, is the disappearance of the "equality of conditions" that Alexis de Tocqueville thought was the most outstanding trait of American democracy and James Madison thought was crucial to the success of an enlightened republic. (In "The Federalist No. 10," Madison knew that human societies are always divided between the haves and have-nots, but it was the function of the Republican government to mediate and attenuate the resulting social tensions.) Describing "landed monopoly" as "the greatest evil," Thomas Paine called for a social security system that indemnifies those who lease humanity's common heritage—land, and, one might add today, air and water—to those who grow rich from its exploitation.[57] Even Benjamin Franklin, the hard-headed realist and astute reader of public sentiments, the quintessential American and Renaissance man who turned his life into a parable, didn't seem to foresee the social extremes of wealth and poverty that would become a feature of America life. (Black slaves and Native Americans were, of course, never included in the picture.)

By the time the hold of classical Puritanism on America was loosening, Franklin composed a new sermon of freedom for the age, a self-help manual on how to become economically independent. In "The Way to Wealth" (1758), Franklin warned against idleness and pride, as both are more taxing than taxes; declared industriousness a major virtue; cautioned against the dangers of procrastination; praised frugality as freedom from tyranny and the best way to manage one's money (he cited colonial Spain as an example of disastrous profligacy); and finally warned about the danger of succumbing to artificial wants, since such wants lead to a vicious and endless cycle of ever-escalating needs.[58]

Franklin was clear about what prospective European immigrants should expect in America. In "Information to Those Who Would Remove to America," published in London and France in 1784, Franklin wrote that birth confers no privilege in America, where only "a general happy mediocrity . . . prevails." Only farmers and craftsmen or artisans who behave well will have a place and be respected. "America," he continued, "is the land of labor, and by no means what the English call *Lubberland,* and the French Pays de Cocagne, where the streets are said to be paved with half-peck loaves, the houses tiled with pancakes, and where the fowls fly about ready roasted, crying *come eat me.*" The abundance of cheap land available for farming in a still agrarian society prevents the kind of poverty found in Europe, he said, although he seemed to have predicted that, once all the land was occupied, such conditions might not prevail forever. Still, for now, the "general mediocrity of fortune that prevails in America" imposes a spirit of industriousness, which in turn preserves morals and the virtues of the nation. Except for atheism and infidelity (beliefs that are best kept secret), religion, in all its various denominations, is tolerated and respected.[59]

America's foremost public citizen, the founder of learned societies, libraries, fire stations, and universities; the writer, urban planner, scientist, and inventor who refused to patent his discoveries ("as we enjoy great Advantages from the Inventions of Others, we should be glad of an Opportunity to serve others by any Invention of ours, and this we should do freely and generously," he said),[60] redefined America as the land of industriousness and self-fulfillment through a secular education. Never a traditional believer (his beliefs were somewhere between those of a deist and an atheist, since at one time he even refuted the existence of virtue and vice, an "erratum" that he later corrected), he was wary of orthodoxy and valued the virtue that comes from doing, not preaching. On May 12, 1784, he wrote Reverend Samuel Mather, the son and grandson of the distinguished ministers at the Second Church in Boston, "I have always set a greater value on the character of a *doer of good,* than on any other kind of reputation." Less than six years later, in response to a query from Ezra Stiles, the president of Yale College, Franklin said he believed in abstract, broad Christian principles, combined with some doubt about the divinity of Jesus, although he saw no harm in those who chose to believe in the latter, as long as their beliefs led to doing good. He further explained that he had no problem with the various sects and religions in the United States, but then the wizened reader of America's mores asked Stiles not to share his views.[61]

If major American periods are defined by sermons, or sermon-like speeches, one could consider Franklin's "The Way to Wealth" the moment that defines America's major transformation from a Christian to a secular nation, from a religion-based morality to an ethic of industriousness and public service, and, as we have seen in the previous chapter, from a Puritanical tradition to one that blends Protestantism and the Enlightenment into a unique American formula. American republicanism is built on the foundations of good public works and fair trade, not religious orthodoxies, for strong religious beliefs always hinder easy interaction with people and nations of different faiths. Franklin, like Jefferson and Madison, had abandoned early colonial beliefs, but, like Winthrop, he still assumed self-fulfillment in labor and a certain condition of social equality.

Yet by the first decade of the twenty-first century, the equality of conditions was severely eroded, as the pursuit of wealth (increasingly through credit, a ruinous policy in the eyes of Franklin) had become the main engine that shaped public policy. For just as Republicans and Democrats were sparring over tax policies and the country's economic future in 2004, Peter G. Peterson, the fiscally conservative chairman of the Blackstone Group, the Council on Foreign Relations, the Institute for International Economics, and president of the Concord Coalition, published a book titled *Running on Empty*, explaining how both "the Democratic and Republican Parties are bankrupting our future."[62] The U.S. economy, Peterson argues, is in a state of crisis because of its chronic and escalating budget and current-account deficits—the so-called "twin deficits." The U.S. government's indebtedness is spiraling out of sight, promising creditors to pay back what observers thought it couldn't afford to collect in tax revenues. In early 2004, the International Monetary Fund had calculated that the U.S. government "would require an immediate and permanent 60 percent hike in the federal tax, or a 50 percent cut in Social Security and Medicare benefits." Not only that, but the American economy itself was "increasingly owned by, or indebted to, foreigners" (the so-called "current-account deficit," or what will come due to foreigners, either in payback or interest)—importing $4 billion every working day in 2003. The situation was so bad that former chair of the Federal Reserve Paul Volcker gave the United States a 75 percent chance of a crisis within five years (counting from 2004), while former Secretary of the Treasury Bob Rubin was predicting a "day of serious reckoning." So grim was the outlook that Warren Buffett, the legendary investor and second-richest man in America and the world (according to the 2004 edition of *Forbes* magazine), started buying foreign currencies to hedge his bets. In 2005, the U.S. trade deficit had reached a record $726 billion, with China and Japan leading the list of nations lending money to Americans to sustain their profligate lifestyles. And by 2006, the White House was asking Congress to raise the so-called "debt ceiling" (that is, how much the United States is authorized to borrow) from $8.184 trillion to the almost mythical figure of $8.961 trillion, mostly to finance military outlays and a dysfunctional health care system, and to subsidize agribusiness and other programs that have no direct benefit to the welfare of American society.[63]

Peterson shows that the cost of Social Security, Medicare entitlements, and interest on debt obligations is expected to "consume all federal spending by 2030." Because Social Security and Medicare are financed through a "Ponzi-scheme method" (Robert Reich, the former Secretary of Labor, sees the pay-as-you-go system in a more positive light, calling it a "compact between generations"),[64] with each new contributor paying for the previous one, and because of the relentless Republican crusade for ongoing tax cuts combined with escalating defense spending, the Bush administration is in fact presiding "over the biggest, most reckless deterioration of America's finances in history," including "a feast of pork, inequitable and profligate tax cuts, and a major new expansion of Medicare that is unaccompanied by any serious measures to control its exploding cost." The only way out for the United States is to save by exporting more and importing less, while other developed countries must consume more and export less. Meanwhile, other countries' populations are aging, and their retirement benefits are expected to consume "between a quarter and a third of their GDP by 2040," leaving those societies even less money to buy American goods and services.[65]

America, with its "birth dearth" and expanding life spans, is aging, too, a situation that is bound to increase federal spending on the old (Social Security, Medicare and Medicaid, nursing homes) and impose more stress on a shrinking pool of workers. The answer to such a challenge is economic growth, but the growth of the gross domestic product is not enough. To stimulate economic growth under existing paradigms, America needs more workers and would need to let five million immigrants into the country annually, but this solution is not politically acceptable; inflation (printing money) is unworkable; cutting health care costs is unlikely, since expectations, driven by the promise of science and technology, are too high, and besides, the growth of a "medical-industrial complex that now spends more than $110 billion in research and construction each year" is too powerful and daunting (there are "more M.R.I. units in Greater Atlanta than in all of Canada").[66]

Militarization is not an answer either. Chalmers Johnson, an Asia spe-
cialist who once advised the CIA, says as much in *The Sorrows of Empire,*
also published in 2004.[67] To Johnson, the United States has become an
"empire of bases, not of territories,"[68] with a martial culture that includes
"military machismo, sexual orthodoxy, socialized medicine for the chosen
few, cradle-to-grave security, low pay, stressful family relationships (including the murder of spouses), political conservatism, and an endless harping
on behaving like a warrior, even though many of the wars fought in the
last decade or more have borne less resemblance to traditional physical
combat than to arcade computer games." Because of this "military Key-
nesianism," by September 2001, the United States had an acknowledged
725 foreign bases in thirty-eight countries and "was deploying a total of
254,788 military personnel in 153 countries." It also had 969 bases in the
fifty states, and more were being built.[69] After its invasion of Iraq, the
United States has established at least four "super-bases" in that country
with amenities and services, including fast food outlets like Burger King
and Pizza Hut, that give them the feel of small U.S. towns or suburbs. The
U.S. embassy in Baghdad, under construction at the time of this writing,
is reported to be a city within a city, a 104-acre, self-contained complex of
buildings on the Tigris River, making it far and away the biggest embassy
in the world, six times the size of the United Nations compound in New
York. Such places give "gated communities" a brand-new meaning since
their residents rarely see Iraqis, let alone experience the violence outside
their gates.[70]

Because of the high-tech nature of weaponry, the government has
become totally dependent on the military-industrial complex. Lockheed
Martin, the U.S. leading weapons manufacturer in recent years, ahead
of Boeing, Northrop Grumman, and General Dynamics, builds so much
of the U.S. military arsenal that the "Pentagon and the Central Intelligence Agency might have difficulty functioning without the contractor's
expertise." Not only does Lockheed Martin exercise significant influence
in Washington, but by locking in lucrative military contracts for next-
generation warplanes and other military and informational devices, its
chief executive could confidently say that "our industry has contributed to
a change in humankind."[71]

Presidents George Washington's and Dwight D. Eisenhower's warnings
about the influence of the military were not without foundation. In his

farewell address of September 17, 1796, Washington stated, "Overgrown military establishments are under any form of government inauspicious to liberty, and are to be regarded as particularly hostile to Republican liberty."[72] The main author of the U.S. Constitution, James Madison, said that "of all enemies to public liberty, war is, perhaps, the most to be dreaded, because it comprises and develops the germ of every other. War is the parent of armies; from these proceed debts and taxes; and armies, and debts, and taxes are the known instruments for bringing the many under the domination of the few."[73] In "The Federalist No. 41," Madison explained:

> Not the less true is it, that the liberties of Rome proved the final victim to her military triumphs; and that the liberties of Europe, as far as they ever existed, have, with few exceptions, been the price of her military establishments. A standing force, therefore, is a dangerous, at the same time that it may be a necessary, provision. On the smallest scale it has its inconveniences. On an extensive scale its consequences may be fatal. On any scale it is an object of laudable circumspection and precaution. A wise nation will combine all these considerations; and, whilst it does not rashly preclude itself from any resource which may become essential to its safety, will exert all its prudence in diminishing both the necessity and the danger of resorting to one which may be inauspicious to its liberties.[74]

Almost two hundred years after George Washington's warning, President Eisenhower echoed the same fear in his own farewell address of January 17, 1961:

> The conjunction of an immense military establishment and a large arms industry is new in the American experience. . . . In the councils of government, we must guard against the acquisition of unwarranted influence, whether sought and unsought, by the military-industrial complex. The potential for the disastrous rise of misplaced power exists and will persist. We must never let the weight of this combination endanger our liberties or democratic processes. We should take nothing for granted.[75]

The German American philosopher Hannah Arendt echoed all three presidents in her classic *The Origins of Totalitarianism*, when she said that although an occupying power may not need the consent of the foreign people it rules over, "it can stay in power only if it destroys first of all the national institutions of its own people."[76] Thus, as Chalmers Johnson phrases it, the United States has "mounted the Napoleonic tiger" without the slightest idea on how to dismount.[77]

America's "war on terror" and its imperial reach are, according to Peterson, too costly. The numbers are staggering when one looks at itemized expenditures. For instance, the sun and sand in Iraq have done "more damage to the equipment than ambushes by insurgents. Each Bradley in Iraq needed new tracks every sixty days, at $22,576 per vehicle. Apache attack helicopters, in perpetual need of maintenance, single-handedly devoured an amazing $1.3 billion in spare parts in fiscal year 2003." And "just keeping two divisions engaged in 'stability operations' in Iraq for one week costs $1 billion; keeping them engaged a full year would cost the entire GDP of New Zealand." Maintaining so-called homeland security is also enormously expensive, with much of the price tag still unknown. To have an adequate first-responder operation; fully equipped and ready health care system; proper inspection of cargoes, borders, and visitors; and a critical infrastructure is nearly impossible to imagine. By early 2006, the cost of the war on terror was close to half a trillion dollars, about the same amount the United States spent on its thirteen-year war in Vietnam, while a conservative estimate, in a study by Joseph Stiglitz and Linda Bilmes, of the "true costs" of the war in Iraq has been projected to be $1 trillion by 2010, a sum that could have been better used for a "mega-mega-mega-Marshall Plan" in the Middle East, or, for only half the price tag, to fix the U.S. Social Security system for the next seventy-five years. (By October of that year, Stiglitz and Bilmes revised their figures and concluded that the "the total costs of the war" were likely "to exceed $2 trillion," a figure that was consistent with the findings of the Iraq Study Group about two months later.) Not to forget, too, that the U.S. government, building a new generation of high-tech submarines and aircraft carriers, is also getting ready for some potential showdown with the rising power of China.[78]

The United States is committing itself to global security while it borrows $540 billion a year to finance its lifestyle and service its debt. Under these circumstances, the best outcome for the United States would be if foreigners bought all the assets they needed or cared about and stopped investing in bonds and stocks. (Foreigners already own nearly $10 trillion in U.S.

assets.) Americans will have to adapt to a less exuberant lifestyle because, as Warren Buffett puts it, America's credit card "is not limitless." Some say foreigners have no choice but to invest in the United States, but their societies are aging fast and their populations declining steadily, so that, sooner or later, they would have to reallocate their surpluses to pay for benefits before they, too, start piling up deficits of their own. The point to remember is that other countries are in effect financing the U.S. war— multilateralism is not a political choice but an economic necessity. The United States simply cannot afford to take care of its citizens, let alone run a worldwide empire. Harvard economist Benjamin Friedman put it succinctly: "World power and influence have historically accrued to creditor countries."[79]

A bedrock principle of the Founding Fathers, and basically every president at least until the 1950s (FDR wasn't comfortable with his deficit-financed New Deal), has always been aversion to debt. Thomas Jefferson cautioned against it, and Madison called public debt a "public curse." Deficit spending has been resorted to only in extremis—mostly in times of war—but from the mid-1960s to the mid-1980s, a new social attitude toward debt emerged. Peterson thinks that Johnson's Great Society programs and Reagan's Opportunity Society led to an "entitlement revolution," or the "Me Decades." The result is that there were almost as many deficit years between 1960 and 2004 as in all previous U.S. history (except in times of war and major recessions). All the while, this fiscal irresponsibility has been accompanied by growing acrimonious politics—the rise of national parties that vote the party line or risk excommunication (the Republican Party now extracts oaths from members of Congress that they will not oppose tax cuts), growing public distrust of government and politics, the alienation of voters, and the reduction of public affairs into a spectator sport.[80]

Peterson's is a sobering book, leaving the impression that an economically and politically unchanged America is heading toward inevitable decline. Yet, to be fair, Americans can only do so much to remedy the situation since their economy is thoroughly implicated in the world system and depends on so many other variables that are beyond the control of most citizens and politicians. If Japan and Europe were to sell less to the United States and buy more U.S. products, the problem would be merely reversed, since by outselling the Americans, foreigners also save enough money to invest in U.S. stocks and bonds, thereby infusing more cash into the American economy. The 2004 Democratic presidential candidate, John Kerry, ran on a campaign promising to cut down outsourcing and restore good manufacturing jobs in America, but the reason the U.S. manufacturing sector is less productive today than it was in the decades following World War II is that other national economies have caught up with the United States and are now producing and selling the same products (such as cars, planes, and electronics) in the global market.[81] In other words, the share of the global market for U.S. manufactured goods is in constant decline because new producers of the same products are being added, further undercutting the U.S. manufacturing sector. (And no one knows what will happen when China adds its homemade brand of cars to the world market.)[82] The United States is therefore trapped in a situation that is beyond its control. In *Running on Empty,* Peterson says that the only option left for Americans is to live within our means, which could actually be quite enriching for both ourselves and for our children, but how would one do that without a radical change in our economic thinking?[83]

American thinkers have in fact always warned about the dangers of materialism and the pursuit of riches at the expense of the well-being of souls and communities. The drafters of Pennsylvania's state constitution were wary of the concentration of wealth and saw it as a threat to freedom.[84] Banks and corporations were already being seen as a menace to society. Banking establishments were, to Thomas Jefferson, "more dangerous than standing armies," a sentiment that was shared by John Adams, who said, "Our whole banking system I ever abhorred, I continue to abhor, and I shall die abhorring."[85] William Henry Harrison, the American war hero and president who died thirty days after assuming office, knew that "all the measures of the Government are directed to the purpose of making the rich richer and the poor poorer."[86] Abraham Lincoln reflected the same spirit when he warned against the power of corporations and, like Karl Marx in Europe, preferred labor to capital: "Labor is prior to, and independent of, capital. Capital is only the fruit of labor, and could never have existed if labor had not first existed. Labor is the superior of capital, and deserves much the higher consideration."[87] In 1890, the Populist Mary Ellen Lease, who urged Kansans to "raise less corn and more hell," said, "Wall Street owns the country. It is no longer a government of the people, by the people and for the people, but a government of Wall Street, by Wall

Street and for Wall Street." Teddy Roosevelt acknowledged this reality in 1912 when he said, "we hold it a prime duty of the people to free government from the control of money," while Woodrow Wilson had no illusions about who controlled the political process: "The masters of the government of the United States are the combined capitalists and manufacturers of the United States."[88] In a 1933 private letter, FDR, whose Wealth Tax Act of 1935 was inspired by his objection to inherited wealth, wrote that "a financial element in the larger centers has owned the government ever since the days of Andrew Jackson."[89]

By the end of 2005, democracy seems to have become a rich man's sport, with New York City's billionaire mayor, Michael Bloomberg, spending more than $77 million to be reelected (compare this to the royal sum of $31 million spent by the entire British Labor Party in the May 2005 elections), a figure that amounts to around $103 per vote.[90] So conspicuous and matter-of-fact has wealth become in the running of the republic that the specter of the "corporatocracy" has spawned a successful literary genre, spearheaded by hired guns (divided, according to author John Perkins, into "economic hit men" who bribe to achieve their mission, and "jackals" who help kill or overthrow heads of state when bribery fails) who have broken ranks with their employers and confessed their role in the sinister machinations and influence of corporations.[91] Given this multigenerational consensus on the dangers of corporations and accumulated wealth on the republic, the first economic text written in the United States, by the nineteenth-century economist Daniel Raymond, described corporations as "detrimental to national wealth. They are always created for the benefit of the rich, and never for the poor. . . . The rich have money, and not being satisfied with the power which money itself gives them, in their private individual capacities, they seek for an artificial combination, or amalgamation, so that its force may be augmented."[92]

Yet with the decline of industry and the rise of finance in the twentieth century, corporations and even individuals amassed wealth that was greater than that of dozens of countries combined. "Of the trillion dollars of currency made daily in the global market of the late 1990s," writes Kevin Phillips, "only 2 to 3 percent had to do with actual trade in goods and services." In this climate, indentured servitude seems to be making a comeback. Nannies, gardeners, and servants became, in some quarters, "among the fastest-growing occupations." Despite their slipping wages, Americans work the longest and hardest, while foreign ownership of U.S. manufacturing assets, including research and development, and finance is steadily increasing. Eric Foner has shown that by the 1950s, freedom has come to be associated with consumer choices; "economic Spartanism," in the words of the vice president of Chrysler Corporation, was denounced as socialism; and now, in this new reality, the fate of American democracy hangs on consumer sales.[93]

Those who wonder about the impact of rampant commercialism on the future of America will find their worse suspicions confirmed in Morris Berman's *The Twilight of American Culture,* published at the turn of the twenty-first century.[94] Everything, the author repeats over and over again, is "drowned in the universal solvent of kitsch and consumerism" and a false sense of egalitarianism. Berman documents how corporate capitalism has turned the United States into a Third World society with mind-boggling social disparities in wealth and shows how Americans have become ignorant of the most basic facts of life, partly because of an educational system that vilifies rigor as an elitist, nondemocratic relic. Consequently, the level of cultural illiteracy has resulted in people living in a foreign culture, unable to grasp basic historical and cultural references, while educators have been pressured into the role of entertainers and babysitters. In such an environment, knowledge has turned into a mere commodity, students are treated as consumers entitled to feeling good about the product they are purchasing, most Americans never read a book, "infantilism" has become an ideology, and people think only in terms of (commercially produced) slogans and are condemned to live in what George Steiner called a "systematic suppression of silence." "We live," says Berman, "in a collective adrenaline rush, a world of endless promotional/commercial bullshit that masks a deep systemic emptiness, the spiritual equivalent of asthma."[95]

Berman finds the current situation eerily similar to the final days of the Roman Empire (massive inequalities and declining cultural standards), which eventually collapsed (while the Byzantine Empire survived partly because such inequalities didn't obtain there). Europe sank into what is known as the Dark Ages (500–1150) until a convergence of factors enabled the new Renaissance that energized European cultures. For such a condition to be contemplated in our own future, a "commitment to individualism" and the repairing or refilling of human interiorities (dissolved by the consumer ethos) will be necessary to counter our "herd culture."[96] The solution is not in the wholesale repudiation of the Enlightenment, only of the commercial culture that converged with science in the twentieth century and made the two twin elements in this catastrophic march of global capitalism. For Berman, commercialism, not science, is the culprit, a practice whose unsalutary effects were noted even by Adam Smith himself: "Another bad effect of commerce is that the minds of men are contracted, and rendered incapable of elevation. Education is despised, or at least neglected."[97] Thomas Paine knew as much in 1776, when he wrote in *Common Sense* that "commerce diminishes the spirit, both of patriotism and military defence," which is how "England hath lost its spirit."[98]

"Zones of intelligence" and a commitment to unstructured monastic nomadism are essential to plant the seeds of future hope.[99] The aristocratic intellectual tradition (falsely labeled elitist) is a central tenet in Berman's outlook. As Pierre Clastres (a French anthropologist) put it, "Thought is loyal to itself only when it moves *against the incline*."[100] In other words, the monastic option entails rejecting "a life based on kitsch, consumerism, and profit, or on power, fame, and self-promotion." Visibility "is something to be avoided; the activity will remain authentic by being its own reward." Pursuing this path with a little dose of postmodern thinking (not allowing oneself to believe in one's certainties or truths) could eventually lead, in the aftermath of collapse, to a New Enlightenment. In the end, only a community-centered economic system and a rigorous educational tradition can provide solutions to this massive crisis.[101]

Berman's suggestions may sound too radical for mainstream America, but with the death and safe burial of Soviet-style Communism, more writers are sharing this view. William Greider, a prominent writer and journalist with a good grasp of the American economic scene, wrote a book in 2003 about the "soul of capitalism" and "opening paths to a moral economy."[102] Unlike Peterson, Greider starts with the startling assertion—because it's so obvious it simply doesn't register, or because human nature simply hasn't adapted to the fact—that the "United States has solved the economic problem." Well, not quite. It's the "fortunate minority who live in the most advanced nations" that no longer worry about an "economic threat." This is remarkable, as if the conditions the British economist John Maynard Keynes expected in his famous letter to his grandchildren have come to pass, but without their corollary human emancipation. Thus we live in a culture of excess—of "more"—without experiencing a corresponding effect on our emotional lives. In other words, life is getting worse even as we produce more. Meanwhile, the middle class that has been able to keep up with consumer patterns through longer hours of work and accumulating huge amounts of debt will not have both at its disposal in the next twenty years. This abundance in the midst of scarcity compels us to go back to the question of capitalism, one that was made taboo for decades and that can now be safely reopened since the specter of Communism is long gone. "American capitalism," in Greider's view, is due for a reevaluation.[103]

Greider doesn't see hope in the government, so beholden is it to big money and so hopelessly trapped in its big ways that hope could only emerge from the fringes of society. Yet we have Nobel economists such as Amartya Sen, who in *Development and Freedom* states that the solution to the problems of inequality "will almost certainly call for institutions that take us beyond the capitalist market economy."[104] This is not a new idea. More than seventy years ago, the Protestant theologian Reverend Emil Brunner of the Swiss Reformed denomination described the market economy as "irresponsibility developed into a system."[105] In his 1944 book *The Great Transformation,* economist Karl Polanyi warned against the threat to culture and tradition if market economies are not kept under control:

> To allow the market mechanism to be sole director of the fate of human beings and their natural environment, indeed, even of their purchasing power, would result in the demolition of society. For the alleged commodity "labor power" cannot be shoved about, used indiscriminately, or even left unused, without affecting also the human individual who happens to be the bearer of this peculiar commodity. In disposing of a man's labor power the system would, incidentally, dispose of the physical, psychological, and moral entity of "man" attached to that tag. Robbed of the protective cover of cultural institutions, human beings would perish from the effects of social exposure. . . . Nature would be reduced to its elements, neighborhoods and landscapes defiled, rivers polluted.[106]

The United States doesn't seem to have much of an alternative but to summon its best will and call on its legendary sense of ingenuity to change the economic model underpinning its social and cultural fabrics, if only to keep its ancestral spirit of dissent alive. "These are rough times for the American dream," wrote *New York Times* columnist Bob Herbert a few days before Thanksgiving in 2004, following reports on hunger and poverty in the United States.[107] With the ascendancy of the "gospel of wealth" privileging the subsidy of the rich (through advantageous tax schemes and other forms of redistributing public wealth) over the welfare and buying power of the middle class and the future of American democracy, as Norton Garfinkle outlined in a thorough analysis of the American economy in the second half of the twentieth century, the American dream in fact is all but declared dead by now.[108] During the past few years, *Washington Post* reporter T. R. Reid and futurist Jeremy Rifkin both looked at the promise of the new rising Europe and saw it overtaking the United States on practically every level of human development.[109] As Americans work harder for less, European states are steadily doing better by their people, giving them a better quality of life, a safer environment, and freedom in community, not in isolation. The British commentator Timothy Garton Ash has insisted that it is Europe, not the United States, that is spreading freedom by enlarging its borders and inviting more nations into its prosperous community.[110]

Meanwhile, Americans are losing faith in their own system. "For the first time," writes Rifkin, "the American Dream no longer serves as the rallying point for everyone in America." The dream has turned into "a cruel hoax, a myth without any real substance. . . . With only our religious fervor to hold on to, we have become a 'chosen people' without a narrative—making America potentially a more dangerous and lonely place to be."[111] *Newsweek* ended a long article titled "Dream On America" synthesizing the verdict on the American dream and concluded by saying, "The true danger is that Americans do not realize [the world's preference for different political and economic models], lost in the reveries of greatness, speechifying about liberty and freedom."[112] A task force of the American Political Science Association also reached a similar conclusion, noting that persistent inequality is undermining democracy at home, even while the U.S. government is promoting it abroad.[113]

Kevin Phillips, the longtime conservative strategist for the Republican Party, has by this time not only given up on his party but has written a book outlining in minute detail and in stark numbers the fast decline of the United States, entrapped as it is in the toxic climate of dependency on a fossil fuel (oil) that is fast being depleted; the displacing of manufacture and the production of goods by the new economy of financialization (what he prefers to call the "debt-and-credit industrial complex"); and the rise of rapture theology (to soothe the angst of consumers). In this new apocalyptic scene, rapture preachers, "fiscal gunslingers," and "paper entrepreneurs" run the show while the great mass of Americans is further alienated from the foundations of their republic.[114] So worrisome has the state of democracy in the United States become that recently retired, Reagan-appointed U.S. Supreme Court Judge Sandra O'Connor, speaking to lawyers at George Washington University, noted the mounting attacks on the independence of the judiciary and encouraged Americans to "speak up" for their constitutional rights if the country is not to slide into a dictatorship.[115] After detailing the crumbling infrastructure of the United States, from highways to education, while colossal amounts of money are being systematically diverted to the rich through tax cuts and other schemes, Bill Moyers, addressing a gathering of educators in San Diego on October 27, 2006, warned that the American dream "is on life support."[116]

Having been reduced to the glitter of material success and dazzling images on screens, the real American dream, like many other places on the American landscape, has been left to rot and await new saviors. The utopian visions that had inspired generations of Americans to forge a new society of boundless optimism are withering away on the debris of the consumer products that had been supposed to liberate human energies.[117] The inability of the United States of America—and of the world, for that matter, because the modern world would not have been the same without the practical spirit of the Founding Fathers, and of those who shared their vision—to snap out of the inertia that seized it with the advent of consumer culture, exacerbated now by economic insecurity for most and spiritual confusion for many, is almost tragic.

It is worth recalling that in less than a decade and a half American leaders were able to draft the blueprints of a society that put limits on the forces that made living, for most people, a Hobbesian affair and gave individuals, regardless of their faith, or even lack of one, the opportunity to live in the dignity of their labor. For the first time in history, people were invited to govern themselves and to do so regardless of their religious background. The founders of the United States did their best to rise above the common sensibilities and prejudices of their time, looking as far as they could see into the distant future (while very mindful of the past), and giving us (Americans and non-Americans alike) a trust for the ages. This was the egalitarian world that impressed Alexis de Tocqueville during his visit, an intoxicating freedom wedged precariously amid the lurking ambitions of biblical literalism, nativist fear-mongering, and economic domination. The Jeffersonian vision is the true American dream—poetic in its vision, local in its effects, and global in its scope. Yet because it had been exchanged for the ephemeral wealth of a few, and the mindless entertainment of all, it has lost its revolutionary touch. Europeans, too, are beholden to the economic paradigm of economic domination *avant tout,* but as the celebrated German filmmaker Wim Wenders expressed in a moving speech, they are still trying to preserve their "soul" embodied in their rich and diverse cultural traditions. Europe is still a place where the President of the European Commission could declare: "Europe is not only about markets, it is also about values and culture," and that "in the hierarchy of values, the cultural ones range above the economic ones. If the economy is a necessity for our lives, culture is really what makes our life worth living."[118] Perhaps this is the reason that T. R. Reid and Jeremy Rifkin see the future in that continent, not in the United States.

The hopes and fears for the American dream were also shared by Ian Buruma, a longtime, self-described Americaphile who had grown disillusioned by the U.S. abandonment of its promise and myths. Writing for the *New York Review of Books* on the eve of the 2004 presidential election, Buruma said that "if America can no longer offer the hope of freedom, refuge from persecution, or a second chance in the lives of millions, the whole world will be worse off. And we cannot blame al-Qaeda for that."[119] Around the same time that Herbert, Buruma, Reid, and Rifkin were noting and lamenting the erosion of opportunities in the United States, the rock musician Bruce Springsteen, who often sings about the angst of the working class in contemporary America, decided to take a stand and contribute an op-ed article for the *New York Times:* "Over the years, I've tried to think long and hard about what it means to be American: about the distinctive identity and position we have in the world, and how that position is best carried." A strong believer in economic, social, and political justice, the singer had always asked himself, "Why is it that the wealthiest nation in the world finds it so hard to keep its promise and faith with the weakest citizens? Why do we find it difficult to see beyond the veil of race? Why does the fulfillment of our promise as a people," Springsteen wondered, in an echo of J. Hector St. John de Crèvecoeur, Bob Dylan, Walter

McDougall, Eric Foner, and American "renunciants" seeking freedom else-where, "always seem to be just within grasp yet forever out of reach?" Springsteen concluded, as if in a musical finale, by saying that "our gov-ernment has strayed too far from American values. It's time to move for-ward. The country we carry in our hearts is waiting."[120] Some readers, utterly moved by Springsteen's faith in his nation, wrote to the newspaper editor to express their renewed hope in their nation. "The values and ideals to which most Americans aspire," one person from Salt Lake City wrote, "are alive and well," and "it is heartening indeed to know there are those who will stand vigilant and safeguard what it truly means to be American."[121]

The voices of hopeful artists, writers, and scholars notwithstanding, the freedoms that inspired English dissenters almost four hundred years ago and led to the creation of the first republic with "divided sovereign-ties" in human history continue to be eroded, as an increasingly prosecu-torial state, always on edge and unable to snap out of a ruinous economic model, drifts along the ocean of uncertainty, more disoriented than the handful of Pilgrims who boarded the *Mayflower* and crossed the forbid-ding Atlantic in 1620. Winthrop's "city upon a hill" and Jefferson's "em-pire of freedom" had become shadows of themselves, recollected to suit economic programs and ideological agendas that might have shocked the founders. (Ironically, Alistair Cooke's question about the future of Amer-ica was answered, literally, on his dead body: long after the ninety-five-year-old man, sick and ravaged by illness, died and was safely buried in a Brooklyn cemetery, his remains were unearthed and sold to tissue pro-cessing plants.)[122]

Yet it is this nation that is setting out to rescue Islam from its decline and own fundamentalist excesses. It is a rather odd sight to behold: a civ-ilization that is losing its moorings coming to the rescue of a long-sunken one. If it is abundantly clear that war and capitalist development are not solutions to the crises they engender, what, then, is to be done? The only answer is to make a last-stand defense of the life-affirming legacies of heresy and free thought (indispensable assets to any democracy that is worthy of its name) as our best hope to glimpse a new horizon of human solidarity out of the ruins of the present.

chapter 6

Vital Heresies

You cannot serve God and Money.

—MATTHEW 6:24

I am not, personally, a believer or a religious man in any sense of
institutional commitment or practice. But I have enormous respect for
religion, and the subject has always fascinated me, beyond almost all others
(with a few exceptions, like evolution, paleontology, and baseball). Much
of this fascination lies in the historical paradox that throughout Western
history organized religion has fostered both the most unspeakable horrors
and the most heartrending examples of human goodness in the face of
personal danger.

—STEPHEN JAY GOULD, "Nonoverlapping Magisteria"

The furor over Danish cartoons satirizing the Prophet Mohammed, Iran's
undeterred quest for nuclear technology, the victory of Hamas in the
Palestinian elections, President Bush's State of the Union address, and the
escalating budget for security and the military in the president's proposed
budget were, to take examples from the first few weeks of 2006, symptoms
of the further deterioration of both Islamic and American societies, although both nations (in the broader sense of the term) were vigorously
defending their traditions and trying to defend them against destructive
alien influences. Even as he was proposing a military and security budget
that approximates half a trillion dollars and scaling back on already poorly
funded social programs, President Bush's anxiety over his nation's economy
being overtaken by China and India, the unsatisfactory performance of
American students compared to those of many other nations worldwide,

the loss of ground in basic scientific research, and his uncertainty over the future of America, given the many challenges facing it, was palpable. Could the president of the United States himself have been entertaining the notion of his country's decline, or perhaps collapse, as major American authors like Kurt Vonnegut were doing around the same time? Political rallying speeches are not meant for such ruminations, but the president did exhort his fellow Americans (with much of the world listening in) that "we must never give in to the belief that America is in decline or that our culture is doomed to unravel. The American people know better than that. We have proven the pessimists wrong before, and we will do it again."[1]

That the president was increasing funding for national security even as he was aware of the possibility of the decline or even unraveling of his nation's power is not surprising: the quest for security and the insistence on ideological orthodoxy, both in the United States and in Muslim nations, is often the corollary of perceived weakness, not the reflection of self-confidence and control. In such uncertain times, almost no state or ruler remembers that it is far better to empower freethinking and "dissensus," not impose a stifling culture of fear and consensus. Nothing can ensure the revitalization of both cultures more than protecting dissent from all orthodoxies, for without a robust tradition of heresy, or *zandaqa,* as the term was used in the early centuries of Islam, neither civilization has much chance to overcome its slow but steady decline. When a Kansan like David Kensinger, former chief of staff to ultraconservative Senator Sam Brownback and chair of the Shawnee County Republican Party, tells a reporter that "there is a Romanesque rot about American culture," and "I think that there's a sense among Kansans that the country's gone to hell," one grasps the extent to which the consciousness of decline has permeated the American mainstream.[2] Muslims, meanwhile, will not only turn a deaf ear to the lessons of American history (most of which are drummed out by the sound and fury of warmongering), but they will also shut out the dissenting voices of their own (distant) history, the very voices that might help them acquire the confidence they need in their pursuit of what some Muslim scholars (as shown in a previous chapter) have called modernity.

Around the time that Bush was running for reelection and Sam Harris was publishing his book on the end of faith, Susan Jacoby, a prominent author and director of the Center for Inquiry, a think tank in New York

City dedicated to rationalist thought, and Elaine Pagels, the Harrington Spear Paine Professor of Religion at Princeton University, published treatises (*Freethinkers* and *Beyond Belief*, respectively) reminding us that nations and religions greatly impoverish themselves when they repress and dismiss dissenting voices.[3] Jacoby's account of atheists or, "freethinkers," in the United States leaves little doubt as to how embattled reason has become in her country. Like Muslims, Americans do not look kindly on disbelief, or atheism, even though a few dozen million Americans may be "unchurched," and even though some of the Founding Fathers and national icons such as Abraham Lincoln pose particular challenges to those who want to read America's history and destiny in purely Christian terms. The legacy of Robert Green Ingersoll (1833–1899), "the most famous orator in late-nineteenth century America," is all but forgotten now because of his unshakable secularist outlook.[4]

Although, as explained in the previous chapter, prominent members of the Revolutionary generation assumed that republicanism would work best if it rested on a Christian foundation, that didn't prevent leaders, such as Jefferson and Washington, both of whom, as we have seen, expressed those sentiments, from treating non-Christians as equals in the new nation. Virginia's landmark 1786 Act for Establishing Religious Freedom, separating state and church, initially drafted by Thomas Jefferson in 1777 and later strongly championed by James Madison, was supported by minority Protestant religions, such as the Baptists, Quakers, Presbyterians, Methodists, and Lutherans not because they shared Jefferson and Madison's sympathies for Enlightenment rationalism or the effort to keep religion out of government, but because they feared Episcopalian domination. The interests of "Enlightenment rationalists" and evangelical groups coincided to such an extent that "lawmakers overwhelmingly defeated a move to acknowledge Jesus Christ rather than a nonsectarian deity. The rejection of any mention of Jesus, Jefferson would recall thirty years later, proved that the law was meant to protect not only Christians, and not only religious believers, but nonbelievers as well."[5] The result of protecting religious pluralism had far-reaching effects:

> Be it enacted by the General Assembly of Virginia that no man shall be compelled to frequent any religious worship, place, or ministry whatsoever, nor shall be enforced, restrained, molested, or burthened in his body or

goods, nor shall otherwise suffer on account of his religious opinions or belief; but that all men shall be free to profess, and by argument to maintain, their opinion in matters of religion, and that the same shall in no wise diminish, enlarge, or affect their civil capacities.[6]

The Virginia Act, the first secular constitution in the world, "unprecedented in both American and world history," immediately translated in French and Italian and spread throughout Europe, would become the basis of the U.S. Constitution. (Other states, such as Massachusetts, required proof of membership in some Protestant church, as Catholics in most states were often excluded from public office.) Supported by secularists and evangelical Christians (because the latter feared the hegemony of established churches), the Constitution established "the world's first secular government," emphasizing how crucial it is for governments to stay out of people's private business—particularly their spiritual matters, since one of the principal signs of tyranny is coercing people into belief systems. To be sure, Article 6, Section 3, requiring no religious test for public office, raised objections in places like Massachusetts where some worried that Muslims, Jews, Catholics, and others could legally become president of the United States, but it was the secular message of the document (God is not mentioned even once in it) that carried the day.[7] In 1790, the year after he was elected president, George Washington, in response to a letter from Moses Seixas, warden of the Hebrew Congregation of Newport, Rhode Island, welcoming the new president to town, echoed the language in Seixas's letter, referring to Jews and Christians as children of the "Stock of Abraham" and announcing a new era of equal rights:

All possess liberty of conscience and immunity of citizenship. . . . It is now no more that toleration is spoken of, as if it was by the indulgence of one class of people, that another enjoyed the exercise of their inherent natural rights. For happily the Government of the United States, which gives to bigotry no sanction, to persecution no assistance requires only that they who live under its protection should demean themselves as good citizens. . . . May the children of the Stock of Abraham, who dwell in this land, continue to merit and enjoy the good will of the other inhabitants, while every one shall sit in safety under his own vine and fig tree, and there shall be none to make him afraid.[8]

Yet George Washington, who was proud of the equal rights of all religions under the Constitution and was himself suspected of not being a believing Christian—"I do not believe," opined Bishop William White, "that any degree of recollection will bring to my mind any fact which would prove General Washington to have been a believer in the Christian revelation"[9]—didn't look kindly on the atheism of Thomas Paine, the man who wrote the first document of American liberation (*Common Sense*), and shored up the spirit of his troops with the immortal lines, "These are the times that try men's souls. The summer soldier and the sunshine patriot will, in the crisis, shrink from the service of their country."[10] The fate of Paine—an English tax collector who defended the rights of Jews and exploited colleagues in England, denounced slavery, British colonialism and religious obscurantism in America, and secular tyranny in France—is emblematic of the reaction against Jefferson and Madison's secularism. By the end of his life, he was vilified as an atheist, abandoned by all—except Jefferson and a number of loyal New York City Republicans—and died miserably at age seventy-two.[11]

Having inspired the American Revolution, Paine saved his most revolutionary work to the end of his life because he knew full well the consequences of questioning revealed religion:

> It has been my intention, for several years past, to publish my thoughts upon Religion. I am well aware of the difficulties that attend the subject; and, from that consideration, had reserved it to a more advanced period of life. I intended it to be the last offering I should make to my fellow-citizens of all nations; and that at a time, when the purity of the motive that induced me to it, could not admit of a question, even by those who might disapprove the work.

The Jacobin Terror following the French Revolution, however, led him to write *The Age of Reason* earlier than he had expected, partly because he feared for his life, and partly as an argument against the violence that he witnessed in France. Paine proclaimed his belief in one God and dismissed the revealed religions of Judaism, Christianity, and Islam as human institutions set up to exploit and oppress people. These religions were revealed exclusively to their founders—Moses, Jesus, and Mohammed—while these men's followers had to believe what was transmitted to them through hearsay. In fact, in Paine's reading, Christianity appears as a constellation within the ancient Greek universe of mythology, one in which the gods copulated with humans and the world was full with demigods. Further, Paine believed that Christianity is a form of atheism, or "man-ism," since it interposes the person of Jesus between the individual and God.[12]

Needless to say, such views gave Paine a lot of trouble. In 1802, after he had been maligned by the American public, Samuel Adams wrote to his old comrade chiding him for defending "infidelity":

> Do you think that *your pen,* or the pen of any other man can unchristian- ize the mass of our citizens, or have you hopes of converting a few of them to assist you in so bad a cause? We ought to think ourselves happy in the enjoyment of opinion without the danger of persecution by civil or ecclesi- astical law.
>
> Our friend [Thomas Jefferson], the President of the United States, has been calumniated for his liberal sentiments by men, who have attributed that liberality to latent design to promote the cause of infidelity. This, and all other slanders have been made without a shadow of proof. Neither reli- gion, nor liberty can long subsist in the tumult of altercation, and amidst the noise and violence of faction.

To which Paine replied implying that disbelief is often the first step toward a new order (Paine had hoped that the American political revolution would be followed by another revolution in people's thoughts and beliefs):

> The case, my friend, is, that the world has been over-run with fable and creeds of human invention, with Sectaries of whole nations, against all other nations, and sectaries of those sectaries in each of them against the other. Every sectary, except the Quakers, had been a persecutor. Those who fled from persecution persecuted in their turn, and it is this confusion of creeds that has filled the world with persecution and deluged it with blood. Even the depredation on your commerce by the Barbary powers, sprang from the crusades of the church against those powers. It was a war of creed against creed, each boasting of God for its author, and reviling each other with the name of infidel. If I do not believe as you believe, it proves that you do not believe as I believe, and this is all that it proves.[13]

The fortunes of Tom Paine are a powerful illustration of the brevity of the late eighteenth-century legacy of the Enlightenment and the American Revolution in U.S. history. Religion came roaring back, and only the brave and committed stood their secular ground, at great cost to their careers, if not their lives.[14] (Thomas Jefferson, as Samuel Adams suggested above, was often charged with infidelity by his opponents.) Abraham Lincoln, who read Paine's *Age of Reason,* cleverly navigated the tension between America's unofficial Christian faith and the secular ideals of the Revolution. Although he was skeptical and had no church affiliation, he spoke like a theologian, the cadence of his style making speeches sound like sermons. "What makes Lincoln a compelling figure to religious believers and nonbelievers alike," Jacoby remarks, "is that his character was suffused with a rare combination of rationalism and prophetic faith in almost perfect equipoise."[15]

By the second half of the nineteenth century, evolution had become a lightning rod for this tension between Christian literalists and secularists. Darwin's *The Origin of Species* (1859) and *The Descent of Man* (1871) elicited spirited public debate that has lasted to the present day. Americans, particularly the rich and the clergy, were, however, more comfortable with Herbert Spencer's brand of social Darwinism—it was Spencer who coined the expression "survival of the fittest"—although Spencer deplored the very notion of public education. Freethinkers soldiered on, rarely flinching, despite the usual premature deaths of children and loved ones.[16]

Robert Green Ingersoll ("Injuresoul," as his critics called him) is, besides Paine, probably the most influential secularist dissenter in U.S. history. A self-taught man who read Shakespeare throughout his life, he eventually became a licensed lawyer in Illinois, and was, briefly, state attorney general, preaching tirelessly on behalf of reason and gender equality and against organized religion and corporal punishment, earning the constant scorn of people and the media everywhere he went. Though never a socialist—despite the fact that he was for taxing estates and against taxing earned incomes—he had a major influence on the socialist Eugene V. Debs, Robert H. LaFollette (the progressive governor of Wisconsin), and Clarence Darrow, the famous lawyer of Scopes trial fame. To those who accused him of having no alternative, he replied:

We are laying the foundations of the grand temple of the future—not the temple of all the gods, but of all the people—wherein, with appropriate rites, will be celebrated the religion of Humanity. We are doing what little we can to hasten the coming of the day when society shall cease producing millionaires and mendicants—gorged indolence and famished industry—truth in rags, and superstition robed and crowned. We are looking for the time when the useful shall be the honorable; and when REASON, throned upon the world's brain, shall be the King of Kings, and God of Gods.[17]

Ingersoll knew all too well the historic significance of the Founding Fathers' Constitution:

They knew that to put God in the Constitution was to put man out. They knew that the recognition of a Deity would be seized upon by fanatics and zealots as a pretext for destroying the liberty of thought. They knew the terrible history of the church too well to place in her keeping, or in the keeping of her God, the sacred rights of man. They intended that all should have the right to worship, or not to worship; that our laws should make no distinction on account of creed. They intended to found and frame a government for man, and for man alone. They wished to preserve the individuality of all; to prevent the few from governing the many, and the many from persecuting and destroying the few.[18]

Ironically, as in the postrevolutionary decades, Ingersoll's fame and the golden age of free thought (roughly between 1875 and 1914) coincided with growing church membership—mostly as a result of the enfranchisement of blacks and Catholic immigration. (Many Eastern European and German Jews remained secular, agnostic, or socialist.) American freethinkers were interested in culture and science and opposed to the parochial school system being established by the Catholic Church.[19] Except for a few cosmopolitan blacks—such Massachusetts-born W. E. B. Du Bois, author of *The Soul of Black Folks*—blacks were not ready for freethinking, since church and religion had given them strength and community in their struggle against slavery. Atypical in his education at Fisk University (an all-black institution), Harvard College (where he was a protégé of William James), and in Germany (where, by this time, he had grown into a freethinker), Du Bois found religion to be a purely aesthetic experience (as a child he was raised as "a liberal New England Congregationalist," not a Baptist, as most African Americans were):

> Religion helped and hindered my artistic sense. I know the old English and German hymns by heart. I loved their music but ignored their silly words with studied inattention. Grand music came at last in the religious orato- rios which we learned at Fisk University but it burst on me in Berlin with the Ninth Symphony and its Hymn of Joy. I worshipped Cathedral and ceremony which I saw in Europe but I knew what I was looking at when in New York a Cardinal became a strike-breaker and the Church of Christ fought the Communism of Christianity.

Du Bois, who grew fond of socialism and even joined the Communist Party before he died at age ninety-three, would have a lasting impact on American culture.[20]

The 1848 Seneca Falls convention and its *Declaration of Rights and Sentiments,* and later the questioning of clerical rule of all known faiths by secular women activists and their freethinking allies, gradually paved the way to universal suffrage and more rights.[21] Freethinkers also challenged obscenity laws and censorship, particularly the Comstock Law of 1873 (whose intent was to prohibit information on birth control devices and sexually transmitted diseases), decades before the advent of the American Civil Liberties Union (ACLU). Walt Whitman's *Leaves of Grass,* first pub- lished in 1855, could not be reissued by a commercial press until 1881, and, even then, was quickly "banned in Boston" (an expression inspired by a 1675 law prohibiting Native Americans from entering Boston for fear they might expose the white population to "mischief"),[22] despite early endorse- ments by Ralph Waldo Emerson and Henry David Thoreau and later by Ingersoll and Ezra H. Heywood. Whitman was censored for his robust humanism and unflinching progressive ideals in poems such as "Song of Myself," "I Sing the Body Electric," "A Woman Waits for Me," and "To a Common Prostitute," all testimonials to human connectedness and the bonds of social solidarity. In the latter poem, Whitman approaches the prostitute as an equal and sees her as part of his natural universe:

> Be composed—be at ease with me—I am Walt
>   Whitman, liberal and lusty as Nature;

Not till the sun excludes you, do I exclude you;
Not till the waters refuse to glisten for you, and the
    leaves to rustle for you, shall my words refuse to
    glisten and rustle for you.[23]

Whitman's work was surely inspired by his humanism, not religion, as his preface to the first edition of *Leaves of Grass* amply testifies:

There will soon be no more priests. Their work is done. They may wait awhile. . . . perhaps a generation or two . . . dropping off by degrees. A superior breed shall take their place . . . . the gangs of kosmos and prophets en masse shall take their place. A new order shall arise and they shall be the priests of man, and every man shall be his own priest. The churches built under their umbrage shall be the churches of men and women. Through the divinity of themselves shall the kosmos and the new breed of poets be interpreters of men and women and of all events and things. They shall find their inspiration in real objects today, symptoms of the past and future. . . . They shall not deign to defend immortality or God or the perfection of things or liberty or the exquisite beauty and reality of the soul. They shall arise in America and be responded to from the remainder of the earth.[24]

The Red Scare of the 1910s set in motion repressive policies. By the 1920s, the great freethinkers of the Gilded Age had become a dying breed, their cause replaced by organizations fighting for free speech, abortion rights, and other causes. (The ACLU was officially founded by Roger Nash Baldwin, a protégé of Emma Goldman, later deported on January 20, 1920.) The Scopes trial in 1925 pitted two aging progressives (William Jennings Bryan and Clarence Darrow), and although Darrow caught Bryan off-guard and won the intellectual argument, fundamentalism found a new life in the culture of advertising and radio. Bruce Barton, who coined the company names General Electric and General Motors, reinvented Jesus Christ as a charismatic CEO. The new popular medium of the radio, designed to appeal to emotion, displaced the long lectures that allowed freethinkers to tour the country and make the case for their views.[25] The age of the sound bite had dawned, and it wasn't friendly to dissent.

During the Depression and World War II, the Catholic Church—hitherto a minority religion in an overwhelmingly Protestant nation, although

by the 1920s it was a significant player in "centers of Catholic population"—
emerged as the most powerful and best organized religion in America,
exerting tremendous influence on censorship, birth control, and anticommunism. Catholics boycotted theaters, forced Hollywood to enact a
viewing code, and pressured unions to speak against contraceptives. In a
way, the church's crusade against communism helped it to consolidate its
American credentials. According to Jacoby, the Catholic Church

> would prove to be unprecedented both in its duration and its influence
> throughout American society. Catholic opposition to "godless commu-
> nism," disseminated both in its duration and its influence throughout the
> tumultuous thirties to radio audiences of millions, laid the groundwork for
> increasing church influence that would reach the highest levels of govern-
> ment during the Cold War era.

During the 1930s, priests like Fulton Sheen and Charles E. Coughlin, mixing demagoguery with faith, and using the new electronic pulpit of the
radio, attacked both reason and communism, "blazing a trail for Protestant
evangelicals, like Billy Graham, who would rise to prominence after the
war as well as for the more recent electronic spokesmen of the Christian
far right." By encouraging people to sniff out Communists in their midst,
they also paved the way for Joseph McCarthy. Wartime patriotism intensi-
fied the persecution of minorities like the Jehovah's Witnesses, who refused
to salute the flag and recite the Pledge of Allegiance, written by Francis
Bellamy, a former Baptist and critic of capitalism, in 1892. Such were the
times.[26]
    The postwar period and the Red Scare kept the anticommunist crusade
alive, while Billy Graham held marathon sermons at Madison Square Garden (the same multipurpose site that hosted Bob Dylan's thirtieth anniversary musical gala in 1992 and the 2004 Republican National Convention).
The Civil Rights movement of the 1960s brought together all faiths—
the religious and nonreligious—but the clergy of white mainstream denominations, including Judaism, were strongly opposed to desegregation,
or they kept a low profile on the issue. The feminism that took off was
mostly secular, since, "at its core, feminism can only be understood as
an attack on the sacralization of man-made customs governing relations
between the sexes." The feminist movement culminated in the landmark

Supreme Court *Roe v. Wade* decision in 1973, upholding a woman's right to abortion; but as with the victory of science over religion in the Scopes trial of 1925, it was this ruling that galvanized Christian fundamentalists into further and more determined activism as they vowed to overturn the Court's un-Christian decision in due time.[27]

With Supreme Court justices like Antonin Scalia openly declaring their belief in the power of God, school boards preventing the teaching of evolution in their curricula, and the promotion of faith-based social initiatives, by 2004, fundamentalists seemed to be getting ever closer to altering the constitutional formula the Founding Fathers considered so crucial to the health of the republic and the protection of public freedoms. Fundamentalists rally to their cause with passion, whereas secular humanists, like the so-called moderate Muslims, come across as embattled, speaking in measured distant tones, not knowing what to call themselves. Susan Jacoby, who avoids the combativeness of Sam Harris in *The End of Faith* (although she eagerly introduced him to and facilitated his talk at the New York Society for Ethical Culture in the fall of 2005), recommends reviving the term *freethinker* and the tradition of Ingersoll, whose moving eulogy for Whitman on March 30, 1892, could be an example of the passion and humanism that the world so badly needs.[28]

Whether it is Thomas Paine, Robert Green Ingersoll, Walt Whitman, the countless progressives who roamed the social landscape of American history, or even the Founding Fathers, American freethinkers have always contested the historical forces of might and wealth by relying on America's old dissenting and prophetic traditions to awaken a great nation to its infinite spiritual potential. Ralph Waldo Emerson (1803–1882) preached against dead dogmas and Christian rituals and insisted that Americans reach deep into their natural souls to be inspired and experience a full life. He wanted his fellow Americans to be self-reliant, not dependent on somebody else's inspirations. He thought that progress and industrialization were dehumanizing, that property and possessions were the enemy of enlightened individualism.

Henry David Thoreau (1817–1862) took these ideas seriously and set out at once to challenge any system that seemed to degrade human life. In February 1848, he told an audience at the Concord Lyceum that it was best not to have a government at all, since it is mostly a hindrance at best, and a major promoter of oppression and injustice at worst. As an institution that seemingly represents the majority, the government doesn't care about justice, only about laws that turn men into agents of injustice. So "it is not desirable to cultivate a respect for the law, so much as for the right." Men who work for the state, including those esteemed to be good citizens, often abdicate their conscience for such a trivial honor; they value free trade over freedom and voting (a form of gaming) over acting. They gladly conform and, in their patriotism, become obstacles to reform. So it is better to act on one's principles and break the law than to participate passively in injustice (slavery and the Mexican War were Thoreau's contemporary examples). If an honest man goes to prison for not paying taxes, that is better than seeking wealth to support the state. "It cost me less in every sense to incur the penalty of disobedience to the State," he wrote, "than it would to obey." In any case, the State can only control a man's body through the use of brute force and coercion, not necessarily through a superior morality. In fact, Thoreau refused allegiance to the State, and even wondered whether democracy is compatible with human rights and justice:

> The progress from an absolute to a limited monarchy, from a limited monarchy to a democracy, is a progress toward a true respect for the individual. Is a democracy, such as we know it, the last improvement possible in government? Is it not possible to take a step further towards recognizing and organizing the rights of man? There will never be a really free and enlightened State, until the State comes to recognize the individual as a higher and independent power, from which all its own power and authority are derived, and treats him accordingly.[29]

To Thoreau, people cannot have a good life as long as they are beholden to material possessions and caught in the frenetic pace of an industrial, commercial civilization. To him, those who work hard to buy a good life are laboring "under a mistake," for "it is a fool's life, as they will find when they get to the end of it, if not before." They are so alienated from nature's simplicity that they make themselves sick and "lead lives of quiet desperation." There is a price for everything, and the cost of slaving now for a better future is trading one's life for an illusory promise. He thought that the cult of hard work was rather deadly, for "I am convinced, both by faith and experience, that to maintain one's self on this earth is not a hardship but a pastime, if we live simply and wisely." Wealth, he insisted, is found not in the accumulation of possessions, but, on the contrary, in relinquishing them, "for a man is rich in proportion to the number of things which he can afford to let alone." Thoreau wanted people to cultivate poverty "like a garden herb, like sage," not to trouble themselves with novelties.[30]

Armed with these principles, Thoreau denounced slavery and the complicity of his fellow New Englanders in the slave trade. To him, Americans may have freed themselves from colonial England, but they remained slaves of "an economical and moral tyrant," overly busy with trade and trivial news, unable to connect with the essence of life itself. Better for him to live without principle than be part of such a system.[31] With such calls for simplicity and self-reliance, a reclusive poor writer from Massachusetts influenced some of the greatest revolutionary leaders of modern history, like Leo Tolstoy (who wrote a letter to Americans urging them to reclaim Thoreau's noble principles), Mahatma Gandhi, and Martin Luther King Jr.[32]

Thoreau's wisdom is part and parcel of the American tradition. Every generation has its own prophets, rebuking and denouncing their fellow citizens for not living up to the ideals of America's forgotten founders. In 1998, during the Clinton presidency, Andrew Delbanco, a professor of German Jewish ancestry at Columbia University, delivered a major lecture at Harvard and reminded his audience that Americans labor under the weight of dual, contradictory hopes, furiously seeking security in wealth and endlessly worrying about not being able to attain it, or if they do, keep it.[33] He also noted what we have seen before that racism and exclusion are as integral a part of America's story as the ceaseless pursuit of freedom, justice, and integration.[34] But to Delbanco, the scope of America's vision has been steadily narrowing since the age of the Puritans, shrinking from the divine principle of God, through the grand secular notion of nation, then collapsing in on the self. The American history of hope is "one of diminution. At first, the self expanded toward (and was sometimes overwhelmed by) the vastness of God. From the early republic to the Great Society, it remained implicated in a national ideal lesser than God but larger and more enduring than any individual citizen. Today, hope has narrowed to the vanishing point of self alone." We now live in the age of wealth but of symbolic deprivation, an age in which the cult of the body has replaced the divinities of old.[35] Under this form of alienation, despotism could very well erode America's great heritage. Delbanco quotes Tocqueville:

I seek to trace the novel features under which despotism may appear in the world. The first thing that strikes the observation is an innumerable multitude of men, all equal and alike, incessantly endeavoring to procure the petty and paltry pleasures with which they glut their lives. Each of them, living apart, is as a stranger to the fate of all the rest; his children and his private friends constitute to him the whole of mankind. As for the rest of his fellow citizens, he is close to them, but does not see them; he touches them, but he does not feel them; he exists only in himself and for himself alone; and if his kindred still remain to him, he may be said at any rate to have lost his country.[36]

Speaking before the 2000 and 2004 elections (during which the issues of faith and morality occupied center stage), Delbanco expected some new faith to rise and take hold of Americans' imagination, but what that new faith is remained unanswered.[37] When I read this, I couldn't help thinking of Emerson, who, 160 years earlier, delivered a similar sermon to the senior class at Harvard's Divinity College, telling his congregation that organized religion, especially the Christian Church, had imposed an implacable tyranny on the soul, alienating it from its natural essence and confining it to the repetition of empty rituals. By establishing Jesus as a God over and above human beings, and attributing his divinity to an unrepeatable miracle, "historical Christianity" has turned Jesus into an enemy (a myth), not the inspiring provocateur and liberator he was. Under the rigid doctrines of the Church, the revelation appears as a frozen moment in history, "as if God were dead." Sermons have therefore become dull, impersonal, and unimaginative. The Puritans, with their struggle for freedom, were a much better example of vibrant Christian practice, but "their creed is passing and none arise in its doom."[38]

Thus both Emerson and Delbanco see the need for faith, but Emerson knew that such faith has to remain personal and cannot be imitated, since all genuine inspiration is irreproducible anyway. Yet one of the conditions for personal and social felicity is the return to nature, or the natural ways of primitive cultures. Emerson, Delbanco notes, knew that Americans, though living in abundance, were sadder than the less fortunate "Indians and Saxons."[39] It was the same conclusion reached by J. Hector St. John de Crèvecoeur's farmer in *Letters from an American Farmer* (1782) and preached as the only solution to Americans by Thoreau. The frenzy of commercialism not only alienates human beings: it is also what ultimately destroys nations and empires. English-born Thomas Cole's Gibbon-inspired, five-piece painting *The Course of Empire,* produced two years before Emerson gave his Harvard speech (around the same period Alexis de Tocqueville was publishing his book on America), was a powerful visual confirmation of what happens in the course of nation- and empire-building, when small communities start out as idyllic places, grow into hustling commercial societies, before they succumb to hubris and consume themselves in strife and war. The fear persists, but there has been no mass response to Emerson and Thoreau's calls for freedom, or to the warnings of the Puritan elders and the Founding Fathers.

That orthodoxies weaken the spirit of nations and impoverish the faith of religions has been made abundantly clear by Elaine Pagels's book on the Gnostic Gospel of Thomas, published in 2004, a sequel to her earlier and well-received exposition of the Gnostic Gospels, thereby resetting not only the history of Christianity but also inadvertently contributing to the attempt to break the stranglehold of the orthodoxy on free thought—what Sam Harris says is needed to save Muslim societies. Drawn back to church following her son's struggle with what turned out to be a fatal illness, and still remembering the exclusivist theology of the evangelical church she had attended as a teenager, the highly educated religion scholar learned Greek and Coptic to better understand the founding texts of Christianity. In the process, she studied and made available the Gnostic Gospels, the thirteen papyri buried on the cliff of Jabal al-Tarif, near Nag Hammadi in Upper Egypt, following the rise of intolerance in the Christian tradition and the zealous extirpation of the gospels that didn't fit the ones chosen by the founding fathers of the Christian church in the second century.

The discovery of the Gnostic Gospels in December 1945 by an Egyptian peasant set in motion an Indiana Jones sort of tale of rather cosmic significance, if for no other reason than what a French-language newspaper in Cairo wrote on June 10, 1949: "[The documents have] to do with one of the most powerful discoveries preserved until the present by the ground of Egypt, surpassing in scientific interest such spectacular discoveries as the tomb of Tutankhamen." What was found were fifteen-hundred-year-old Coptic translations of still older gospels (older perhaps than even the main Gospels in the New Testament) that were buried to avoid persecution of the "catholic" (universal) church, which arose by 200 A.D. and which had deemed all different or alternative views of Jesus and early Christianity as heresy.

Thus, the fifty-two texts found at Nag Hammadi, ranging "from secret gospels, poems, and quasi-philosophic descriptions of the origin of the universe, to myths, magic, and instructions for mystical practice," variously seen as embodying the philosophical and world views of Hellenism, Platonism, Zoroastrianism, Hinduism, Buddhism, and Judaism, have come to be termed *Gnostic,* from the mystical art of self-knowledge (not the rational science of facts and mathematics), implying that to know oneself is to know god. (The term *Gnosticism* is now contested by scholars, but that debate doesn't affect this line of argument.) In such gospels, we get, for instance, the maligned serpent's point of view, a female god, and an uncompromising duality, as one poem, "Thunder, Perfect Mind," features a divine power saying that she is "the whore and the holy one," "the wife and the virgin." Such texts talk about a "living Jesus" who is more of a spiritual guide than the son of an abstract god, a view akin to Buddhism and probably influenced by it during contacts from 80 to 200 A.D. The Gnostics were the few among the hoi polloi (the many), deviators from the "truth faith" of the catholics, showing that Christianity as we know it is the outcome of politics and power. As often happens with state ideologies, scholars had known about the Gnostics and their gospels through the attacks levied against them by Church authorities throughout the millennia and through tiny fragments of the Gnostic literature that had come to light before the Egyptian peasant broke the jar and took its contents home. Despite what had been irretrievably destroyed, the thirteen papyri that survived provided the first instance in which the world got to hear directly from Christianity's early heretics.[40]

First, there was the question of Jesus's resurrection, whether it is real or metaphorical. The Gnostics believed it was metaphorical. Although several New Testament accounts present different versions and forms of the resurrection, and although Jesus himself in the Gospel of Mark divides the world into those with access to the mysteries of life and those who must be told, Luke's account of Christ returning from the dead physically and eating broiled fish became a central policy of the Church in the second century, the litmus test of the faith itself. (The formidable writer Tertullian left no doubt as to what the church meant when he stated that the

physical resurrection "must be believed" precisely "because it is absurd.")
The Twelve Apostles to whom Jesus appeared, witnesses to his posthu-
mous forty-day sojourn among the living, became the ultimate authority
on doctrinal matters. Thus, the New Testament with its approved gospels
became the canon ("guideline").[41]

The Christian creed asserting belief in "one God, Father Almighty,
Maker of heaven and earth" was therefore a political ploy in the second
century to establish a spiritual hierarchy with a bishop as "monarch" (or
"sole ruler"); Ignatius of Antioch nicely summed up the policy as "One
God, one bishop." Yet the Gnostics, the "pneumatics" (or "those who are
spiritual"), rejected this new catholic god as a mere creator (*demiurgos,* in
Greek), himself created by the loftier Father, accessible not through some
institutional and political scheme, or some rigid theology, but through
gnosis, insight, or self-knowledge. This catholic god was, furthermore, a
boastful, arrogant, mad, and jealous master, envious of Adam; as the Gnostic Marcion said, this god created suffering, disease, and even mosquitoes.
The Gnostics saw through the orthodoxy's lust for power through religion, while leaders of the orthodoxy, such as Bishop Irenaeus and Tertullian, denounced the Gnostics' social, political, and spiritual egalitarianism
as sure signs of heresy and hypocrisy![42]

The Nag Hammadi texts are by no means uniform on the question of
gender equality, but they do offer tantalizing visions of an androgynous
god, both male and female, a view strikingly at odds with the unremit-
tingly masculine god of the three monotheistic religions. Some texts see
paradise as the womb, while the Mother, wisdom (Sophia) and source of
life, rebukes the creator (demiurge) for his unwarranted pretentiousness.
Moreover, this primal feminine power speaks with the voice of humil-
ity, embracing in herself all human behavior, excluding no one: "I am the
first and the last," says the poem "Thunder, Perfect Mind." The poem
continues:

> I am the honored one and the scorned one. I am the whore, and the holy
> one. I am the wife and the virgin. I am (the mother) and the daughter. . . .
> I am she whose wedding is great, and I have not taken a husband. . . .
> I am knowledge, and ignorance. . . . I am shameless; I am ashamed. I
> am strength, and I am fear. . . . I am godless, and I am one whose God
> is great.[43]

Almost two millennia later, we would hear echoes of this all-inclusive spirit in the poetry of Walt Whitman.

Jesus was crucified at a time of Roman occupation, when relations between Jews and Romans were tense, so the messiah ("anointed king") was the hope for some Jews and the fear of others, who thought such hope may lead the Romans to destroy their city. Early Christians were persecuted by Roman authorities, forced to renounce their faith or be beheaded, executed, or subjected to orgies of torture. They were accused of being "atheists" who didn't "swear by the *genius* [divine spirit] of the emperor." But many Christians refused to surrender and willingly, even joyfully, became *martyres,* the plural for *martus,* which in Greek means witness. Yet the very Christians who suffered cruel persecutions and were accused of being atheists hurled the same accusation at the Gnostic Christians, accusing them of cowardice, even though the Gnostics simply found the belief in a "human sacrifice" absurd, since it made God appear as a cannibal. In fact, many Gnostics saw the crucifixion of Jesus much as Muslims see it, that is, the crucified body was not Jesus's, either literally or metaphorically. (In April 2006, reports were published that another Gnostic codex, written in Coptic and found in Egypt in the 1970s, casts an entirely new light on Judas Iscariot, long the synonym for betrayal in Christian mythology. The twenty-six-page Gospel of Judas relates that Jesus had selected his disciple to betray him to the Romans as a supreme act of faith, not treason.)[44] In the Acts of John, Jesus appears to John and tells him, "I have suffered none of the things which they will say of me; even that suffering which I showed to you and to the rest in my dance, I will that it be called a mystery."[45]

The catholic Church's insistence on agreement was, however, a practical solution to uniting a global institution around a set of common beliefs. While Gnostic Christians compared their orthodox detractors to "dumb animals" and "dealers in bodies" attached to literal readings, the church needed objective criteria for a global organization; it needed a *systema* (or constitution), not the Gnostics' communalism and rejection of meaningless rituals, like baptism. Philosophers do not make for a good, docile polity, as Tertullian knew: "Away with all attempts to produce a mixed Christianity of Stoic, Platonic, or dialectical composition! We want no curious disputation after possessing Christ Jesus, no inquiring after enjoying the gospel! With our faith, we desire no further belief."[46]

To the Gnostics, the religious quest implied the pursuit of self-knowledge through a long, elaborate process of ascetic practices—much like in Buddhism—and the reliance on mind and reason; in this way, the source of suffering is conquered and the Kingdom of God comes within sight. They saw in Jesus a deeply inspired solitary wanderer without possessions as the guide in a world of torment. Needless to say, such esoteric monasticism ran against the dominant belief that salvation was only attainable through the agency of Jesus Christ. Admittedly, a global organization with order and rituals could not have been founded on such elusive philosophies, let alone survive for millennia, but the price of survival—an uncompromising insistence on orthodoxy—came at a cost to Christians themselves, for "the process of establishing orthodoxy ruled out every other option. To the impoverishment of Christian tradition, gnosticism, which offered alternatives to what became the main thrust of Christian orthodoxy, was forced outside."[47]

This is the main lesson of Pagels's remarkable book on the Gnostic Gospels: it is to remind readers that any attempt at enforcing a doctrine on the masses is bound to impoverish the very organization that seeks to benefit from such indoctrination, whether this organization is a religion, or, as I am trying to argue, a nation (in this case, the nation born out of the American Revolution, whose main gospels remain the Declaration of Independence and the Constitution). So just when she was undergoing one of the most trying moments in her life (having a child with a life-threatening illness), Pagels chose to further elaborate on the notion of belief, clearly showing that the ascetic, communalist, profoundly humanitarian theology of the Gnostics was more suitable to her than the empty and self-serving doctrines of the Church. (One must quickly note that Pagels's approach is more nuanced than what I am presenting here; this is partly my deduction. Pagels knows well that organizations don't survive without extracting a certain degree of uniformity from their members. Wisdom here, though, is in achieving the right balance.)

What is also emphasized in her more recent book, *Beyond Belief,* is that early Christians were in the same position in relation to the pagan Roman state as the Gnostics were in relation to the orthodox Church in the following centuries.[48] Early Christians were radical egalitarians, communalists, and willing martyrs for an ideology of love. Justin Martyr, baptized in 140, records how his faith meant extending love to all others, for "we, who valued above everything else acquiring wealth and possessions, now bring what we have into a common fund, and share with everyone in need;

we who hated and killed other people, and refused to live with people of another tribe because of their different customs, now live intimately with them." To these Christians, baptism meant leaving the old behind and being born anew into this culture. Even Tertullian, the harsh denouncer of heretics, said, "What marks us in the eyes of our enemies is our practice of loving kindness." But once they settled on the synoptic Gospels of Mark, Matthew, and Luke, and added that of John, they rejected the mystical Gospel of Thomas (not a real name, but the designation for [Jesus's] "twin" in Aramaic, a powerful collapsing of two people into one), partly because Thomas's Jesus would insist that "the kingdom of the Father is spread out upon the earth, and people do not see it," or, more commonly, is "within you," a dictum that Tolstoy would use in a book title almost two thousand years later. Thomas's "living Jesus" is inside and outside, one who is in plain sight of those who see. But the Gospel of John disparages this Thomas as a "doubting" disciple, not worthy of the rank of apostle, since he was skeptical of Jesus's otherworldly claims. Thus, he branded who might have been his rival as "Doubting Thomas," thereby obscuring a legacy that could have infused more light into the Christian faith.[49]

Christianity could have taken a different turn had not orthodox leaders like Irenaeus worked to discredit the open-endedness of the faith. A Zen Buddhist told Pagels that "had I known the Gospel of Thomas, I wouldn't have had to become a Buddhist!" Yet in the early days of Christianity, Christians with *charismata* ("power to heal, to exorcise, to prophecy, even to raise the dead"), or charismatic Christians, nowadays best represented by Pentecostalists, believed that the "gift of prophecy" was available to all who sought it, that it was not exclusive to Jesus Christ. Such prophecies, however, were denounced by the orthodox as false and satanic. It was these threats that led Irenaeus to build the edifice of Christianity on the four gospels, the "four formed gospels"—just the right number for such a construction project—although even such a move did not guarantee the control of textual interpretation (always an impossible task). The conversion of the Roman Emperor Constantine to Christianity in the fourth century and the institutionalization of the faith as a state religion in Nicaea (in today's Turkey) in 325 further drove unofficial expressions of the faith underground.

What strikes the reader of such histories is the transferability of epithets and slanderous designations, terms such as *atheist* and *heretic* once applied to Christians for willfully refusing to obey the gods of Rome, then to nonorthodox Christians (whether dualist or not), terms wielded to silence troubling critics and opponents, punish freethinkers, and eliminate dissent from the body politic. Atheism was Thomas Paine's worst offense against the republic he had helped create, just as it was an ever-haunting menace to the unorthodox Jefferson. Yet the quest for the "luminous *epinoia*," what Pagels defines as roughly the "'creative' or 'spiritual' consciousness"—a life that doesn't necessarily negate the dictates of rational inquiry but relies on self-knowledge (gnosis) and freedom through renunciation and solidarity with the poor and marginal as the way to the good life—has never ceased.[50]

I mention this episode in the history of early Christianity not only to show what could have been (although such contemplations can certainly enlighten us about the archaeology of faiths, of the ways in which the divine is construed by prevailing narratives), but also to map out a sort of geography of ideas, to question the popular association in Muslim societies of atheism with the secular West. There was no secular West in this account of early Christian history, and most of the players in the formative years of Christianity were Middle Eastern, to use a crude cultural designation. The orthodox and the heretics, atheists and worshippers of the right god, in this drama were from places like Turkey, Syria, Egypt, and Tunisia. In fact, the dualism that all three monotheistic faiths condemn as heresy predates all three religions and dates back, as Yuri Stoyanov has shown in his masterful study of dualism, to ancient Egyptian and Persian religions that allowed for twin opposite forces to coexist in the same deity. Notions of Adam and Eve, good and evil, God and Satan, Paradise and Hell, the Day of Judgment, and various other motifs were developed by Zoroastrianism, "the only religion," in the words of R. C. Zaehner, "ever produced by the Aryan race," also known as Mazdaism, after the worshippers of Mazda. Such views eventually found their way into Islam and made a brief resurgence in the Islamic world with the Ismaili creed, a mixture of Neoplatonic, Gnostic, and Shiite doctrines, embraced by the Fatimid dynasty and the Qarmatians in Bahrain, who, in 930, the fifteen-hundredth anniversary of the supposed death of Zoroaster, "sacked Mecca and took away the Black Stone of the Kaaba to herald the end of the era of Islam." In fact, a young Persian ruler in Bahrain went as far as to abolish Islam and reinstate Zoroastrian forms of worship.[51]

The communist Qarmatians (who espoused the esoteric philosophy of the *batinya,* meaning that exterior reality has a correspondent inner one), according to Haytham Manna, preached the critical examination of religious texts and the supremacy of philosophical thought over revealed religions. And they were not the only ones to have questioned Sunni orthodox dogma. The radical Babakiyya movement also stands out as the ultimate expression of what might have been had the murderous arm of the *mihna* (inquisition) not nipped them in the bud. Founded by the enigmatic Babak during the reign of the Abbasid caliph Al-Ma'mun (813–833), the Babakiyya, influenced by Mazdaism, seem to have espoused a culture of strict egalitarianism, as the communal sharing of possessions and the redistribution of wealth from the rich to the poor were major aspects of this highly spiritual culture. Babak, like many *zindiqs,* was accused of not observing religious practices (*tark al-fara'id*). From their stronghold in Azerbaijan, Babaks revolted against the regime of Al-Ma'mun in 816 before they were defeated in 837, during the reign of the following caliph, Al-Mu'tassim. Babak was subsequently killed when his body parts were amputated, his face slapped with his severed arms, and his head was decapitated and displayed in Baghdad. (Such gruesome state-sponsored murders were not uncommonly applied to condemned heretics. The reputed eighth-century literary luminaries Bashar ibn Bord and Ibn al-Muqaffa' were also brutally executed.) Yet when the geographer Al-Muqaddassi visited Babak's region in the tenth century, he found a community of clean, gentle, and peaceful people, the very embodiment of what the executed Babak had championed.[52] Were the Babakiyya and Qarmatians agents of the United States or of the modern West? Of course not. They were people who simply disagreed with the Sunni orthodoxy, itself, like the Catholic Church, built over the ashes of heretics, the *zanadiqa,* many of whom were the legatees of the same Gnostic tradition buried by the Church's founding fathers.

The Moroccan weekly *TelQuel* was right to point to an all-but-forgotten tradition of heresy (*zandaqa*) that flourished in the early centuries of Islam, because what is hampering Muslims' progress to a culture of indigenous dissent is the lack of a vocabulary that doesn't come loaded with Eurocentric and imperialist assumptions. The scholars, Muslim or not, who make the case for modernity as a universal attribute would still have to qualify what counts as modern and what doesn't, whether such modernity is the effect or the handmaiden of the rapacious economic system that is destroying much of the world's social and cultural fabrics. One might make a good case for a secular constitution (the gift of the United States to the world), but not for a secular Muslim society, since Muslims, like most people throughout history, are unlikely to give up the pursuit of spiritual fulfillment. Muslims who think that their worst critics are the "secular" modernists in their midst, those who are so thoroughly colonized by the colonizer's culture that they don't even have a clue about their own, better know about the Iraqis of the eighth and ninth centuries, the heretics and atheists from Kufa, Basra, and Baghdad who had no time for revealed religions, including Islam, and had contempt for the uncouth masses who embraced such irrational creeds.

Recent studies of *zandaqa* and freethinking in Islam produce the same feelings Pagels experienced upon discovering and commenting on the long-lost Gnostic Gospels. She had to unlearn much of what she believed and then feel freer to pursue her faith outside rigidly prescribed bounds. In Syrian scholar Melhem Chokr's magisterial study on the subject of heresy in Islam, we come to learn that *zandaqa* emerged as a "dangerous crime" punishable by death in the second century of Islam, during the reign of the Abbasid caliph Abu Abdallah al-Mahdi (775–785), justified by the attempt to go back to the real, pure Sunni Islam of the Umayyads and bring an end to the proliferation of cults that had characterized the previous decades. It was an attempt to enforce orthodoxy, legally and ideologically, as the Mu'tazilites made the doctrine of the unicity of God (*tawhid*), based on criteria such as the advent (*huduth*) of the world, the authenticity of prophecy, bodily resurrection, and Judgment Day, the sine qua non of the faith. Anyone who espoused a different system of thought, hid their faith (*nifaq*), renounced it (*ridda*), as well as anyone who behaved contrary to prescribed Islamic ethics (heteropraxy, blasphemy) was labeled one, thereby lumping a broad range of views and disparate social elements into the tightening net of orthodoxy.[53]

The expansion of Islam and the collapse of the Umayyad order following the death of Hisham 'Abd al-Malik was a period of efflorescence for all sorts of non-Muslim religions in Babylonia and Khurassan, including Buddhists, dualists (such as the Gnostics, notably Marcionites), all critical of Islam and its literalism. Practitioners of *kalam,* Shiites, and libertines of all sorts were free to do pretty much as they pleased. Even a few caliphs who succeeded Hisham 'Abd al-Malik were known libertines or *zanadiqa.*

In fact, the Abbasid caliph Al-Mansur's entourage, known as *sahaba,* was similarly inclined, many of whose children would later be persecuted as *zanadiqa.* With the rise to power of Al-Mahdi, the persecution started in earnest, with an office for an inquisitor—*sahib* or *'arif al-zanadiqa,* and a Book of *zanadiqa*—established for the purpose of ferreting out the culprits through tricky tests. By the end of the eighth century (second century of the Hijra), the *zanadiqa* had, for all practical purposes, disappeared into oblivion in a structurally orthodox regime.[54]

The heterogeneous group of *zanadiqa* questioned the existence, unicity (*tawhid*), and justice of God, as well as God's relationship with His creatures (*at-tadbir*). The picture of the Qur'an's deity didn't impress them at all: the God of the Qur'an punishes, fights, terrorizes, mistreats people, inflicts pain and suffering on the innocent to test their faith, brags of having destroyed entire communities, even nations, in ancient times; it's a mercurial (good and bad at the same time), violent, and capricious god who openly displays resentment (*qayd*) and resorts to ruses (*makr*). The *zanadiqa* saw no purpose in life, believing that the world—eternal and uncreated—was delivered to chance (*ihmal*); it could not have come into existence through divine fiat (*kun*), for one orders only what already exists. Not unexpectedly, they found a multitude of contradictions and inconsistencies in the text of the Qur'an, as when God allows men in the famous passage on polygamy to marry up to four women if they can treat them equitably and then adds that they cannot do so. Because the Qur'an both challenges doubters and promises their failure to imitate its stylistic quality—a double gesture that forecloses the success of any attempt to do so— anyone who attempted a *mu'arada* (discrediting through imitation), as in the case of Ibn Abi al-Awja', Ibn al-Muqaffa', Salih ibn 'Abd al-Quddus, and others, was accused of this type of *zandaqa.*

Needless to say that for the *zanadiqa* there was no prophecy, only able, savvy, and intelligent philosopher-kings, like Mohammed, who founded human laws (*namus*). The ninth-and-tenth-century mystical poet Abul 'Ala' al-Ma'arri expressed this attitude beautifully in the following lines:

> Mohammad or Messiah! Hear thou me,
> The truth entire nor here nor there can be;
> How should our God who made the sun and the moon
> Give all his light to One, I cannot see.[55]

Such heresies were obviously rebutted by the defenders of the *tawhid* and persecuted.[56] Even the *mutakallimun,* the theologians who relied on the tenets of reason-based *kalam,* were accused of *zandaqa* by their traditionalist rivals (*muhadditun*) because, as the saying went, *man talaba al-din bi l-kalam tazandaqa* (Anyone who seeks to know religion through the use of reason falls into heresy).[57] In short, the list of eighth-century *zanadiqa,* which Chokr derives from a wide range of scholarly sources, included anyone who was a highly cultivated, cosmopolitan, and charming companion (*dharif*); any hedonistic, epicurean, or heedless indulger in all sorts of rhetorical and material pleasures; anyone accused of being an adulterer, inveterate connoisseur of wine, or outlaw; any sinful person without proper religion (*fasiq*); any insolent debaucher who knew nothing about the Qur'an and didn't observe religious rituals; any disciple of Satan and Iblis (the patron saint of the *zanadiqa*); any master of the art of blasphemy; and any lover of music and dance (*lahw wa tarab*). Many *zanadiqa* also rejected the existence of God, the creation of the world ex nihilo, and the afterlife.

Sarah Stroumsa's equally authoritative study of the *zanadiqa* or *malahida* (another attribute of heresy, often related to atheism) shows that demonized Muslim dissenters were not atheists in the strict modern sense, as their views didn't necessarily negate God's existence, only prophecy and revelation. Neither were they deists or materialists. They are best described as freethinkers who advocated "autonomous reflection on the major metaphysical and human issues, with no commitment to the monotheist tradition." No matter how contentious figures like the "ninth century theologian Ibn al-Rawandi and the tenth-century philosopher Abu Bakr al-Razi" (known as Rhazes in Latin) were, freethinking even in "its radical form was a typically Islamic phenomenon, a heresy whose particular character developed in response to the centrality of the concept of the prophecy in Islam."[58] The latter was a consuming issue, the subject of an unprecedented literary genre dealing with "proofs of prophecy," as in Al-Jahidh's *kitab hujaj al nubuwwa* and 'Abd al-Jabbar al-Hamadhani's *tathbit dala'il al-nubuwwa,* which dealt with Christian and Jewish dismissals and the challenges posed by the *barahima* (Brahmins) or "Hellenizing philosophers." Al-Jahidh's *hujaj al nubuwwa* even comes up with a sign called *khabar qahir,* or indisputable tradition, a great expression that may very well sum up the tyranny of all tradition! Al-Jahidh also enumerates other criteria for determining prophecy, such as *kitab natiq* (revealed book), *khabar mujtama* *alayhi* (widely accepted tradition), *hujjat* *aql* (intellectual argument), and *ijma* or *ijma'min al-umma* (consensus of the people). In short, proving prophecy was a major preoccupation for the Mu'tazilites in early Islamic history.[59]

There were figures like Al-Warraq, probably a Manichaean and author of *The Book of Lament over Animals* (*kitab al-nauh* *ala al-baha'im*) and the blasphemous sentence "He who orders his slave to do things that he knows him to be incapable of doing, then punishes him, is a fool,"[60] and his disciple Ibn al-Rawandi, a (sometimes) self-declared apostate or atheist (*mulhid*) associated with Shiism, Aristotelian philosophy (*dhahriyya*), and radical atheism and who was accused by one author of establishing "irreligious ideas" (*tathbit al-ilhad*), negating God's unity, denying prophecy, and vilifying prophets and imams. In fact, Ibn al-Rawandi's famous *Book of the Emerald* (*kitab al-zumurrud*) seems to have been written in the form of a dialogue with Al-Warraq himself, one standing for a heretic, the other defending orthodoxy. What adds to the provisional positions taken in this book (Al-Warraq dismisses prophecy, while Ibn al-Rawandi makes a feeble attempt to defend it, until he moves beyond his interlocutor's position and rejects all religions as equally absurd) is his longstanding habit of presenting arguments only to systematically refute them in a later work, a practice that one scholar, Josef van Ess, defined as a "péché mignon," a form of "intellectual coquetry." To write a book and refute it is, as Sarah Stroumsa puts it, to speak with "two voices." Ibn al-Rawandi's *zumurrud* was probably a "potpourri of arguments" making the case for the "sufficiency of human intellect" and innate knowledge (*ilham*) and against "prophetic revelation." As with the other *zanadiqa*, Ibn al-Rawandi was not impressed by the Qur'an, with its faulty Arabic and contradictions, or the traditions with their account of angels helping the Prophet in one battle (as in Badr) and somehow not showing up for him in another (as in Uhud). The miracles were merely "products of legerdemain" and "fraudulent tricks" (*makhariq*). Prayer and ritual had no significance, while the hajj (pilgrimage to Mecca) was absurdity itself: the ritual of "throwing stones, circumambulating a house that cannot respond to prayers, running between stones that can neither help nor harm" doesn't make any sense to him, leading him to ask "why the Ka'ba is any better than any other house,"[61] a not-uncommon sentiment among the *zanadiqa*, as one might find in the following poetic lines, also from Abul 'Ala' al-Ma'arri:

Fortune is (so strangely) allotted, that rocks are visited (by
   pilgrims) and touched with hands and lips,
Like the Holy Rock (at Jerusalem) or the two Angles of Quraysh,
   howbeit all of them are stones that once were kicked.[62]

Or even more explicitly:

And stranger still that Muslims travel far
To kiss a black stone said to be divine:—
Almighty God! Will all the human race
Stray blindly from the Truth's most sacred shrine?[63]

Although *zandaqa* was mortally weakened by the end of the eighth
century, the legacy of Al-Warraq and Ibn al-Rawandi, among many other
zanadiqa, survived in the work of figures like Abu Bakr Razi (865–925),
arguably the most famous physician and freethinker, iconoclast, and probably heretic in all of Muslim history. "With the possible exception of
Avicenna and Averroes," wrote Arthur J. Arberry in 1950, "no man so
powerfully affected the course of learning in the Middle Ages and the early
Renaissance as Rhazes." (He is mentioned in Chaucer's *Canterbury Tales*
as one of the Doctor of Physic's masters, and Razi's treatise *On Smallpox
and Measles,* highly praised for its accuracy, was reprinted as late as 1866.)[64]
Razi's "anti-prophetism," based on his insistence on rational and empir-
ical thought, traits that are indispensable in medicine and science, clashed
with the "proofs of prophecy" literature of the period. In his *Book on the
Prophets' Fraudulent Tricks* (*kitab makhariq al-anbiya*), written in the form
of a question-and-answer debate, he questions why some people are chosen for prophethood and others not, and argues that it would be far better
for social harmony and peace if all people were to be so inspired. He also
sees religion as perpetuated by blind imitation and habit, and the religious
as persecuting rational thought whenever and wherever they are challenged
by its premises. Of course, Razi treated all religions the same, as he simply rejected the claim to miracles at the foundation of all such myths—
bad myths at that, too. To him, the Qur'an is bad mythology, full of
contradictions, and could in fact have been written better. Such views
were described by one scholar as "the most violent polemic against religion
in the course of the middle ages." He also differed from the Mu'tazilites in

his insistence on "the sufficiency and universality of the intellect" without any supernatural help to guide humans in their lives on earth. Because he was a thoroughgoing rationalist, he thought that "the notion of prophecy is not only superfluous, but also biologically and logically false." For Razi, people are endowed with equal intellectual opportunities, even though most do not take advantage of them, particularly of philosophy, which is the only form of contemplation that purges people "from the turbidity of this world." Despite his views, and unlike the theologian Ibn al-Rawandi, Razi seems to have enjoyed an untroubled life, living and dying in peace, a fact that raises the issue of whether the dogma of the infallibility of the Qur'an had not yet crystallized, or whether Islam was still able to engage such views, no matter how shockingly offensive they may have appeared to the orthodox.[65] No wonder the philosopher Abdel Rahman Badawi concluded his study of atheism in Islam by lamenting the absence of the spirit of that age in our own.[66]

In addition to questioning prophecy, the arbitrariness of God's master plan is something that bothered the *zanadiqa*. Ibn al-Rawandi wondered how a wise and compassionate god could inflict so much suffering and poverty on His slaves, and then ask for obedience when He knows people will disobey. So Al-Rawandi concluded, according to one account, that "He who punishes the infidel and disobedient in eternal fire is a fool (*safih*). He is not wise, nor does He know the [appropriate] measures of punishment for sins."[67] Even Iblis (the devil), according to an account by Shahrastani, had this say:

> Since God knew in advance what would become of me, he asked, what is the wisdom of His having created me? Since He created me according to His wish and will, why did He (then) command me to know and obey Him? And what is the wisdom of this command (*taklif*), since He neither benefits from obedience nor is He harmed by disobedience? Since He created me and made me . . . compelled [me to act in the way I did] . . . . why did He curse me and drive me out of Eden? Why did He let me tempt Adam and his consort? It would have been better for them and more appropriate to His wisdom to create them having inborn knowledge of the right behavior (*'ala al fitra*), without leading them into temptation. And lastly, why was I allowed to pester humanity? Would it not have been better to have a world free of evil?[68]

Razi, who believed that social solidarity can only be built on a system of reason (*mujtama' al-ta'awoon wal ta'adhud al-'aqli*),[69] may also have seen the world full of evil and mounted a strong challenge to "monotheistic theodicy," but his goal was to rescue God (who endows gnosis, or inspiration [*ilham*] to His creatures and lets His creation unfold) from the so-called "revealed religions [that] cause fanaticism and thus encourage strife and wars." To Razi, "the good, merciful God must have had a better idea for the salvation of humankind." Such *zanadiqa* regarded all religions as the same, rejected rituals and the tendency to support every opinion by a quote from the Qur'an or some other hallowed tradition.[70] They were sometimes charged with being unoriginal thinkers, or with trying to rival or parody the language of the Qur'an (as in the case of the dualist Ibn al-Muqaffa'); they were called names—*jahil* (ignoramus), *safih* (fool), *khabeeth* (wicked), *majin* (impudent), *la'een* (cursed)—but they bravely persevered in the face of an orthodox program of demonization.

Philosophically, Muslim *zanadiqa* like Ibn al-Rawandi and Razi were similar to the Christian heretics who refused the single vision of an almighty god ruling despotically over his creation. They may "represent a direct continuation of what Pierre de Labriolle has called "the pagan reaction against Christianity in antiquity," but they were also influenced by and incorporated the rationalism of the *barahima* (a generic term, like *sumaniyya, asshab al-budud,* or *al-bidada,* for Indian religions). Probably deployed as a topos testifying to Muslim-Indian contact, the *barahima* supported the *zanadiqa*'s "anti-abrogationist" views (a perfect God doesn't make up His mind and change it repeatedly, or send a prophet with a revelation only to abrogate and update it later). The mysterious Sabeans may have had an influence on Razi, too, since both the *barahima* and the Sabeans did not exclude the notion of "original guidance or inspiration, while rejecting the idea of revelation in its historical sense."[71]

And Ibn al-Rawandi's influence may have trickled further down the slopes of history, influencing the art of rhetoric and keeping the anxiety over prophecy alive, however latent it may have been, in the works of such luminaries as Al-Ghazali and Ibn Taymiyya, who rejected Sufi views, particularly Ibn 'Arabi's, as well as in Avicenna's philosophy. Being an excellent dialectician, the author of *kitab adab al-jadal* (On the art of disputation), "probably one of the earliest books written in Islam [before his heretical phase] about dialectics," Ibn al-Rawandi, either through those who emulated him or those who rejected his techniques of presenting a case and arguing against it, pioneered the high art of dialectical argumentation. Despite his heretical stance, there was no doubt, as Tawhidi recorded in his *kitab al-basha'ir*, that Ibn al-Rawandi "makes no mistakes and his speech is free of dialectical barbarism. For he is a superb theologian, a discerning critic, an inquisitive dialectician, and a persevering observer."

Such sharp minds, refined scholars, accomplished physicians, and later, the Sufis, who would be suspected of "harboring antinomian ideas" and "denying prophecy" suffered from the strong arm of a Sunni orthodoxy that decapitated not only the heads of *zanadiqa,* as sometimes happened, but also the source of innovation in Muslim civilization. The Abbasid inquisitors were inflicting a damage so severe on the body of the nascent Islamic civilization that its effects are still haunting us today. Freethinking would thereafter be integrated into the larger Islamic legacy and conveyed in "philosophical parables like Ibn-Sina's, or poetry like Al-Ma'arri's and Jalal al-Din al-Rumi's."[72] Al-Farabi (c. 870–950), known as "the second teacher" (after Aristotle), believed that a physical afterlife was a metaphor designed to make sense to the masses and that an intellectual elite could do without such literalism. Meanwhile, the famous Aristotelian metaphysician Ibn Sina (980–1037), known in the West as Avicenna, author of *al-qanun,* "which in its Latin translation [canon] became the standard medical work in Europe until the seventeenth century," developed Neoplatonic doctrines that Al-Ghazali found "incompatible with Islamic beliefs."[73] Even a titan like the Moorish Aristotelian Abu al-Walid Ibn Ahmed Ibn Rushd (better known as Averroës and the "Commentator," on Aristotle's philosophy) couldn't jump-start the freethinking tradition. As Daniel Gimaret, who wrote the preface to Chokr's study, put it, it needs no reminding that such a movement—eclipsed by the "deadly heritage of Hanbalism"—is still badly needed today.[74]

Mohammed ʿAbed al-Jabri, the renowned Moroccan philosopher of Islam, would agree that Muslims need to seek their modernity through tradition, for if we imagine modernity as a rupture with our past, the most arduous efforts will come to naught. Used separately, neither fundamentalist nor Western-based modernist approaches will do, but if modernity is used as a method to reactivate the slumbering genius of the Islamic past, to renew the Arab-Muslim tradition (*turath*), Muslims and Arabs may have a chance at entering the world stage and using their own modernities to engage the world's multiple modernities (indeed, there are multiple modernities, according to Al-Jabri).[75] Muslims need an "epistemological break": not renouncing tradition but the Muslims' "traditional understanding of tradition," which are two very different things. They need to be disjointed from it through a structuralist, historical, and ideological approach to its texts (a project that is made much more difficult by the sacral, unchanging nature of the Arabic language, whose immutability proves, if anything, that cultures are captive to their structures, not vice versa). A certain distance from and a "meticulous dissection" of texts are therefore vital to the project of renewal. Once approached through this rigorous, modern scientific method, they may then be rejoined to tradition under "a new relationship," one that addresses their contemporaneity. It would allow them to understand why Arab philosophy, both in its medieval guise and in the modern period, is almost obsessively concerned with "reconciling reason and transmission," although one senses that a number of great Islamic philosophers, ranging from Al-Ghazali to Al-Farabi and Razi, had access to truths they couldn't "divulge" to those who couldn't handle them—an ironic example, I might add, of how Islamic thought was confined to well-guarded boundaries that limited the range of philosophical expression.[76]

Looking back at the Abbasid period, Al-Jabri says that

> philosophy was never a luxury within Islamic society: it was in fact, ever since its birth, a militant ideological discourse. Abu Yusuf Yaʿqub ibn Ishaq al-Kindi (c. 800–870), the first Aristotelian Muslim philosopher, was directly involved in the ideological conflict that existed during his lifetime between the Muʿtazilites, then representing the state's ideology, on the one hand and the Gnostics and the "Sunnites," on the other.

Though Al-Kindi tried to reconcile reason and revelation, he had harsh words for those who use religion to discredit reason: "He who commodifies religion no longer has a religion, and he who refuses to acquire knowledge of the truth about things and denounces it as impiety (*kufr*) deserves to lose his title of 'religious.'" But the "Philosopher of the Arabs," as Al-Kindi was known, who was sponsored by three Abbasid caliphs, was persecuted under the reign of Al-Mutuwakkil, following what Al-Jabri calls the "Sunnite 'coup d'etat' against the Muʿtazilites."[77]

Al-Jabri locates hope in the peripheral and autonomous Moroccan-Spanish (Andalusian) tradition, which, until the total eclipse of Islamic philosophy, had tried to resurrect the Aristotelian legacy of reason. (Al-Jabri considers gnosticism a form of unreason and therefore part of the obscurantist tradition responsible for the decline of Islam.) Andalusian philosophy was supported by the study of the "ancient sciences" (mathematics, astronomy, logic, and so on) without the anxiety of having to reconcile faith and reason. Ibn Tufayl (d. 1158), author of *hayy ibn yaqdhan* (Alive, son of the one who is awake), put it well when he wrote:

> The people of superior minds who grew up in Al-Andalus before the spread in this land of the sciences of logic and philosophy devoted their lives to the mathematical sciences in which they reached a high level. After them, came a generation of men who, in addition, possessed rudiments of logic; they studied this discipline, which did not lead them to real perfection. . . . After them came another generation of men who were more skillful in theory and who came closer to the truth.[78]

Ibn Hazm's (994–1063) *dhahrist* (exoterist) philosophy was more than an intransigent textual literalism, but a critique of Shiite and Sufi illuminist philosophies and the Muʿtazilites' adventurous reasoning *hors texte*. He strongly opposed imitation. "No one is allowed," Ibn Hazm asserted, "to imitate someone else, living or dead, but each must perform to the best of his ability, an interpretative effort (*ijtihad*)." It's even wrong and unjustified to imitate a mufti or even the prophet's companions and the founders of the main schools of Islamic Sunnite jurisprudence: "Let anyone who imitates a companion, a follower, a Malik, an Abu Hanifa, a Shafiʿi, a Sufyan [al-Thawri], an Awzaʿi, an Ahmad (Ibn Hanbal), or a Dawud (al-Isfahani)—may God be satisfied with them—know that all of the above people 'wash their hands' of him, in this world as well as in the other world." Ibn Hazm relied on reason and evidence, allowing that things preceding the fact, such as the way nature is made, people are shaped, or what constitutes prayer, fall outside the scope of reason since they appear as faits accomplis.

The Almohads, the ruling dynasty at the time, inspired by Ibn Hazm's *dhahirism*, encouraged the study of "ancient sciences," especially under the reign of the highly cultured and avid reader of philosophy Yaʿqub al-Mansur. Thus, Al-Mansur commissioned Ibn Rushd (Averroës) to make Aristotle's philosophy more accessible. Averroës had to begin by theorizing away "the Avicennian 'conciliationism' and its gnostic residues and counter Ghazali's offensive against philosophy and philosophers" and eventually come up with his own system of conciliation, allowing religion ("legislator's intent") and philosophy ("natural causes" or the "principle of causality") to operate in their own independent spheres, converging, as they do, on the same quest for truth and virtue. (The late Jewish agnostic scientist Stephen Jay Gould, whose statement opens this chapter, famously dubbed the attempt to keep both spheres separate as NOMA, short for "nonoverlapping magisteria," a concept that Sam Harris in *The End of Faith* rejects as a false compromise.)[79] This kind of thinking would affect the legal sphere—in the work of Shatibi, for instance, whose philosophy of legislation was based on grand principles and echoed the Aristotelian methodology, as did the work of the Maghrebian historian Ibn Khaldun and his general principles.[80]

Al-Jabri's sweeping view of the Islamic philosophical tradition leads him to conceive of only one option for Arabs and Muslims alike: the future can only be Averroist. Tradition is not immutable or something that happened long ago and has no effect on the present. It builds on its record, so to speak, one philosophy building on, and thereby canceling, a previous one (as the early Muslims did with the Greeks), and just as Averroës did with Avicenna's "oriental" gnostic philosophy of "Sunni Sufism," unsupported by the prophetic tradition. Averroës simply rejected the search for conciliation "between reason and transmission" and offered a "carry-on spirit" to conceptualize the Muslim tradition in relation to its Other—which, in our present, might mean a Western-inspired modernity. For Averroës had no problem using non-Muslim methodologies, liberally seeing human sciences as part of a universal heritage, regardless of faith or tribal affiliation. And so, according to Al-Jabri, "to adopt the Averroist spirit is to break with the Avicennian 'oriental' spirit, a gnostic one that promotes *gloom* thinking." To him, this is not a chauvinistic move but the only logical one, given that modern universality can only be experienced from "within a tradition not outside it."[81]

In a way, Al-Jabri's call for the revival of Averroës's philosophy has been echoed more recently by Richard E. Rubenstein, who explores the remarkable impact of Aristotle on the three monotheistic faiths, and why it behooves us to rediscover his legacy today.[82] Consistently rational, student and colleague of the more idealistic Plato at the Academy, founder of the Lyceum, intellectual elitist who died at sixty-three, Aristotle believed neither in an omnipotent creator nor in a meaningless universe, but in a purposeful cosmos. For him, things had essences (soul), and (self-)actualization through knowledge was perhaps the ultimate mission in life. When his work was found in Muslim Spain, translated and commented on in Arabic by Arab and Jewish scholars, it was one of the most dramatic cultural events of the High Middle Ages. "No intellectual discovery before or after had anything like the impact of this remarkable find," says Rubenstein. The event didn't pit faith against reason, as one might surmise today, but led to the negotiation of the two principles, and how to blend them without taking away from one's fundamental commitments and beliefs. Unlike Islam, the Catholic Church did more to promote the philosophy of reason than people realize.[83]

Aristotelian philosophy gave ammunition to the critics of the Catholic Church. It inspired the morally upright but persecuted Cathars under the leadership of the *Perfecti*—vegetarian, asexual, pacifist antimaterialists who were avid readers and against capital punishment, who fasted to death (*endura*) when old and ill—to establish an unofficial "counter-Church" in Languedoc (southern France), Provence, and northern Italy. When the Spanish Domingo de Guzmán was dispatched to dispute them in France, the future founder of the Dominican order wanted his side to emulate the Cathars in their manners and lifestyle; but Pope Innocent III still ordered their extermination in an all-out crusade, leading to gruesome massacres of thousands of civilians, Cathars and Catholics alike, women and children. Meanwhile, universities were spreading throughout Europe, even as Church leaders forbade the teaching of Aristotle's treatises on the natural sciences and metaphysics, first in Paris, as well as the works of other Aristotelians, possibly including Ibn Rushd (Averroës) himself.[84]

The Belgian philosopher Siger de Brabant (b. 1240), a master of the arts faculty at Paris (he was not a theologian), and his followers, the mostly northern European and Scandinavian Sigerists, relying on the works of the philosopher and on his Muslim commentator, Averroës, espoused a radical, "uncompromising," rationalist outlook and "seemed to relish the discontinuities between Aristotelian *scientia* and Christian faith," a position that would, six centuries later, be formulated by "ascetic Dane Søren

Kierkegaard" as "Either/Or." Siger and other radicals relied on the commentaries of Avicenna and Averroës, particularly the latter's "monopsychism" (the theory of a collective intellect that survives the death of the body). His critics believed that he was teaching the "scandalous doctrine of Dual Truth" (one secular, the other faith-based, and therefore to be "soft on secularism," as one might put it today). For this reason, "Siger and his 'Averroistic' friends" were condemned and had to answer to the Inquisition, while the bishop of Paris, once again, banned the teaching of certain Aristotelian principles in the Condemnations of 1270. By doing his best to refute Sigerist thesis, Thomas Aquinas relied on the same logic, but the net effect was even more reliance on rational thinking and logic, and it wouldn't be long until, in the 1320s, Jean de Jandun "gained a large following in Paris by teaching the separation of reason and faith, church and state, and by collaborating with Marsilius of Padua on the treatise *Defensor Pacis,* a notorious attack on the doctrine of papal supremacy." The Dominican Thomas Aquinas would later be canonized and his teaching adopted by the Church; Siger de Brabant is said to have been stabbed to death in Italy, by his secretary who had gone mad.[85]

By the fourteenth century, the papacy, despite its pomp and claims, was losing ground to increasingly independent secular rulers. The French (Philip the Fair) or Bavarian (Ludwig) kings even attacked the pope and removed him from office. Meanwhile, post-Thomist Franciscan intellectuals, such as William of Ockham, were calling for "an entirely new map of knowledge," allowing for the unhindered pursuit of scientific work, while arguing that it was impossible to apply reason to understand God or His motives, that everything unfolds in nature according to an inscrutable divine plan. Eventually, William of Ockham was accused of heresy and summoned to Avignon for a hearing, the same place where German mystical Dominican Meister Eckhart headed to answer similar charges. William of Ockham was subsequently given protection by King Ludwig and moved to Munich, the destination of persecuted scholars. A mystical evangelical movement, espoused by the "friends of God," flourished in the Rhineland, giving "a strong foretaste of the coming Protestant movement, with its inwardness and evangelical zeal, its communities of 'saints,' its intense focus on Scripture, and its relative lack of interest in scientific reasoning."[86]

The "collapse of the Aristotelian consensus" began when the likes of the Augustinian monk Martin Luther and the atheist Thomas Hobbes launched vicious attacks against the philosopher's work and his legacy ("scholastic theology"), giving a free hand to fundamentalist literalism ("scripture alone") and state absolutism without the tempering impact of Aristotelian ethics. Again, Rubenstein: "Fundamentalist literalism, in other words, was not a feature of the medieval worldview from which modern rationalists had to be 'liberated.' It came into the world as a result of the same attack on Aristotelian-Christian thinking that produced secular science." Yet by trying to reconcile the two main (pre)occupations of humans, while lending his work to multiple "corrections" and commentaries, Aristotle's legacy of integrating faith and reason, allowing them to live in a state of "creative tension," is what the world needs to restore peace and harmony. The conundrum, as Rubenstein realizes, is that Aristotle is more congenial in times of growth and stability, while Plato, like monotheism, emerges in times of confusion, disarray, trouble, and doubt.[87] Which is why I started this book by showing how the current global economic system, which produces vast inequalities within nations and around the world, is not conducive to a more peaceful world order.

There is no doubt that the sort of monotheisms that have governed people's lives and influenced the course of history have diminished people's ability to experience the divine, however conceived, directly. Though it is not something that can be described with any degree of precision, the divine is the experience of being part of one's natural environment, vibrating with its energy, connected to all, without having to erect imaginary boundaries between the Self and the Other. It is the state of nonalienation, as Karl Marx would have it, the condition of being fully realized as a human being through one's activities, not enslaved by the despotism of false wants or dehumanizing beliefs. To be alive—fully alive—is to be divine, for that is the optimal state of creation. Only when our natural faculties are dulled by oppressive social conventions do we lose touch with our essence and seek answers through the mediums of religion, nationalism, physical prowess, or any other substitute that is bound to disappoint us and lead us down the path of more misery.

There is, in fact, a long American tradition, stretching from Thomas Paine and Thomas Jefferson to Emerson and Thoreau, reaching all the way to the present, that has tried to unshackle spiritual elevation from the iron grip of religious faith. Jefferson even wrote his own gospel, which consisted largely of taking out the miraculous from the King James Bible and compiling a multilingual book of wisdom called *The Life and Morals of Jesus of Nazareth* (titled *The Jefferson Bible* by Beacon Press). Jefferson's list of virtues, when outlined by an essayist, appears like the quintessence of early Christianity, the one encoded in the long-lost Gnostic Gospel of Thomas, or in the spirit of early Christianity itself. Justice, compassion, the uncompromising pursuit of peace, the reconsideration of what is valuable in life and what is not (as an epicurean, Jefferson seems to have believed that all good things in life are come by easily), nonjudgment of others, modesty, and unpretentiousness are all virtues that are best upheld in a simple agrarian economy of self-reliance and self-sufficiency. When the Gospel of Thomas, Jefferson's Bible, and Ralph Waldo Emerson's teachings are combined, Erik Reece says we get "a truly American gospel," one that brings the Kingdom of Heaven down to earth.[88] Such vision, as shown in the previous chapter, didn't come to pass, with the rise of industry, the frantic pursuit of riches, the quest for security in arms, the spread of dependency, the collapse of the social fabric, and the politicization of religion. A superorthodoxy, fusing un-Christian economic practices with selective biblical literalism and generating counterorthodoxies elsewhere, as in the lands of Islam, or even in Islamic thought itself, has gained the upper hand and is now influencing much of the course of history. This American "way of life" eventually clashed with the ossified orthodoxy of Sunni Islam, the ideology of Umayyad caliphs, and the backbone of the prosecutorial Abbasid state that drove *zandaqa* underground and wrapped the social polity in the dark colors of legalism and political despotism. As it is, the clash of Islam and America is more like the *danse macabre* of civilizations drained of their creative energies, unable to see their ways out of habits that do nothing but exacerbate the human predicament.

It is true that Muslims cannot open up on their own, for history has shown over and over again that a people that perceives itself to be under siege recoils into core beliefs—however imagined or problematic such beliefs may be—and doesn't gravitate toward the sage wisdom of Aristotle, adopt the dynamic intellectual traditions of the *zanadiqa,* or even ponder the mystical ways of, say, Jalal al-Din Rumi, the thirteenth-century mystic and founder of the Mevlana order, with its *sama'* ceremonies (shall we call them *danses célèbres,* for they are definitely not macabres, even though transcendence is their goal?), joyfully performed by what we have come to know as the Whirling Dervishes. (This book is being published in what the United Nations has designated the Year of Rumi.) If the United States and the rest of the world don't change their own orthodoxies, the Muslim condition is unlikely to change, at least not in any meaningful way. Times of trouble and chaos favor the gods of monotheism and the guardians ("bishops," as Tertullian would say) of orthodoxy, and such gods do not look down benignly on freedom of thought and liberty of conscience.

Yet the freethinking traditions of the United States and Islam constitute the only hope both cultures have to revitalize themselves and brighten the splendor of their stars and crescents. Not only that, but we may do well to remember that both Muslims and Americans started out as dissenters from despotic beliefs or states, vowing to make their new doctrines the shield and abode of the downtrodden and overlooked, the meek and weak among us. America has long been engraved in world opinion as the "asylum" for humanity, a sentiment that has echoed throughout the ages and is immortalized by the Jewish writer Emma Lazarus's poetic lines:

> Give me your tired, your poor,
> Your huddled masses, yearning to breathe free,
> The Wretched refuse of your teeming shore.
> Send these, the homeless, tempest-tost to me,
> I lift my lamp beside the golden door.

These lines are inscribed on the pedestal of Frédéric-Auguste Bartholdi's sculpture *The Statue of Liberty*, probably the best welcoming sign a nation has displayed at its gates. Within this mainstream dissenting spirit, other dissenters, such as the ones catalogued by Susan Jacoby, have kept the country's moral compass firmly in (not on) the right, insisting that whenever one's founding principles are forgotten, whenever the spirit of ancestors is trivialized, the wrath of god descends on their progeny. To reclaim America's revolutionary heritage, as imperfect as it was and still is, is not to go back in time but to move forward, toward the Whitmanesque universe of human solidarity at its best.

The *zanadiqa* of Islam, as well as Islam's persecuted or neglected philosophers, are also Islam's only hope to break free, finally, from the tyranny of Sunni orthodoxy and carry on the work that had long been cast in Islam's golden trash heap of history. For modernity, in its Islamic sense, is no more than embracing the right critical method and ensuring a society that doesn't punish difference or proscribe intellectual pluralism. Being modern doesn't have to be about mimicry—for that would be a lost cause, as is well known by now—but rediscovering the spirit of inquiry in its most radical form. Some may question dogma and champion a narrow vision of modernity without straying out of the faith, but others (always a minority in any society) may choose to step out of the boundaries of the faith altogether, believing, as Ibn al-Rawandi, Razi, and others did, that prophecy and religious rituals are mere aids for spiritual novices and the intellectually unenlightened, or as the Sufis did, who dismissed rituals and formal Islamic law, even "conventional morality and social custom," as superfluous.[89] After all, then and now, the mind struggles to see the connection between ritual practices and existential truth. As Christopher Hart commented on a post–9/11 British law criminalizing the criticism of religion as hate speech, "the difficulty is rather that all the religions on offer are so patently preposterous, if not downright unpleasant," because "all religions without exception are fallible human creations, in parts beautiful and profound and in parts ridiculous and repellent. To protect them from criticism is bad for our society and, even more importantly, bad for our souls."[90]

Far better is to know oneself through meditation or to think rationally about the creation than to chain one's beings to orthopraxy. Ibn al-Rawandi's dismissal of hajj rituals as absurdity itself finds echoes even today, as would-be pilgrims, like the Princeton-based Moroccan anthropologist Abdellah Hammoudi, are required to submit more than thirty photographs, a seemingly infinite number of documents, and bribe a multitude of clerks in order to perform the obligatory ritual. (It must be noted, however, that Hammoudi, a U.S. resident, complicated his case by insisting on joining the Moroccan contingent.) As hundreds of pilgrims were dying in stampedes in 2004 and 2005, fancy hotels in Mecca, like Le Meridien Towers, advertised their luxurious shared-ownership apartments ("six nights, $12,000; five nights within the first 20 days of Ramadan, $21,000; 30 nights during the hajj, $170,000") with religious punch lines about the rewards of pilgrimage.[91] The frenzy of commercial development in and around Mecca is turning the holiest city into a Las Vegas look-alike temple for the consumption of brand-name goods, while the high-rise buildings sprouting up around the Kaʿaba, the most sacred site in Islam, are allowing wealthy condo owners to join in prayers without leaving their suites.[92] Even Ramadan, the holy month of fasting, is gradually turning into a commercial ritual, with greeting cards, sweepstakes, advertising campaigns, and even displays with "an uncanny resemblance to a Nativity scene, complete with moving camels, a village elder reading stories and a desert scene" in a shopping mall in Dubai.[93] The Gnostics and *zanadiqa* of old would rather stay home than turn human creations, land plots, and artifacts of everyday use into fetishes, for the Kingdom of Heaven is right here and now, within and around us, a sacred trust not to be negligently confused with theological mandates and wasted for the elusive benefits of material riches or political power. Al-Jabri and Rubenstein are also right to think that Aristotle and his famous commentator, Averroës, are our common link to modernity, for they guide the way to free inquiry, politely separating the realms of what Karen Armstrong calls mythos and logos and Stephen Jay Gould terms the two "nonoverlapping magisteria."

Monotheism, to end where I started, may have long outlived its usefulness and may no longer be suitable for a tightly globalized planet without much room for exclusivist convictions, but since one cannot reasonably expect faith to fly back into the heavens any time soon, the best we can do is keep faith and intellectual inquiry, religion and politics (which, at its basic level, means no more than the management of human affairs and the neutral arbitration of differences) apart, until Muslims, like all the world's monotheists, eventually reach a new synthesis, one that is closer to Gnosticism than to caliphal orthodoxies. The *zanadiqa,* like American freethinkers, were and may still be more likely to nudge their fellow citizens toward more enriching economies of the spirit and the mind, ones that are contemptuous of crude materialism, elevating the finer, more aesthetic aspects of human activity, including philosophical inquiry, above all else. Even the scriptures of orthodox monotheism insist that the life of the spirit and the worship of mammon, the quest for human plenitude and a life of material abundance cannot coexist in the same person and place without one of the two being seriously undermined, an axiom obvious enough to be clearly postulated by Matthew in the Bible.

In 1993, the Parliament of the World's Religions, held in Chicago, made a strong and unambiguous plea for a global ethic based on capacious theologies of love and solidarity, sustained by the timeless dictates of the Golden Rule and a robust culture of tolerance, and nurtured in a healthy natural environment. It is a moving declaration, but its realization, the authors knew, depends on establishing an equitable economic system:

> Where extreme poverty reigns, helplessness and despair spread, and theft occurs again and again for the sake of survival. Where power and wealth are accumulated ruthlessly, feelings of envy, resentment, and deadly hatred and rebellion inevitably well up in the disadvantaged and marginalized. This leads to a vicious circle of violence and counter-violence. Let no one be deceived: There is no global peace without global justice![94]

In his first encyclical meditating on the fundamental obligation for love in its most sublime sense, Pope Benedict XVI said that while the Catholic Church is not interested in replacing the secular state, it "cannot and must not remain on the sidelines in the fight for justice."[95] For, as he pronounced on his 2006 Christmas address from St. Peter's Basilica, the human condition in the third millennium, an age of high-tech wonders, is still in shackles to hunger and spiritual emptiness:

> People continue to die of hunger and thirst, disease and poverty, in this age of plenty and of unbridled consumerism. Some people remain enslaved, exploited and stripped of their dignity; others are victims of racial and religious hatred, hampered by intolerance and discrimination, and by political interference and physical or moral coercion with regard to the free profession of their faith. Others see their own bodies and those of their dear ones, particularly their children, maimed by weaponry, by terrorism and by all sorts of violence, at a time when everyone invokes and acclaims progress, solidarity and peace for all. And what of those who, bereft of hope, are forced to leave their homes and countries in order to find humane living conditions elsewhere? How can we help those who are misled by facile prophets of happiness, those who struggle with relationships and are incapable of accepting responsibility for their present and future, those who are trapped in the tunnel of loneliness and who often end up enslaved to alcohol or drugs? What are we to think of those who choose death in the belief that they are celebrating life?[96]

Pope Benedict's diagnosis of the human condition in our already troubled millennium is certainly accurate, but the pursuit of doctrinal orthodoxies is not, in my opinion, part of the answer. The concern for human welfare was expressed by Amos, Isaiah of Jerusalem, and Micah, among others, who were far more interested in social justice and compassion for all humans than in empty and self-serving sacrifices meant to please God. Arthur J. Bellinzoni has powerfully reminded us that the Christianity of meaningless rituals is bound to collapse and could only survive (in what shape is not clear) if it renews the philosophy of justice and resistance to slavery and oppression in all their forms, since that is what Jesus (if he ever existed), just like the Hebrew prophets before him, fundamentally preached. For this to happen, Church doctrine (both Catholic and Protestant) must be radically reconceptualized. The Nicean Creed, hammered out in 325 to stipulate that the Son and the Father are part of the same substance, a concept that was later (in 451, at Chalcedon, Turkey) refined to mean that Jesus was both "*wholly* human and *wholly* divine" no longer makes sense in light of the knowledge at our disposal. Similarly, while the "Roman Catholic Church's outrageous claim of infallibility" is clearly the outcome of political infighting, the Protestant fundamentalist insistence on the "literal inerrancy of the scriptures" counters a Catholic myth with another, since the books of the Bible, "produced over a period of more than a thousand years," are clearly the product of human literary imagination, a process of reading back into the past and investing distant events with religious and ideological significance. Just as God, in Bellinzoni's account, is not a vain sadist or a "real estate broker," religion is no more than "the doing of justice and righteous[ness] and the loving of mercy and kindness."[97]

But how does one envision this world of global justice without fundamentally replacing a global economic system that is continually expanding the gap between the haves and have-nots with human-scale economies, ones that are driven not by the avaricious appetites of moguls but by the ascetic requirements of mystics like Rumi?[98] If the current model of globalization persists unchanged, Muhammad Yunus, the Bangladeshi who won the Nobel Peace Prize in 2006 for loaning tiny amounts of money—pocket change in countries like the United States—to the poor, sees no hope for the world's masses. When one surveys the vast global wasteland of plenty and deprivation, the contrast of opulence and wretched misery, it's hard to see any alternative to scaling back through a new global political economy of "degrowth," or *décroissance,* in Serge Latouche's expression.[99]

Mainstream Muslim thought, let alone its fundamentalist variant, has done nothing to contribute to a more equitable and harmonious human civilization, preoccupied as it is with cultural authenticity and the purity of faith above any other consideration. Trapped in the gilded cage of embellished histories and the mores of long-perished societies, most contemporary Muslims have confined their horizons to the pursuit of autonomy based on an idealized past, not to a genuine rethinking of the structures of global civilization or world history. Sometimes, the Muslim quest for authenticity can lead to the absurd, as when, in 2005, a Syria-based company gave birth to a fully robed version of the Barbie doll, Fulla, which became instantly popular in countries like Morocco, not least because it gave the impression that one could buy into consumer-culture icons and deal a blow to the West's cultural hegemony at the same time.[100] Similarly, beating the drums of war and patriotism in the face of complicated geopolitical realities; maligning leftists, atheists, liberals, or members of another faith; and locking up the nation in a plethora of security systems will not attenuate the breakdown of the social fabric in the United States. Chauvinism, whether cultural, political, or economic, may smooth out thorny contradictions, but it cannot provide long-term answers to the crises besetting Islam, the United States, and much of the world under the blind forces of globalization. It is merely a form of avoidance that will only worsen the fate and future of our children and grandchildren.

In the end, there is simply no alternative to harnessing all the educational and cultural tools at our disposal to rethink the foundations of our current world order. We seem to go through years and decades of education as if in a state of amnesia. Religions that cannot stand basic intellectual examination are honored as the basis of our moral edifice, while economic systems that are ravaging the global habitat, diminishing our humanity, and endangering peace and coexistence for the ephemeral benefit of a handful of people and states are taken for granted by leaders who see no way out of our conundrum. What's worse, and even more distressing, resignation in the face of the daunting challenge to imagine solutions often turns well-meaning people into militant apologists for existing religious and economic regimes, as if both religion and capitalism were part of a divinely decreed natural order, not the outcomes of particular historical processes and human intervention. Yet, however hard we try to argue over the meaning of history or human nature, we can't afford to wait too long for badly needed alternatives to our conceptions of faith and the economy. The world is in bad shape and is getting worse by the day. This is why we need freethinkers and *zanadiqa,* the daring few who can break away from mainstream thought and imagine new possibilities for our embattled lives. Any attempt to repress the voice of life-affirming dissent under the cloak of economic, political, and religious orthodoxies, or through the dead weight of force, will simply prolong our agony and deprive future generations from the chance to make our long-suffering world anew.

NOTES

INTRODUCTION

First epigraph quoted in Jon Meacham, *American Gospel: God, the Founding Fathers, and the Making of a Nation* (New York: Random House, 2006), 28. Second epigraph quoted in Arthur J. Bellinzoni, *The Future of Christianity: Can It Survive?* (Amherst, N.Y.: Prometheus Books, 2006), 47.

1. For the ways in which nationalism depends on establishing and maintaining a sense of the sacred to keep a people together, see Paul D. Smith, *Chosen Peoples: Sacred Sources of National Identity* (Oxford: Oxford University Press, 2003).

2. See Marshall G. S. Hodgson, *The Venture of Islam: Conscience and History in a World Civilization. Vol. 1. The Classical Age of Islam* (Chicago: University of Chicago Press, 1974), 58–60.

3. See Walter A. McDougall, *Freedom Just around the Corner: A New American History 1585–1828* (New York: HarperCollins, 2004), 245, 340; Pauline Maier, *American Scripture: Making the Declaration of Independence* (New York: Knopf, 1998); George Monbiot, "America Is a Religion," *Guardian,* July 29, 2003. Although Clifford Longley's thesis in *Chosen People: The Big Idea That Shapes England and America* (London: Hodder and Stoughton, 2002) may not come as a surprise to those who are intimately familiar with the patterns of American history, the author provides fascinating insights into the effects of the "Chosen People Syndrome" on race and ethnic relations in the United States.

4. Timothy Marr, *The Cultural Roots of American Islamicism* (New York: Cambridge University Press, 2006), 21, 25, 39, 35, 65, 69; Robert J. Allison, *The Crescent Obscured: The United States and the Muslim World, 1776–1815* (New York: Oxford University Press, 1995).

5. Marr, *Cultural Roots,* 94.

6. Ibid., 296.

7. Sam Harris, *The End of Faith: Religion, Terror, and the Future of Reason* (New York: Norton, 2005).

8. Ibid., 39.

9. Ibid., 43.

10. See Kwame Anthony Appiah, "Toward a New Cosmopolitanism," *New York Times Magazine,* January 1, 2006; and his book, *Cosmopolitanism: Ethics in a World of Strangers* (New York: Norton, 2006).

11. Harris, *End of Faith,* 30.

12. Ibid., 11–49.

13. Ibid., 67.

14. Ibid., 79.

15. Quoted in ibid., 86.

16. Ibid., 80–107. The section on the mistranslation of the word *alma* is on pages 94–95. The biblical scholar Arthur J. Bellinzoni attributes the mistranslation to Matthew's reliance on the Greek translation of the Old Testament, undertaken between 250 and 150 B.C. by the Hellenized Jews of Egypt, who no longer knew Hebrew. Thus, the passage in Isaiah 7:14, "Look, a young woman is with child and shall bear a son, and shall name him Immanuel," spoken in eighth century BC and meant to encourage Judah's King Ahaz to see in such signs the portent of his victory against Assyria, eventually led to the doctrine of Mary's perpetual virginity, a fact that also sweeps Joseph's paternity and Jesus's siblings, alluded to in the gospels of Matthew and Mark, under the rug of orthodoxy. See Bellinzoni, *Future of Christianity,* 92–97, 129.

17. Harris, *End of Faith,* 109.

18. Ibid., 115.

19. Ibid., 117–23, 137.

20. Ibid., 127, 132.

21. Ibid., 134.

22. Ibid., 157, 153–69.

23. Ibid., 194.

24. "UN Calls for Guantánamo Bay to Close," *Guardian,* February 16, 2006. For the complete UN report, see http://www.ohchr.org/english/bodies/chr/docs/62chr/E.CN.4.2006.120_.pdf.

25. See Randy Kennedy, "An Atheist *Can* Believe in Christmas," *New York Times,* December 17, 2006.

26. Harris, *End of Faith,* 221.

27. Ibid., 215.

28. Ibid., 294, note 12.

29. Ibid., 295, note 12.

30. Ibid., 231.

31. Michel Onfray, *Traité d'athéologie: Physique de la métaphysique* (Paris: Bernard Grasset, 2005). Onfray's project is to trace, and erase, the deeply entrenched monotheistic motifs that run through the fabric of everyday life and morals, even when people

don't believe in the scriptures. The project is essential if we are to reclaim our full and fragile humanity and not postpone the good life to the time after death. It is the postponement of life that turns monotheistic religions into death cults, since such religions prevent us from building structures of human well-being on the only habitat and time we have on earth.

32. Sam Harris, "God's Dupes," *Los Angeles Times,* March 15, 2007.

33. See Malek Chebel, *L'Islam et la Raison: Le combat des idées* (Paris: Perrin, 2005).

34. On February 16, 2004, hundreds of people in France signed the *Manifeste des libertés* (Manifesto of Freedoms) to announce their open opposition to the stifling forces of Islamism, often entailing "islamessence," or the essentializing of Muslim identity into the narrow confines of orthodoxy. The manifesto makes the distinction between "Islam" (with a capital *i*) and "islam" (with a lowercase *i*), the first (like Hodgson's notion of the "Islamicate") connoting a civilization with diverse tendencies and irreducible differences, including non-Muslim faiths, and the second restricted to Islamic religious practice. Benslama's reflections on the making of this movement and why this culture of insubordination is needed is one of the most fascinating and original analyses I have seen in recent years. The manifesto has also inspired the establishment of an Internet-based *Université des libertés* (University of Freedoms). See Fethi Benslama, *Déclaration d'insoumission: Á l'usage des musulmans et de ceux qui ne le sont pas* (Paris: Flammarion, 2005). The manifesto can be found at www.manifeste.org. The notion of dissensus, as opposed to consensus, is a vital democratic practice, without which democracy has no meaning or content. The West, for instance, has never been and is not now unified, as the "clash of civilizations" discourse would have us believe. See, for instance, Anne Cécile Robert, "Occident contre Occident," *Le Monde diplomatique,* May 2006, 3.

35. Meacham, *American Gospel,* 84–86, 245–46, 135, 181.

36. Marx had written on behalf of the Central Council of the International Workingmen's Association to congratulate President Lincoln for his reelection. His letter to President Lincoln can be found in *Marx and Engels on the United States* (Moscow: Progress Publishers, 1979), 168–69. Both Marx's letter and Lincoln's response through Ambassador Adams are online at http://www.marxists.org/history/international/iwma/documents/1864/lincoln-letter.htm.

37. Quoted in Bernard Lewis, *Islam in History: Ideas, People, and Events in the Middle East,* rev. ed. (Chicago: Open Court, 1993), 289. "In legal parlance," writes Lewis, "the *zindiq* is the criminal dissident—the professing Muslim who holds beliefs or follows practices contrary to the central dogmas of Islam and is therefore to be regarded as an apostate and an infidel. The jurists differ as to the theoretical formulation of the point of exclusion, but in fact usually adopt the practical criterion of open rebellion" (287). Given this definition, the Kharijites, defending the Bedouins' culture of consensus against the new "encroaching state," and the Shiites, who championed the rights of non-Arab converts (the *mawali*) against the chauvinistic Arab dynasties in the early phase of Islam, could qualify as heretical. See Lewis, 278–80, and the whole chapter "The Significance of Heresy in Islam" (273–93).

38. Juan Goytisolo, "Les boucs émissaires de l'Espagne européenne," *Le Monde diplomatique,* October 1992, 12 (my translation).

1. DEATH IN CANCÚN

1. World Health Organization, "Suicide Huge but Preventable Public Health Problem, Says WHO," September 11, 2004; Jamie Stockwell, "Va. Violent Deaths Are Mostly Suicide," *Washington Post,* October 12, 2005; Robert Roy Britt, "The Odds of Dying," www.LiveScience.com, January 6, 2005. In the United States, for instance, there is a well-established pattern, going back to the 1980s, of disgruntled postal workers shooting their colleagues before turning their guns on themselves. The annual number of murder-suicides (killing others before turning the gun on oneself) in the United States may reach, according to the Violence Policy Center, two thousand fatalities a year, while people continue to die for the most trivial reasons. To cite but one random example from 2006 of the precariousness of life in the United States, a sixty-six-year-old man in Ohio shot his neighbor's fifteen-year-old teenager dead simply because he walked across his lawn on his way home. "I shot him with a goddamn 410 shotgun twice," the killer told the emergency services operator. Indeed, one might consider the United States, with its 30,136 deaths by firearms in 2003, as a war zone comparable to the worst areas in the globe. See Steve Chawkins and Michael Muskal, "Ex-Postal Worker Kills 6, Commits Suicide in Goleta," *Los Angeles Times,* January 31, 2006; *American Roulette: The Untold Story of Murder-Suicide in the United States,* Violence Policy Center, http://www.vpc.org/studies/amercont.htm; Julian Borger Washington, "Gunned Down: The Teenager Who Dared Walk across His Neighbour's Prized Lawn," *Guardian,* March 22, 2006.

2. Arjun Appadurai, *Fear of Small Numbers: An Essay on the Geography of Anger* (Durham, N.C.: Duke University Press, 2006), 32–33.

3. Pablo Fajnzylber, Daniel Lederman, and Norman Loayza, "Inequality and Violent Crime," *Journal of Law and Economics* 45, no. 1 (2002): 1–40.

4. Paul Collier, *Economic Causes of Civil War and Their Implications for Policy* (Washington, D.C.: World Bank, 2000). Accessed at http://econ.worldbank.org/files/13198_EcCausesPolicy.pdf.

5. World Health Organization, "First Ever Global Report on Violence and Health Released," www.who.int/mediacentre/releases/pr73/en/.

6. Elizabeth Becker and Ginger Thompson, "Poorer Nations Plead Farmers' Case at Trade Talks," *New York Times,* September 11, 2003.

7. James Brooke, "Farming Is Korean's Life and He Ends It in Despair," *New York Times,* September 16, 2003 (picture on A1).

8. Christine Ahn, "Death at the WTO," www.CommonDreams.org ("Views"), September 12, 2003; "Suicide at WTO Meeting Highlights Farmers' Plight," www.CommonDreams.org ("Headlines"), September 12, 2003; Somini Sengupta, "On India's Despairing Farms, a Plague of Suicide," *New York Times,* September 19, 2006; "Sahitya Akademi Award: Arundhati Roy Rejects Honor," *Deccan Herald* (Bangalore, India), January 16, 2006.

9. "Suicide Bomber Strikes in Bolivia," *Taipei Times,* April 1, 2004; Jane Perlez, "Aborigines Say Australia Pushes Their Plight to Sideline," *New York Times,* April 18, 2004.

10. Jon Peter, "Protests Force Bolivian Leader to Resign," *Washington Post,* October 18, 2003; Keith Slack, "Poor vs. Profit in Bolivian Revolt," *Los Angeles Times,* October 19, 2003; Larry Rohter, "Bolivia's Poor Proclaim Abiding Distrust of Globalization," *New York Times,* October 17, 2003; William Powers, "Bolivia, the Poor Little Rich Country," *International Herald Tribune,* June 13, 2005.

11. Larry Rohter, "Mapuche Indians in Chile Struggle to Take Back Forests," *New York Times,* August 11, 2004; Alain Devalpo, "Opposition pacifique des Mapuches chiliens," *Le Monde diplomatique* (February 2006): 18–19; Carolina Ariaga, "Chile Rediscovers Native Mapuche Remedies," www.Yahoo!News.com, March 25, 2007.

12. Larry Rohter, "Once Secure, Argentines Now Lack Food and Hope," *New York Times,* March 2, 2003; Larry Rohter, "For Argentina's Sizzling Economy, a Cap on Steak Prices," *New York Times,* April 3, 2006; Larry Rohter, "Argentina's Economic Rally Defies Forecasts," *New York Times,* December 26, 2004; Larry Rohter, "A Widening Gap Erodes Argentina's Egalitarian Image," *New York Times,* December 25, 2006.

13. Simon Romero, "São Paulo Becomes the Kidnapping Capital of Brazil," *New York Times,* February 13, 2002; James C. McKinley Jr., "With Beheadings and Attacks, Drug Gangs Terrorize Mexico," *New York Times,* October 26, 2006.

14. Juan Forero, "Latin America Graft and Poverty Trying Patience with Democracy," *New York Times,* June 24, 2004.

15. Historically, and as polls continue to show, Russians have tended to be more comfortable with authoritarian systems. See Seth Mydans, "Give Me Liberty, but Not Too Much: This Is Russia," *New York Times,* April 21, 2004. For democracy and electoral politics in Russia, see Michael McFaul and Nikolai Petrov, "Russian Democracy in Eclipse: What the Elections Tell Us," *Journal of Democracy* 15, no. 3 (July 2004): 5–19.

16. "Chavez Calls U.S. 'Immoral,'" *Chicago Tribune,* January 29, 2006; Luis Hernandez Navarro, "Socialismo o muerte de la especie humana, la disyuntiva: Hugo Chávez," *La Jornada* (Mexico), January 28, 2006.

17. Larry Rohter, "Uruguay's Left Makes History by Winning Presidential Vote," *New York Times,* November 1, 2004.

18. Juan Forero, "Advocate for Coca Legalization Leads in Bolivian Race," *New York Times,* November 26, 2005; Juan Forero, "Coca Advocate Wins Election for President in Bolivia," *New York Times,* December 19, 2005; Juan Forero, "Bolivia's Newly Elected Leader Maps His Socialist Agenda," *New York Times,* December 20, 2005; Juan Forero and Larry Rohter, "Bolivia Leader Tilting Region Further to the Left," *New York Times,* January 22, 2006; Tom Henningan, "Leader Takes Power from Earth God on Ancient Site," *Times* (London), January 23, 2006; Fiona Smith, "Bolivia's Morales Announces Cabinet, Including Marxist Energy Minister," *San Diego Union-Tribune,* January 23, 2006; "Morales da inicio a la rebaja salarial en cargos jeráquicos," *La Rázon* (Bolivia), January 27, 2006; Luis Crespo, "Morales: abajo los sueldos,"

www.BBCMundo.com, January 26, 2006; Maurice Lemoine, "Nationalisations en Amérique Latine," *Le Monde diplomatique,* May 18, 2006; Dan Keane, "Bolivian Senate Oks Sweeping Land Reform," *Washington Post,* November 29, 2006; Simon Romero, "In Bolivia's Affluent East, Anger at Morales Is Growing," *New York Times,* December 26, 2006; David Brooks, "Trade, Oppression, Revenge," *New York Times,* December 25, 2005; Juan Forero, "Indians in Bolivia Celebrate Swearing In of One of Their Own," *New York Times,* January 23, 2006.

19. Patrick J. McDonnell, "Former Political Prisoner Is Chile's New President," *Los Angles Times,* January 16, 2006; "Socialist Bachelet Wins Chilean Presidency," *New York Times,* January 16, 2006; Larry Rohter, "A Leader Making Peace with Chile's Past," *New York Times,* January 16, 2006; Monte Reel, "Bachelet Sworn In as Chile's President," *Washington Post,* March 12, 2006.

20. James C. McKinley Jr., "Leftist Outsider's Campaign Surges in Mexico," *New York Times,* March 19, 2006; Fernando Matamoros Ponce, "L'autre campaigne' des zapatistes," *Le Monde diplomatique* (February 2006): 20; Sam Enriquez, "Masked Marxist, with Marimbas," *Los Angles Times,* January 23, 2006; Ginger Thompson, "On Mexico's Mean Streets, the Sinners Have a Saint," *New York Times,* March 26, 2004.

21. Juan Forero, "Nationalism and Populism Propel Front-Runner in Peru," *New York Times,* April 2, 2006.

22. Jean Hébert Armengaud, "Le frère jumeau d'Aristide" *Libération* (France), February 16, 2006; Ginger Thompson, "Préval's Silence Obscures Quiet Bid to Reunite Haiti," *New York Times,* February 20, 2006.

23. Noam Chomsky, "Latin America Declares Independence," *International Herald Tribune,* October 3, 2006.

24. Silene Ramirez, "Leftist Fiesta in Chile for Bachelet Inauguration," *Reuters,* March 11, 2006; "Ortega Vows to Work with Castro, Chavez," *Chicago Tribune,* November 9, 2006; Guy Hedgecoe, "Ecuador: Protest and Power," www.OpenDemocracy.net, November 28, 2006; Jeanneth Valdivieso, "Ecuador Names 1st Female Defense Chief," *Guardian,* December 27, 2006; Andrew Buncombe, "Chavez Hails Landslide Election Victory as Defeat for 'Devil' Bush," *Independent,* December 5, 2006; Simon Romero, "Chávez Begins New Term Vowing Socialism," *New York Times,* January 11, 2007; Luisa Valenzuela, "What We See in Hugo Chávez," *New York Times,* March 17, 2007.

25. Brian Murphy, "Newsview: Economy Key to Iranian Election," www.Yahoo!News.com, June 25, 2005; Michael Slackman, "Iran Vote: Dark Horse Rises," *New York Times,* June 24, 2005; Karl Vick, "Class Is Pivotal in Iran Runoff," *Washington Post,* June 24, 2005; Michael Slackman, "A New Face in Iran Resurrects an Old Defiance," *New York Times,* January 30, 2006; Alexandre Leroi-Ponant, "L'Iran du president Mahmoud Ahmadinejad," *Le Monde diplomatique* (December 2006): 8–9; Shirin Ebadi (with Azadeh Moaveni), "Reading a Death Warrant in Tehran," *New York Times Magazine,* April 9, 2006; "Nobel Laureate Says Iran Would Defend Self," *Guardian,* April 21, 2006; also, see Shirin Ebadi, "People Hold Promise for Peace," *USA Today,* October 3, 2006. In this article Ebadi warned that if the United

States attacked Iran, "Iranians will unite, forgetting their differences with their government, and they will fiercely and tenaciously defend their country." The awkward English translation of President Ahmadinejad's letter was published on *Le Monde*'s Web site at http://www.lemonde.fr/web/article/0,1-0@2-727571,36-769886@ 51-677013,0.html.

26. "West Attacked over Cancun Collapse," *Times* (London), September 15, 2003; "L'ampleur des désaccords Nord-Sud met l'OMC en échec," *Le Monde*, September 15, 2003.

27. John Cavanagh and Robin Hood, "A Turning Point for World Trade?" *Baltimore Sun*, September 18, 2003.

28. *New York Times*, "The Rigged Trade Game," July 20, 2003. The editorial is part of an occasional series dealing with the West's unfair trade practices with the poor. They are collected under the title of "Harvesting Poverty."

29. Thomas L. Friedman, "Connect the Dots," *New York Times*, September 29, 2003.

30. Joseph Stiglitz, "Distant Voices," *Guardian*, March 12, 2004; Joseph Stiglitz, "Do As the US Says, Not As It Does," *Guardian*, October 29, 2003; Thom Shanker, "Pentagon Hones Its Strategy on Terrorism," *New York Times*, February 5, 2006.

31. Robert A. Pape, "Dying to Kill Us," *New York Times*, September 22, 2003; Shimali Senanayake, "Suicide Bomber Kills 94 in Northern Sri Lanka," *New York Times*, October 17, 2006; Shimali Senanayake, "Suicide Boats Explode in Sri Lanka Port, Killing 16," *New York Times*, October 19, 2006. The escalation of suicide bombings in U.S.-occupied Iraq in 2005 only confirmed Pape's contention. See Robert A. Pape, "Blowing Up an Assumption," *New York Times*, May 18, 2005; on the futility of trying to wipe out Hezbollah, see Robert A. Pape, "Ground to a Halt," *New York Times*, August 3, 2006; on the popularity of Hezbollah's Sheikh Hassan Nasrallah, see Liz Sly, "Hezbollah Chief Wins Admirers," *Chicago Tribune*, August 3, 2006, and Michael Slackman, "And Now, Islamism Trumps Arabism," *New York Times*, August 20, 2006; on the response to the Iraq Study Group's recommendations, see Robert Pape, "We Can Watch Iraq from the Sea," *New York Times*, December 10, 2006; Mike Davis, *Buda's Wagon: A Brief History of the Car Bomb* (London: Verso, 2007), 1–3.

32. Noah Feldman, "Islam, Terror and the Second Nuclear Age," *New York Times Magazine*, October 29, 2006; Alan B. Krueger and Jitka Malecková, "Seeking the Roots of Terrorism," *Chronicle of Higher Education*, June 6, 2003, B10–11.

33. Michael Shermer, "Murdercide," *Scientific American*, December 26, 2005; Nichole Argo, "The Role of Social Context in Terrorist Attacks," *Chronicle of Higher Education*, February 3, 2006, B15. Argo writes that most jihadi forms of suicide bombing occurred after 9/11: "According to a recent study by Bruce Hoffman of the RAND Corporation, 81 percent of human bombs since 1968 occurred in the four years *after* September 11. And, while secular organizations perpetrated approximately half of the human bombs up to 2001, Hoffman says, 31 out of 35 groups perpetrating terror today are jihadi." For the Gallup poll results, see "U.S. Domination Fear Fuels Muslim

Anger," *Wall Street Journal,* May 4, 2006; Mark Mazzetti, "Spy Agencies Say Iraq War Worsens Terrorism Threat," *New York Times,* September 24, 2006.

34. Louis A. Pérez Jr., *To Die in Cuba: Suicide and Society* (Chapel Hill: University of North Carolina Press, 2005), 5–6.

35. "De la madre al hijo," in Jesús Orta Ruiz, *Décima y folclor;* quoted in Pérez, *To Die in Cuba,* 118–19.

36. Kare Zernike, "Violent Crime Rising Sharply in Some Cities," *New York Times,* February 12, 2006; Chistophe Cornevin, "500 agressions gratuites chaque jour en France," *Le Figaro,* February 14, 2006; Piotr Smolar, "Hause de 6.6% des atteintes volontaires à l'intégrité physique," *Le Monde,* February 14, 2006. The rate of such homicides in cities like Hartford, Connecticut, are so high that civic leaders are calling for cease-fires and frightened citizens are willing to give up their civil rights and expand police powers to stem the tide of violence. See Susan Haigh, "Cities Struggling with Increased Violence," www.Yahoo!News.com, June 8, 2006.

37. Ian Buruma, "Killing Iraq with Kindness," *New York Times,* March 17, 2004. See also Ian Buruma and Avishai Margalit, *Occidentalism: The West in the Eyes of Its Enemies* (New York: Penguin, 2004).

38. Susan Sachs, "Poll Finds Hostility Hardening toward U.S. Policies," *New York Times,* March 17, 2004.

39. Dilip Hiro, "The Rise of Political Islam: The Palestinian Election and Democracy in the Middle East," www.TomDispatch.com, January 25, 2006; Steven Erlanger, "Hamas Routs Ruling Faction, Casting Pall on Peace Process," *New York Times,* January 27, 2006. For more on initial reactions to the victory of Hamas, see Simon Freeman, "World Reaction to the Hamas Victory: 'Fasten Your Seatbelt,'" *Times* (London), January 26, 2006; Robert F. Worth, "New Business Blooms in Iraq: Terror Insurance," *New York Times,* March 21, 2006.

40. Quoted in Doug Henwood, *Wall Street: How It Works and for Whom,* rev. ed. (New York: Verso, 1998), 303.

41. Celia W. Dugger, "UNICEF Says Children in Deprivation Reach a Billion," *New York Times,* December 10, 2004; Roger Dobson, "Rise in UK's Child Mortality Rate Is Linked to Inequality," *Independent,* April 1, 2007.

42. *State of the World 2004: A Worldwatch Institute Report on Progress toward a Sustainable Society* (New York: Norton, 2004), 4.

43. Jeremy Rifkin, *The European Dream: How Europe's Vision of the Future Is Quietly Eclipsing the American Dream* (New York: Tarcher/Penguin, 2004), 379.

44. Paul B. Brown, "There Is No Place Like Home," *New York Times,* January 21, 2006; David Kocieniewski, "After $12, 000, There's Even Room to Park the Car," *New York Times,* February 20, 2006; Ian Urbina, "Keeping It Secret as the Family Car Becomes a Home," *New York Times,* April 2, 2006.

45. Emily Arnold and Janet Larsen, "Bottled Water: Pouring Resources down the Drain," Earth Policy Institute, February 2, 2006, http://www.earth-policy.org/Updates/2006/Update51.htm.

46. Ibid., 4–5, 71, 94, 97.

47. Leigh Strope, "Gap between Rich and Poor Widening in Troubled Economy," www.Commondreams.org, August 17, 2004.

48. Ibid., 44, 17, 22–23.

49. See the Worldwatch Institute press release for *State of the World 2006: China and India Hold World in Balance* at http://www.worldwatch.org/press/news/2006/01/11.

50. James Lovelock, "The Earth Is about to Catch a Morbid Fever That May Last as Long as 100,000 Years," *Independent,* January 16, 2006; Michael McCarthy, "Environment in Crisis: 'We Are Past the Point of No Return,'" *Independent,* January 16, 2006; Michael McCarthy, "Why Gaia Is Wreaking Revenge on Our Abuse of the Environment," *Independent,* January 16, 2006; Michael McCarthy, "Climate Poses Increased Threat, Admits Blair," *Independent,* January 30, 2006; Matt Weaver, "PM Issues Blunt Warning on Climate Change," *Guardian,* January 30, 2006.

51. *State of the World 2004,* 13, 14; Cornelia Dean, "Study Sees 'Global Collapse' of Fish Species," *New York Times,* November 3, 2006.

52. *State of the World 2004,* 12–15, 97.

53. Philip Thornton, "US Savings Rate Sinks to Lowest since Great Depression," *Independent,* January 30, 2006; Timothy Egan, "Newly Bankrupt Raking in Piles of Credit Offers," *New York Times,* December 11, 2005; Martin Hickman, "Britons in Debt to the Tune of £1.13 trillion," *Independent,* January 3, 2006; Hilary Osborne, "Bankruptcies and Repossessions Rise," *Guardian,* February 3, 2006; Keren Lentschner and Marie Visot, "Consommation: La belle surprise de fin d'année," *Le Figaro,* December 22, 2005; "Insolvent Britons Set to Rise by 400%," *Guardian,* October 24, 2006.

54. Al Baker, "Crime Numbers Keep Dropping across City," *New York Times,* December 31, 2005.

55. *State of the World 2004,* 17, 29, 29; Tanya Mohn, "The Biggest Little Noticed Hazard," *New York Times,* April 17, 2007.

56. "Meat and Dairy: Where Have the Minerals Gone?" *Food Magazine* (January/March 2006): 10; Felicity Lawrence, "Mineral Levels in Meat and Milk Plummet over 60 Years," *Guardian,* February 2, 2006.

57. "Obesity Called 'Scourge' Afflicting Entire World," *International Herald Tribune,* September 3, 2006; *State of the World 2004,* 10.

58. Jeff Stryker, "Forehead Billboards," *New York Times Magazine,* December 11, 2005; Charles Duhigg, "Late in Life, Finding a Bonanza in Life Insurance," *New York Times,* December 17, 2006; Alicia Chang, "Scientists: Greenland Glaciers Retreating," *Associated Press,* December 8, 2005; Fiona Harvey, "UN Warns of Poverty as World's Lakes Evaporate," *Financial Times,* October 31, 2005.

59. Philip Jenkins, *The Next Christendom: The Coming of Global Christianity* (New York: Oxford University Press, 2002).

60. Laurie Goodstein, "More Religion, but Not the Old-Time Kind," *New York Times,* January 9, 2005; see also Laurie Goodstein, "Pentecostal and Charismatic Groups Growing," *New York Times,* October 6, 2006. For a thorough report on Pentecostalism, see http://pewforum.org/surveys/pentecostal.

61. Jenkins, *The Next Christendom*, 67.

62. Ibid., 76.

63. Ibid., 72–73.

64. See chapter 9 in ibid., 191–201.

65. Daniel J. Wakin, "In New York, Gospel Resounds in African Tongues," *New York Times,* April 18, 2004; Daniel J. Wakin, "Nowadays, New York City Is Prime Conversion Ground," *New York Times,* July 11, 2004; Neela Banerjee, "American Ruptures Shaking the Episcopal Church," *New York Times,* October 3, 2004; "Two Washington Churches Leave the Episcopal Church USA," *Seattle Post-Intelligencer,* October 19, 2004; Laurie Goodstein, "Episcopalians Are Reaching Point of Revolt," *New York Times,* December 17, 2006; Bill Turque and Michelle Boorstein, "7 Va. Episcopal Parishes Vote to Sever Ties," *Washington Post,* December 18, 2006; Lydia Polgreen and Laurie Goodstein, "At Axis of Episcopal Split, an Anti-Gay Nigerian," *New York Times,* December 25, 2006.

66. Simon Romero, "A Texas Town Nervously Awaits a New Neighbor," *New York Times,* August 21, 2005.

67. Jenkins, *The Next Christendom*, 169, 177, 171, 166.

68. Giovanni Arrighi, *The Long Twentieth Century: Money, Power, and the Origins of Our Times* (New York: Verso, 1994), 356.

69. Henwood, *Wall Street*, 23, 26–27, 314.

70. Robert Brenner, *The Boom and the Bubble: The US in the World Economy* (New York: Verso, 2002), 178.

71. Quoted in Henwood, *Wall Street*, 234.

72. Brenner, *The Boom and the Bubble*, 129

73. Ibid., 271; "Could It Happen Again?" *Economist,* February 20, 1999, 19–22; Daniel Altman, "Exporting Expertise, If Not Much Else," *New York Times,* January 22, 2006.

74. James N. Rosenau, *Turbulence in World Politics: A Theory of Change and Continuity* (Princeton, N.J.: Princeton University Press, 1990), quoted in Arrighi, *The Long Twentieth Century,* 79.

75. Arrighi, *The Long Twentieth Century,* 78–79, 355–56.

76. Quoted in Laurie Goodstein, "An Ailing Evangelist Prepares to Come Down from Mountain," *New York Times,* June 12, 2005.

77. Steven Greenhouse, "Forced Labor Said to Bind 12.3 Million People around the World," *New York Times,* May 12, 2005.

78. Ian Buruma, "An Islamic Democracy for Iraq?" *New York Times Magazine,* December 5, 2004.

79. Daniel C. Dennett, "Common Sense Religion," *Chronicle of Higher Education,* January 20, 2006, B6–8.

80. Roberto Giorgi, *Pour une histoire de la zandaka* (Florence: La Nuova Italia, 1989), 9.

81. Benslama, *Déclaration d'insoumission*, 31.

82. Ibid., 31–32.

83. Bellinzoni, *The Future of Christianity*, 19. Bellinzoni's entire book is an eye-opening primer on the biblical concept of God, the authorship of the Bible, and the future of Christianity.

84. See *In the Lands of the Christians: Arabic Travel Writing in the Seventeenth Century*, ed. and trans. Nabil Matar (New York: Routledge, 2003), 197–214.

2. SPECTERS OF ANNIHILATION

1. See Gilles Kepel, *Fitna: Guerre au coeur de l'islam* (Paris: Gallimard, 2004), 211–36.

2. Mohammed Qutb, *jahiliyyatu al-qarn al'ishreen* (The decadence of the twentieth century) (Cairo: Dar a-shuruq, 1992); Sadik J. al-Azm, "Time Out of Joint," *Boston Review* (October/November 2004).

3. Qutb, *jahiliyyatu al-qarn al'ishreen*, 105 (my italics).

4. Ibid., 201.

5. Ibid., 262–63. My translation of the Qur'an is freely based on the version revised and edited by Saudi Arabia's Presidency of Islam Researches, IFTA, Call and Guidance (undated).

6. Qutb, *jahiliyyatu al-qarn al'ishreen*, 31.

7. Ahmad S. Moussalli, *Radical Islamic Fundamentalism: The Ideological and Political Discourse of Sayyid Qutb* (Beirut: American University of Beirut, 1992), 42.

8. Ibid., 26–28. For a complete account of Sayyid Qutb's essay on America, see "'The America I Have Seen': In the Scale of Human Values," in *America in an Arab Mirror: Images of America in Arabic Travel Literature*, ed. Kamal Abdel-Malek, trans. Tarek Masoud and Ammar Fakeeh (New York: St. Martin's, 2000), 9–27.

9. Quoted in Moussalli, *Radical Islamic Fundamentalism*, 60.

10. Ibid., 180.

11. Ibid., 195, 197.

12. Quoted in ibid., 191.

13. Ibid., 200–213.

14. Gilles Kepel, *Fitna: Guerre au coeur de l'islam* (Paris: Gallimard, 2004), 13–20.

15. Karen Armstrong, *The Battle for God* (New York: Ballantine, 2001), vii–xviii.

16. Fletcher, *Cross and the Crescent*, 112.

17. Armstrong, *Battle for God*, 9–10.

18. "Madonna 'Upsets Israeli Rabbis,'" *BBC News*, October 10, 2005; "Rabbinical Rebuke for Madonna Song," *Newsday*, October 10, 2005.

19. Armstrong, *Battle for God*, 23.

20. Ibid., 27.

21. Ibid., 83.

22. Ibid., 98.

23. Ibid., 109.

24. See ibid., 113.

25. Ibid., 123.

26. Ibid., 129–32.

27. Ibid., 145–46.

28. Ibid., 160.

29. Ibid., 199–232.

30. Quoted in ibid., 240.

31. Ibid., 243.

32. Quoted in ibid., 259.

33. Ibid., 270–71.

34. Quoted in ibid., 273.

35. Quoted in ibid., 273–75.

36. Ibid., 278–81.

37. Quoted in ibid., 286.

38. Quoted in ibid., 299.

39. Ibid., 308.

40. Ibid., 299–309.

41. Quoted in ibid., 315.

42. Ibid., 368.

43. See ibid., 370.

44. Wafik Raouf, *L'Europe vue par l'Islam* (Paris: L'Harmattan, 2000), 21–65.

45. Ibid., 134, 33, 136.

46. Ibid., 77.

47. See Benslama, *Déclaration d'insoumission,* 40–41.

48. Fletcher, *Cross and the Crescent,* 1–29.

49. Ibid., 30–66, 116.

50. Ibid., 67–99.

51. Bernard Lewis, *What Went Wrong: Western Impact and Middle Eastern Response* (New York: Oxford University Press, 2002), 25–26, 33. On the Crusades as "armed pilgrimages," see "Le Choc," an interview with Jean Delumeau, in *Le Nouvel Observateur,* December 24, 2003.

52. Raouf, *L'Europe vue par l'Islam,* 86.

53. Ibid., 13; Fletcher, *Cross and the Crescent,* 128–29.

54. Kepel, *Fitna,* 88–89. The *Larousse Gastronomique* (New York: Clarkson Potter, 2001), 372–73, attributes the honor of catching the Ottomans to the bakers of Budapest in 1686. For a brief history of the croissant, see José-Alain Fralon, "Délices universels: Les mystères du croissant," *Le Monde,* August 7, 2004.

55. Lewis, *What Went Wrong,* 50.

56. Ibid., 101.

57. Ibid., 67–153.

58. Ibid., 223, 226.

59. Lizette Alvarez, "Iranian Lawyer, Staunch Fighter for Human Rights, Wins Nobel," *New York Times,* October 11, 2003; Elaine Sciolino, "A Prize, Laureate Says, 'Good for Democracy,'" *New York Times,* October 11, 2003; Craig S. Smith, "In Speech, Nobel Winner Rebukes the U.S." *New York Times,* December 11, 2003; "Iranian Wins Nobel Peace Prize," www.CBSNEWS.com, October 10, 2003.

60. "Nobel Peace Choice 'A Big Mistake': Poland's Lech Walesa," *Channel News Asia,* October 10, 2003.

61. Béatrice Gurrey and Jean-Pierre Tuquoi, "Après trios ans d'attente, Mohammed VI révolutionne le statut de la femme," *Le Monde,* October 12, 2003; Giles Tremlett, "Morocco Boosts Women's Rights," *Guardian,* October 13, 2003.

62. "Le nouveau Code assure une parfaite adéquation entre les valeurs religieuses," *Le Matin du Sahara et du Maghreb,* October 27, 2003.

63. "La quatrième causerie religieuse, animée par une femme," *Le Matin du Sahara et du Maghreb,* November 11, 2003.

64. Stephen O. Hughes, *Morocco under King Hassan* (Reading, U.K.: Ithaca Press, 2001), 44.

65. Eric Fottorino, "Musulmanes," *Le Monde,* October 14, 2003. See a compilation of responses in Arabic in http://www.islamonline.net/Arabic/contemporary/2005/04/article01F.shtml.

66. Fadwa El Guindi, *Veil: Modesty, Privacy and Resistance* (Oxford: Berg, 1999).

67. Quoted in ibid., 150.

68. Ibid., 81, 94–95.

69. Quoted in ibid., 147.

70. Quoted in ibid., 169.

71. Ibid., 31, 33, 134, 167, 172–73.

72. Nadia Yassine, *Toutes voiles dehors,* 2nd ed. (Casablanca: Editions Le Fennec, 2003).

73. Benedict Anderson, *Imagined Communities: Reflections on the Origin and Spread of Nationalism,* rev. ed. (New York: Verso, 1991).

74. The principal propositions of the National Action Plan for the Integration of Women in (the process of) Development (*Plan d'action national pour l'intégration des femmes au développement*) consist of literacy programs and a progressive education that teaches the principles of equality; promoting a positive image of women; instituting health programs that educate and disseminate information; fighting poverty and taking into account household activities; reforming the Mudawwana (marriage age; tutorship; divorce; polygamy; custody and the divorced woman's right to remarry or change residences; a woman's entitlement to alimony, not just the children; dividing property—acquired during marriage—in half after divorce; creating separate family courts); revising the code of nationality (art. 6.2 of the 1958 Nationality Code); the right to a copy of the Civil Status booklet; and giving a fictitious name to a child instead of "unknown Father." These broad outlines of the "*Plan*" (or *Khotta* in Arabic) were accessed through the Web site of the business publication *La vie économique,* November 26, 1999.

75. A good selection of responses is to be found in the book *huququal-mar'a bayna al-azma wa al-badeel: qira' naqdiya fi mashru' al-khuta al-watania li-idmaj al-mar'a fi a-tanmiya* (Women's rights between crisis and alternative: A critical reading of the National Action Plan for the Integration of Women in [the process of] Development), in the series *akhtartu lakum,* no. 4 (Casablanca: Manshurat al-Furqan, 2000).

76. Deborah Sontag, "In Israel, Suddenly Cucumbers Are Not Kosher," *New York Times,* September 10, 2000; Deborah Sontag, "Israel Ponders Constitution with Head Throbbing," *New York Times,* September 17, 2000; Steven V. Mazie, "You Say You Want a Constitution," *New York Times,* March 30, 2006; Nicole Winfield, "Jews Divided over Eating Pork," www.Yahoo!News.com, November 26, 2001. The battles usually pitch recent immigrants from countries like Russia against orthodox and ultraorthodox Jews.

77. On April 8, 2005, the Moroccan online publication *Emarrakech* reported on the case of a thirty-year-old Moroccan nurse in Italy who had formally requested to lead prayers in a mosque but whose request was swiftly and summarily rejected. The congregation also wanted the imam fired for entertaining such a wild notion, one, according to the same article, that had been tried by Amina Wadud, an African American professor, in a Friday prayer held on March 18, 2005, in the Episcopal church in New York, St. John the Divine, in the presence of a coed congregation of 125 people, many of whom were unveiled women. The mufti Sheikh Yusuf al-Qaradawi, "whose edicts range from legitimizing wife beating to the killing of foreigners in Iraq to the shunning of Christians and Jews," the head of Al-Azhar in Egypt, Sheikh Tantawi, and other scholars immediately responded by saying that while women leading prayers is a good thing, women leading both sexes in prayer or in politics has no precedent or legal support in Islamic history, mostly because Muslim prayers entail body movements that may simply interfere with men's concentration, a view supported by Suʿad Salih, dean of Islamic Studies at Al-Azhar. See Hafida Benslimane, "Des femmes imams en Egypte et en Italie," www.SaphirNet.info, April 7, 2005; Youssef M. Ibrahim, "Will the Middle East Bloom?" *Washington Post,* March 13, 2005. Also, see the Egyptian mufti Dr. Ali Jomaa's response, at http://www.islamonline.net/Arabic/contemporary/2005/04/article01F.shtml and associated links; "Sheikh Qaradâwî répond sur la femme imam de New York," www.SaphirNet.info, March 22, 2005. On the Moroccan female leaders, or *murshidat,* see "Morocco Gets First Women Preachers," www.Aljazeera.net, April 28, 2006. Ironically, while these Muslim women are challenging a male-defined orthodoxy, in secular Syria, secret women's groups known as Qubaisiate (named after founder Munira al-Qubaisi) are trying to Islamicize society. See Katherine Zoepf, "Islamic Revival Led by Women Tests Syria's Secularism," *New York Times,* August 29, 2006.

78. See Laurie Goodstein, "Women Taking Active Role to Study Orthodox Judaism," *New York Times,* December 21, 2000; Laurie Goodstein, "Ordained as Rabbis, Women Tell Secret," *New York Times,* December 21, 2000; "Orthodox Women, in a New Day," Letters to the Editor, *New York Times,* December 28, 2000; R. Albert Mohler Jr., "Against an Immoral Tide," *New York Times,* June 19, 2000.

79. Sander L. Gilman, "The Parallels of Islam and Judaism in Diaspora," *Chronicle of Higher Education,* April 8, 2005.

3. ISLAM AND ITS DISCONTENTS

First epigraph quoted in Brooke Allen, *Moral Minority: Our Skeptical Founding Fathers* (Chicago: Ivan R. Dee, 2006).

1. The number of converted or local Christians in Morocco has been estimated in the thousands to around five hundred. See, for instance, "Au coeur du malaise des chrétiens" and "Le Maroc assailli par les néo-protestants US" in *Le Journal Hebdomadaire,* January 8–14, 2005; Dawn Herzog Jewell, "Moderating Morocco," www.ChristianityToday.Com, October 20, 2005.

2. See Ruth Eglash, "Muslim Woman Fights to Convert and Stay in Israel," *Jerusalem Post,* June 25, 2006.

3. Apostasy laws can reach absurd dimensions, as when groups of Muslims begin to charge each other with this mortal sin. By 2005, Muslims in Spain and Morocco who were subjected to global profiling and persecution because of the terrorist deeds of Muslim extremists started fighting back by issuing *fatwas* of apostasy against Osama bin Laden and his organization, Al-Qaeda. In November 2005, when two Moroccan diplomats were kidnapped in Iraq, Moroccan *ulema* warned that their execution by Al-Qaeda would amount to apostasy. See, for instance, David Sharrock, "Muslims Issue Fatwa against Bin Laden," *Times* (London), March 11, 2005; "Al Qaeda Hostages to Be Martyrs If Killed—Morocco's Scholars," *Reuters,* November 5, 2005.

4. Abdessamad Dialmy, "Chosir sa foi: Le grand interdit," *Le Journal Hebdomadaire,* July 16–22, 2005, 21–29. Dialmy's quotation on is page 28.

5. The first name given in the article is "Mouhiedine," which I think might have been confused with the mystic Ibn ʿArabi's first name. The other famous Razi is Imam Fakhr al-Din Razi (1149–1209), whose profile doesn't fit with those of the "libertines" on the list.

6. "Les grands libertines de l'islam," *TelQuel,* May 14, 2005; Abdelwahab Meddeb, *La maladie de l'islam* (Paris: Éditions du Seuil, 2002), 38–42, 50–52.

7. See, for instance, Magdi Abdelhadi, "Accused Morocco Islamist Speaks Out," www.BBCNews.com, September 30, 2005. For a fuller account of Nadia Yassine's challenge to the monarchy, see Craig Whitlock, "Feud with King Tests Freedoms in Morocco," *Washington Post,* February 12, 2006.

8. Rachid Benzine, *Les nouveaux penseurs de l'islam* (Casablanca: Tarik Editions, 2004).

9. Ibid., 39.

10. Ibid., 50.

11. Ibid., 57–85.

12. A similar argument was made by the Sudanese scholar Mahmoud Mohamed Taha, who was executed for his views. See his *The Second Message of Islam,* trans. Abdullahi Ahmed An-Naʿim (Syracuse, N.Y.: Syracuse University Press, 1987).

13. This discussion of Arkoun is drawn from Benzine, *Les nouveaux penseurs,* 87–118.

14. Ibid., 168–77.

15. Youssef Seddik counts that the Qur'an attests twelve times that it is revealed in Arabic. Youssef Seddik, "Dieu à la premiere personne," in "La Bible et le Coran," special issue of the weekly *Le Nouvel Observateur,* December 23, 2003.

16. Bruno Étienne, *Islam, les questions qui fachent* (Paris: Bayard, 2003), 59.

17. Cited in Benzine, *Les nouveaux penseurs,* 213–43.

18. Ibid., 276, 280, 282.

19. Mohamed Talbi, *Réflexions d'un musulman contemporain* (Casablanca: Éditions Le Fennec, 2005).

20. Ibid., 29, 18.

21. Ibid., 20.

22. Ibid., 93.

23. Ibid., 14.

24. Ibid., 108.

25. Ibid., 117.

26. Hichem Djaït, *La crise de la culture Islamique* (Tunis: Cérès Éditions, 2005).

27. Ibid., 19–42.

28. Ibid., 333.

29. Ibid., 15.

30. Ibid., 16.

31. Abdelwahab Meddeb, *La maladie de l'islam* (Paris: Éditions du Seuil, 2002). All translations from this book are mine.

32. Ibid., 10.

33. Ibid., 220–21.

34. Ibid., 12.

35. Ibid., 55.

36. Ibid., 65.

37. Ibid., 69.

38. Ibid., 73–74; Also, see Étienne, *Islam,* 22, 33–34, 118, 122.

39. Meddeb, *La maladie,* 113.

40. Ibid., 121.

41. Ibid., 122.

42. Ibid., 13, 15.

43. Ibid., 76.

44. Ibid., 135.

45. See Marr, *Cultural Roots of American Islamicism,* 113; Meddeb, *La maladie,* 50.

46. Meddeb, *La maladie,* 77–78.

47. Ibid., 144.

48. Ibid., 157; Appadurai, *Fear of Small Numbers,* 16. There is now a dedicated effort to restore at least one of the ruined Buddhas and excavate the treasures of the ancient site. See Carlotta Gall, "From Ruins of Afghan Buddhas, a History Grows," *New York Times,* December 6, 2006.

49. Meddeb, *La maladie,* 49, 167, 16.

50. Étienne, *Islam,* 142–43.

51. All quotations cited in Geisser, *La nouvelle islamophobie,* 57–76.

52. Lewis, *What Went Wrong.*

53. Ibid., 45–46.

54. Ibid., 129.

55. Ibid., 150.

56. Ibid., 114.

57. Ibid., 82–95.

58. Ibid., 159.

60. Ibid., 157.

61. Ibid., 101–2.

62. Ibid., 111.

63. Ibid., 116.

64. Djaït, *La crise de la culture Islamique,* 19–42.

65. Cited in Wafik Raouf, *L'Europe vue par l'Islam* (Paris: L'Harmattan, 2000), 205–17.

66. Quoted in Étienne, *Islam,* 141–42.

67. Armstrong, *Islam,* 187–88.

68. Étienne, *Islam,* 147.

69. Meddeb, *La maladie,* 211.

70. Leïla Babès, *Le voile démystifié* (Paris: Bayard, 2004).

71. Ibid., 12.

72. Ibid., 32. Babès's suspicions were recently justified when Ekin Deligöz, a German legislator of Muslim descent, exhorted young Muslim women to discard the veil to better integrate into German society. She was swiftly compared to a Nazi in Turkey and placed under police protection in her home country. A year earlier, in 2005, Emel Abidin-Algan, a forty-five-year-old mother of six, whose father and husband were active in Islamic groups, and herself once the head of the Islamic Women's Association in Berlin for ten years, removed her headscarf and gave it to a history museum. She reasoned that not wearing the headscarf expands one's options of interacting with different people, including men. The idea of concealing attraction simply doesn't hold anymore. "In my experience," she wrote, "stimuli-overload has made men fairly immune." Unveiled women may be looked at but they are rarely seen by men. Not only that, but the headscarf itself, once a code for Muslim piety, has become banal where the majority of women, such as in Egypt, wear one, leading to the more extreme measure of wearing a *niqab.* See "Police Protection for German Parliamentarian," *Der Spiegel* (English version), October 31, 2006; Emel Abidin-Algan, "Kicking the Headscarf Habit," www.signandsight.com, November 13, 2006; Michael Slackman, "In Egypt, a New Battle Begins over the Veil," *New York Times,* January 28, 2007.

72. Babès, *Le voile démystifié,* 82.

73. Ibid., 43.

74. Ibid., 20.

75. Ibid., 22.

76. Ibid., 88–89.

77. Ibid., 111.

78. Ibid., 47–49.

79. Ibid., 118–19, 71.

80. Ibid., 61–71.

81. See ibid., 50–56.

82. Ibid., 115.

83. Ibid., 117.

84. Ibid., 102–4.

85. Alfred-Louis de Prémare, *Aux origines du Coran: Questions d'hier, approches d'aujourdhui* (Tunis: Cérès Èditions, 2005).

86. Ibid., 7–23.

87. Ibid., 25–41.

88. Ibid., 53–92.

89. Ibid.

90. Ibid., 93–122.

91. Ibid., 123–24.

92. See Toby Lester, "What Is the Koran?" *Atlantic Monthly* (January 1999): 43–56.

93. Cited in Roger-Pol Droit, "Et si les vierges célestes du Coran n'étaient que fruits blancs?" *Le Monde,* May 5, 2003.

94. Lester, "What Is the Koran?" 44, 56.

95. Sadik J. al-Azm, "Time Out of Joint," *Boston Review* (October/November 2004).

96. See Katherine Zoepf, "In Syria, Building a Civil Society Book by Book," *Chronicle of Higher Education,* January 14, 2005.

97. Taha Hussein, *A Man of Letters,* trans. Mona El-Zayyat (Cairo: University of Cairo Press, 1994). The novel was originally published as *Adeeb* in 1935.

98. Ibid., 62.

99. Ibid., 64.

100. See "Aktal-Al," in *Encyclopedædia Britannica* (2006).

101. Hussein, *Man of Letters,* 109.

102. Ibid., 116.

103. Ibid., 119.

104. Ibid., 128.

105. Ibid., 129.

106. Ibid., 138.

107. Ibid., 140.

108. *Min tarikh al-ilhad fi al-islam* (The history of atheism in Islam), ed. and trans. Abdel Rahman Badawi (Cairo: Sina li-annashr, 1993 [1945]), 9–11, 263.

109. Ibid., 5–6.

4. REGIME CHANGE

Second epigraph quoted in Alistair Cooke, *Alistair Cooke's America* (New York: Carroll & Graf, 2002 [1973]), 389.

1. The unofficial translation of the Constitution of the Islamic Republic of Afghanistan was accessed at http://www.afghan-web.com/politics/current_constitution.html. I have used the text of Iraq's draft charter, translated by the U.N., published on the *New York Times* Web site on October 12, 2005.

2. Dinesh D'Souza, *The Enemy at Home: The Cultural Left and Its Responsibility for 9/11* (New York: Doubleday, 2007), 276.

3. Ibid., 2–3, 14, 27, 94.

4. Ibid., 100, 103, 117, 118, 162.

5. Ibid., 121, 130, 135, 146.

6. Ibid., 161, 164, 170.

7. Ibid., 276, 278, 280–81, 292.

8. Andrew Sullivan, "The Mullah," *New Republic,* March 19, 2007.

9. "National Briefing: Southwest," *New York Times,* March 26, 2004; "Mel Gibson: Action Hero Gets Serious," *BBC News,* February 25, 2004; "Gibson Acts over 'Prayer Stalker,'" www.BBCNews.com, October 2, 2004.

10. Frank Rich, "2004: Year of *The Passion,*" *New York Times,* December 19, 2004.

11. Jeffrey Gettleman, "Alabama Judge Defiant on Commandments' Display," *New York Times,* August 21, 2003.

12. See Jeffrey Gettleman, "Alabama Justice on Trial over Ten Commandments," *New York Times,* November 12, 2003; "He'd Do It Again, Says the 'Ten Commandments Judge,'" *New York Times,* November 13, 2003; "Alabama Panel Ousts Judge over Ten Commandments Monument," *New York Times,* November 14, 2003.

13. Cited in "Ten Commandments Judge May Run for Gov.," www.Yahoo!News.com, December 17, 2003.

14. Robert Wright, "Faith, Hope and Clarity," *New York Times,* October 28, 2004.

15. Kate Zernike, "Does Christmas Need to Be Saved?" *New York Times,* December 19, 2004.

16. See http://www.notbored.org/sinead.html (accessed on October 8, 2004).

17. Alexis de Tocqueville, *Democracy in America,* ed. and trans. Harvey Claflin Mansfield and Delba Winthrop; quoted in Mark A. Noll, *America's God: From Jonathan Edwards to Abraham Lincoln* (New York: Oxford University Press, 2002), 6.

18. Ibid., 10.

19. "Britain: Strangers No More," *New York Times,* October 28, 2004.

20. William Bradford, *Of Plymouth Plantation 1620–1647,* ed. Samuel Eliot Morison (New York: Knopf, 2002).

21. John Winthrop, "A Modell of Christian Charity," in *American Sermons: The Pilgrims to Martin Luther King Jr.* (New York: Library of America, 1999), 28–43.

22. *The Norton Anthology of American Literature,* 3rd ed., vol. 1., ed. Nina Baym et al. (New York: Norton, 1979), 29, 47–48.

23. I am here thinking of the profile of Puritan saints in Michael Walzer's *The Revolution of the Saints: A Study in the Origins of Radical Politics* (Cambridge, Mass.: Harvard University Press, 1965).

24. Jonathan Edwards, "Sinners in the Hands of an Angry God," in *American Sermons,* 347–64.

25. Noll, *America's God,* 3–16.

26. Quoted in ibid., 65.

27. Quoted in ibid., 86.

28. Quoted in ibid., 63.

29. Ibid., 88.

30. Quoted in ibid., 91.

31. Ibid., 93.

32. Quoted in ibid., 96–97, 102.

33. Ibid., 74, 92.

34. Ibid., 164–66.

35. Quoted in ibid., 188.

36. See ibid., 184–85.

37. Quoted in ibid., 199.

38. Ibid., 203.

39. Quoted in ibid., 203–4.

40. Quoted in ibid., 204.

41. Quoted in ibid.

42. Quoted in ibid., 207.

43. Ibid., 208.

44. Quoted in ibid., 374.

45. Quoted in ibid., 380.

46. Ibid., 383–85, 396.

47. Ibid., 432.

48. Quoted in ibid., 433.

49. Ibid., 438.

50. Harley Sorensen, "A Fundamental Change in America," *San Francisco Chronicle,* November 29, 2004.

51. Farouz Farzami, "Iran's Lonely Crowd," *New York Times,* November 27, 2004.

52. Mehran Seyed, "Reading (Shh!) in Tehran," Letter to the Editor, *New York Times,* November 30, 2004.

53. Karim Raslan, "The Islam Gap," *New York Times,* February 15, 2006.

54. Ian Buruma, "An Islamic Democracy for Iraq?" *New York Times Magazine,* December 5, 2004.

55. Noah Feldman, *After Jihad: America and the Struggle for Islamic Democracy* (New York: Farrar, Straus and Giroux, 2003), xvi. Also, see Feldman's summary argument in "A New Democracy, Enshrined in Faith," *New York Times,* November 13, 2003.

56. Ibid., xi–xvii.

57. Ibid., 12, 11, 8.

58. Ibid., 37, 32, 54–55, 59.

59. Steven V. Mazie, "You Say You Want a Constitution," *New York Times,* March 30, 2006.

60. Feldman, *After Jihad,* 71.

61. Michael Slackman, "When Tehran Rocks, Discretion Rules," *New York Times,* February 15, 2006.

62. Feldman, *After Jihad,* 112.

63. Ibid., 150, 112, 139, 163.

64. Ibid., 198, 221.

65. Benslama, *Déclaration d'insoumission*, 81.

66. Feldman, *After Jihad*, 124. In November 2006, a new bill transferring rape cases to criminal courts, not Islamic ones regulating family affairs, and outlawing sex with girls before the age of sixteen, passed the lower house of Parliament. It was supported by liberals and Pakistan's president, Pervez Musharraf, but one Islamist leader warned that the bill "will turn Pakistan into a free-sex zone." Its future in the Senate was unclear. See Salman Masood, "Pakistan Moves toward Altering Rape Law," *New York Times*, November 16, 2006.

67. The best way the accused Christian could save himself in Afghani courts was to be declared mentally unfit to stand trial or to recant and revert back to Islam. Upon the release of the news, Abdul Rahman got the backing of the United Nations and other Western nations. President Bush was troubled by the fact that the country he had helped liberate would try to execute a Christian for his beliefs. See Tony Karon, "Being Christian in Afghanistan," www.Time.com (Web exclusive), March 22, 2006; Scott Stearns, "Bush Troubled by Afghan Christian Facing Death," *Voice of America*, March 22, 2006; "In Quotes: Afghan Convert Case," www.BBCNews.com, March 22, 2006. On March 23, the *New York Times* covered the case and ran an editorial titled "Outrage in Afghanistan," pointing out that Afghanistan "is a country that was liberated from the Taliban by American troops and whose tenuous peace is enforced by those troops. If Afghanistan wants to return to the Taliban days, it can do so without the help of the United States." The irony that the *New York Times* and others, including Christian groups, noted would have made sense if the American media and public had strongly objected to the new U.S.-sponsored constitutional arrangements. This incident is a perfect example of why regime change could leave cultural habits intact, and perhaps even strengthen them. Within days of strong Western outrage, and to the consternation of many Afghani Muslims who wanted the man killed, Abdul Rahman's case was dismissed, the defendant was set free, and he was granted asylum by Italy. See Amir Shah, "Afghan Convert Released from Prison," *Washington Post*, March 28, 2006; Ian Fisher and Elisabeth Povoledo, "Italy Grants Asylum to Afghan Christian Convert," *New York Times*, March 30, 2006. The details about Abdul Rahman's previous itinerary and unsuccessful attempts to immigrate to Europe were published in Christopher Sultan, "The Troubled Odyssey of Abdul Rahman," *Der Spiegel* (English version), April 3, 2006.

68. Justin Huggler, "Women's Lives 'No Better' in New Afghanistan," *Independent*, November 1, 2006.

69. Drinan, *Can God and Caesar Coexist?* 40–41.

70. See Jane Perlez, "Once Muslim, Now Christian and Caught in the Courts," *New York Times*, August 24, 2006; Thomas Fuller, "Malaysia's Secular Vision vs. 'Writing on the Wall,'" *International Herald Tribune*, August 30, 2006; "Thai Advocates Islamic Law for Far South," *New York Times*, November 8, 2006.

71. Drinan, *Can God and Caesar Coexist?* 9, 71–72.

72. Ibid., 8–29, 32.

73. Ibid., 67–68.

74. Pope Benedict XVI, *Deus Caritas Est.* Delivered on December 25, 2005. Online at http://www.vatican.va/holy_father/benedict_xvi/encyclicals/documents/hf_ben-xvi_enc_20051225_deus-caritas-est_en.html.

75. Alexis de Tocqueville, *Democracy in America,* trans. George Lawrence, ed. J. P. Mayer (New York: Perennial Library, 1988), 46–47.

76. Ibid., 252.

77. Ibid.

78. Ibid., 254–55.

79. Ibid., 255–56.

80. Ibid., 703.

81. Ibid., 467.

82. Ibid., 435.

83. Ibid., 247.

84. Ibid., 704–5.

85. Ibid., 18–19.

86. Ibid., 374.

87. Fanny Trollope, *Domestic Manners of the Americans* (Gutenberg Project ebook #10345, 2003). Available at www.gutenberg.org/etext/10345.

88. Tocqueville, *Democracy in America,* 455–56.

89. Ibid., xiv.

90. Ibid., 445.

91. Noah Feldman, *Divided by God: America's Church-State Problem—And What We Should Do about It* (New York: Farrar, Straus and Giroux, 2005).

92. See ibid., 19–56.

93. Protestant–Catholic tensions fueled the incipient nativism and led to the Bible riots of 1844 in Philadelphia. The Catholics lost the fight, and the Bible was read in school until after World War II. See ibid., 87–88. Regarding the Mormons, it was assumed that polygamy is associated with the patriarchy and despotism and therefore contrary to "republican democracy." States, after all, cannot allow human sacrifice in the name of religion.

94. Feldman, *Divided by God,* 106–9.

95. Ibid., 112–49.

96. Ibid., 156, 157–58, 161–62. In 1938, Justice Harlan Fiske Stone wrote "the most famous and consequential footnote in American constitutional history" when he made reference to "discrete and insular minorities" (156). Even as religiosity was more openly celebrated in the following decades (the phrase *under God* in 1954; *in God we trust* in 1956, and so on), the Supreme Court strengthened the Establishment Clause, struck down school prayers in New York (in 1962) and Bible reading (in 1963). Thus, in the name of a concept that only recently appeared in America (that is, secularism), and even more recently cleansed from its taint of atheism, the Supreme Court turned secularism into a legal doctrine (in the 1940s), feeding the Christian backlash and giving rise to evangelicalism.

97. Feldman, *Divided by God*, 216–18.

98. Ibid., 229.

99. Ibid., 236.

100. Ibid., 238–39.

101. Ibid., 234.

102. See Warren Hoge, "Rights Groups Fault U.S. Vote in U.N. on Gays," *New York Times,* January 27, 2006.

5. AMERICA AND ITS DISCONTENTS

Second epigraph quoted in Russell Mokhiber and Robert Weissman, "Economic Apartheid in America," www.Znet.org, November 27, 2005.

1. Bryant Urstadt, "Electing to Leave," *Harper's* (October 2004); posted on *Harper's* Web site on November 3, 2004; Sarah Anderson, "Ten Reasons Not to Move to Canada," www.Commondreams.org, November 3, 2004; David Ljunggren, "Unhappy Democrats Need to Wait to Get into Canada," www.Yahoo!News.com, November 3, 2004.

2. See Howard Zinn, *A People's History of the United States* (New York: Harper-Perennial, 1990 [1980]), 176–78, 484; Rick Lyman, "Some Bush Foes Vote Yet Again with Their Feet: Canada or Bust," *New York Times,* February 8, 2005; Andrew Metz, "Canada a Haven Again," *Newsday* (New York), March 2, 2005; John Hagan, *Northern Passage: American Vietnam War Resisters in Canada* (Cambridge, Mass.: Harvard University Press, 2001), xi, 3, 35, 184–88, 14, 176–79; Fred A. Bernstein, "Greetings from Resisterville," *New York Times,* November 21, 2004. The U.S. Army estimates that between October 1, 2003, and April 30, 2006, an average of 192 people deserted every month. See Mark Sommer, "Against the Iraq War, Buffalo Veteran Heads to Canada," *Buffalo News,* June 18, 2006.

3. Richard Sennett, *The Culture of the New Capitalism* (New Haven, Conn.: Yale University Press, 2006).

4. J. Hector St. John de Crèvecoeur, *Letters from an American Farmer and Sketches of Eighteenth-Century America,* ed. Albert Stone (New York: Penguin, 1981), 22.

5. Ibid., 54, 67.

6. Ibid., 67.

7. Ibid., 68–69, 81.

8. Ibid., 72.

9. Ibid., 88.

10. Ibid., 89–90.

11. Ibid., 254.

12. Ibid., 258.

13. Ibid., 262–63.

14. Ibid., 263.

15. Ibid., 173.

16. Ibid., 174.

17. Ibid., 175.

18. Ibid., 212.

19. Ibid., 209.

20. Ibid., 222.

21. McDougall, *Freedom Just around the Corner.* For a good review, see Gordon S. Wood, "Free to Be You and Me," *New York Times Book Review,* March 28, 2004. McDougall "unabashedly writes of Americans and assumes throughout that there is something called an American character," comments Wood, whose work on the radicalism of the American Revolution has had a major impact on my own understanding of the American Revolution. "Only the character he describes may not be what many Americans would want to admit about themselves," Wood continues. "Unlike other national narratives, which he says tend either to celebrate or to condemn America—and in righteous seriousness—his book aims to do neither. Instead, he wants to tell the truth about 'who and why we are what we are,' and to tell it entertainingly. His is thus a 'candid' history. Its major theme is 'the American people's penchant for hustling.' We Americans, he claims, are a nation of people on the make."

22. McDougall, *Freedom,* 322.

23. Quoted in ibid., 510.

24. Ibid., 513.

25. Eric Foner, *The Story of American Freedom* (New York: Norton, 1998).

26. Ibid., xviii.

27. Ibid., 7–8, 11, 35, 32, 36–37, 87.

28. Ibid., 12, 26–28.

29. Ibid., 37, 39–40, 43.

30. Quoted in ibid., 67.

31. Quoted in ibid., 48.

32. Ibid., 50.

33. Ibid., 55, 57.

34. Ibid., 65, 68, 62.

35. Quoted in ibid., 15.

36. Ibid., 76, 77, 92–93.

37. Ibid., 107.

38. See ibid., 115–37.

39. Quoted in ibid., 151.

40. See ibid., 196–218.

41. Quoted in ibid., 223.

42. Ibid., 219–47.

43. Ibid., 250–73.

44. Ibid., 275–305.

45. Ibid., 307–32, 320–24.

46. See Christina Bellantoni, "Hill Fries to Be French Again," *Washington Times,* August 2, 2006; *New York Times* editorial, "Au Revoir, Freedom Fries," *New York Times,* August 4, 2006.

47. David D. Kirkpatrick, "Battle Cry of Faithful Pits Believers and Unbelievers," *New York Times,* October 31, 2004.

48. Pam Belluck, "Letter Supports Anti-Kerry Bid over Abortion," *New York Times,* October 19, 2004; Pam Belluck, "Vatican Says Kerry Stance on Abortion Is Not Heresy," *New York Times,* October 20, 2004.

49. David M. Halbfinger and David E. Sanger, "Kerry's Latest Attacks on Bush Borrow a Page from Scripture," *New York Times,* October 25, 2004.

50. Maureen Dowd, "Slapping the Other Cheek," *New York Times,* November 14, 2004.

51. Eric Foner, "Freedom Belongs to All," *Nation,* February 14, 2005.

52. Allen, *Moral Minority.*

53. Jeff Sharlet, "Though a Glass, Darkly," *Harper's* (December 2006): 33–43.

54. Cited in Allen, *Moral Minority,* 62–63, 67, 78–79, 86.

55. On the growing linkage between abortion and birth control as part of the same un-Christian mind-set, see Russell Shorto, "The War on Contraception," *New York Times Magazine,* May 7, 2006.

56. Cooke, *Alistair Cooke's America,* 388.

57. Thomas Paine, *Agrarian Justice,* in *Paine: Collected Writings* (New York: Library of America, 1995), 396–413.

58. Benjamin Franklin, "The Way to Wealth," in *Norton Anthology of American Literature,* 361–67.

59. Benjamin Franklin, "Information to Those Who Would Remove to America," in *Norton Anthology of American Literature,* 379–84.

60. See *Benjamin Franklin's Autobiography,* ed. J. A. Leo Lemay and P. M. Zall (New York: Norton, 1986), 98.

61. Franklin's letters are quoted in *Norton Anthology of American Literature,* 405–7.

62. Peter G. Peterson, *Running on Empty: How the Democratic and Republican Parties Are Bankrupting Our Future and What Americans Can Do about It* (New York: Farrar, Straus, and Giroux, 2004).

63. Vikas Bajaj, "U.S. Trade Deficit Sets Record, with China and Oil the Causes," *New York Times,* February 11, 2006; Robert B. Reich, "Raising Debt the Wrong Way," www.CommonDreams.org, March 17, 2006.

64. Broadcast on the evening segment of *Marketplace,* National Public Radio, November 17, 2004.

65. Peterson, *Running on Empty,* ix–xxviii.

66. Ibid., 56–79.

67. Chalmers Johnson, *The Sorrows of Empire: Militarism, Secrecy, and the End of the Republic* (New York: Metropolitan Books, 2004).

68. Ibid., 23, 188.

69. Ibid., 26, 32, 154, 188.

70. Thomas E. Ricks, "Biggest Base in Iraq Has Small-Town Feel," *Washington Post,* February 4, 2006; Oliver Poole, "Football and Pizza Point to US Staying for Long Haul," *Telegraph,* February 11, 2006; Tom Engelhardt, "Tomgram: A Permanent

Basis for Withdrawal," www.TomDispatch.com, February 14, 2006; Staff Sgt. Ryan Hansen, "Burger King, Pizza Hut Open Doors at Balad Air Base," www.DefenseLink .mil, October 22, 2006; Peter Spiegel, "Bush's Requests for Iraqi Base Funding Make Some Wary of Extended Stay," *Los Angeles Times,* March 24, 2006; Charles J. Hanley, "U.S. Building Massive Embassy in Baghdad," *Seattle Post-Intelligencer,* April 14, 2006.

71. Quoted in Tim Weiner, "Lockheed and the Future of Warfare," *New York Times,* November 28, 2004.

72. Quoted in Johnson, *Sorrows of Empire,* 39.

73. Quoted in ibid., 44–45.

74. See http://www.constitution.org/fed/federa41.htm. Accessed on November 19, 2004.

75. Quoted in Johnson, *Sorrows of Empire,* 39.

76. Quoted in ibid., 283.

77. Ibid., 284.

78. Julian Borger, "Cost of Wars Soars to $440 Billion for US," *Guardian,* February 4, 2006; the study by Stiglitz and Bilmes is cited in Bob Herbert, "George Bush's Trillion-Dollar War," *New York Times,* March 23, 2006; Nicholas D. Kristof, "Iraq and Your Wallet," *New York Times,* October 24, 2006; *The Iraq Study Group Report,* James A. Baker III and Lee H. Hamilton, cochairs (New York: Vintage Books, 2006), 32; Michael T. Klare, "Not Terrorism—China Drives Up U.S. Military Spending," *Providence Journal,* April 7, 2006.

79. Peterson, *Running on Empty,* 80–106; Buffett is quoted on page 97, Friedman on page 106.

80. Ibid., 170–93.

81. See, for instance, Louis Uchitelle, "Overcapacity Stalls New Jobs," *New York Times,* October 19, 2003.

82. Keith Bradsher, "China's Factories Aim to Fill the World's Garages," *New York Times,* November 2, 2003.

83. Peterson, *Running on Empty,* xxviii.

84. Kevin Phillips, *Wealth and Democracy: A Political History of the American Rich* (New York: Broadway Books, 2002), 6.

85. Jefferson and Adams quoted in ibid., 293, 303.

86. Quoted in Bill Moyers, "America 101," www.TomPaine.com, November 1, 2006.

87. Quoted in Phillips, *Wealth and Democracy,* 298.

88. Lease, Roosevelt, and Wilson all quoted in ibid., 308, 312, 311.

89. Quoted in ibid., 312.

90. Sara Kugler, "N.Y. Mayor's Re-Election Bid Hit $77 Million," *Orlando Sentinel,* December 6, 2005; Alan Cowell, "Hints of Corruption Lead Some to Urge Blair to Resign," *New York Times,* March 18, 2006. I assumed the Labor Party figure from this passage in Cowell's article: "In a statement on Friday, the Labor Party said it had taken loans worth $24.5 million from individuals, more than three times the

$7 million it had previously reported. It did not say who had made the loans, which accounted for most of the $31 million Labor said it spent on last May's elections."

91. Inspired by the legacy of his ancestor Tom Paine, John Perkins's book is a call-to-arms to defend the republic from the "corporatocracy." Very few books match its power to outline the hijacking of America's ideals to the misguided interests of the few. See John Perkins, *Confessions of an Economic Hit Man* (New York: Plume, 2006); Landon Thomas Jr., "Confessing to the Converted," *New York Times,* February 19, 2006.

92. Quoted in Phillips, *Wealth and Democracy,* 310, 208.

93. Ibid., 138, 160, 162, 284–85, 332.

94. Morris Berman, *The Twilight of American Culture* (New York: Norton, 2000).

95. Ibid., 41, 58, 53, 54.

96. Ibid., 88.

97. Quoted in ibid., 123.

98. Paine, *Common Sense,* in *Paine: Collected Writings,* 42.

99. Berman, *Twilight,* 134–35.

100. Quoted in ibid., 138 (emphasis in original).

101. Ibid., 157, 69.

102. William Greider, *The Soul of Capitalism: Opening Paths to a Moral Economy* (New York: Simon and Schuster, 2003).

103. Ibid., 1–22.

104. Quoted in ibid., 34.

105. Quoted in ibid., 35.

106. Quoted in ibid., 45.

107. Bob Herbert, "Shhh, Don't Say 'Poverty,'" *New York Times,* November 22, 2004.

108. See Norton Garfinkle, *The American Dream vs. the Gospel of Wealth: The Fight for a Productive Middle-Class Economy* (New Haven, Conn.: Yale University Press, 2006). Garfinkle provides convincing proof that a Keynesian, demand-side approach to the U.S. economy produces more wealth than supply-side economics, but he pays no attention at all to the global context that increasingly informs economic trends today. The American economy of the early decades of the twenty-first century is substantially different from the one of the 1950s and 1960s. To work, Garfinkle's pre-scription for a government-engineered American Dream must be extended to people around the world, a case that would then raise a whole set of new issues.

109. T. R. Reid, *The United States of Europe: The New Superpower and the End of American Supremacy* (New York: Penguin, 2004); Rifkin, *European Dream.*

110. Timothy Garton Ash, "The Great Powers of Europe, Redefined," *New York Times,* December 17, 2004.

111. Jeremy Rifkin, "Worlds Apart on the Vision Thing," *Globe and Mail,* August 17, 2004; Rifkin, *The European Dream,* 56. It should be noted that, in my view, Europe's economic model is not substantially different from that of the United States, and that whatever social advantages Europe has over the United States in the present

are sure to be eroded if the economic system that regulates European life is not radically altered. The same applies to the rising powers in Asia, such as China and India.

112. Andrew Moravcsik, "Dream On America," *Newsweek International,* January 31, 2005.

113. American Political Science Association, "American Democracy in an Age of Rising Inequality," 2004. Available online at http://www.apsanet.org/imgtest/task forcereport.pdf.

114. Kevin Phillips, *American Theocracy: The Peril and Politics of Radical Religion, Oil, and Borrowed Money in the 21st Century* (New York: Viking, 2006), 283, 270–71.

115. Julian Borger, "Former Top Judge Says US Risks Edging near Dictatorship," *Guardian,* March 13, 2006. Interestingly, O'Connor's address didn't make headlines in major U.S. newspapers. See Jonathan Raban's comment on this event in "Dictatorship Is the Danger," *Guardian,* March 13, 2006.

116. Moyers, "America 101."

117. See Andrew L. Yarrow, "America: Utopia Lost," *Los Angeles Times,* February 25, 2006.

118. Wim Wenders, "Giving Europe a Soul?" www.signandsight.com, December 20, 2006.

119. Ian Buruma, "The Election and America's Future," *New York Review of Books,* November 4, 2004.

120. Bruce Springsteen, "Chords for Change," *New York Times,* August 5, 2004.

121. "Born in the U.S.A., and Changing It," Letters to the Editor, *New York Times,* August 6, 2004.

122. Susan Cooke Kittredge, "Black Shrouds and Black Markets," *New York Times,* March 5, 2006. Grave robbing for human tissue and body parts is part of a long tradition in the lucrative biomedical fields. See Michele Goodwin, *Black Markets: The Supply and Demand of Body Parts* (New York: Cambridge University Press, 2006), 171–79.

6. VITAL HERESIES

Second epigraph quoted from Stephen Jay Gould, "Nonoverlapping Magisteria," *Natural History* 106 (March 1997): 61.

1. David E. Sanger, "Bush Budget Plan for $2.77 Trillion Stresses Security," *New York Times,* February 7, 2006. The transcript of President Bush's State of the Union speech, delivered on January 30, 2006, was accessed at the *New York Times* Web site, http://www.nytimes.com/2006/01/31/politics/text-bush.html. The despair of Kurt Vonnegut, the humanist son of freethinking German American parents, was exacerbated by the policies of President Bush and his entourage. See his memoir, *A Man without a Country,* ed. Daniel Simon (New York: Random House, 2005). Accounts of the book and interviews with the author also appeared in the *Sunday Herald* (Scotland) on February 5, 2006.

2. Rupert Cornwell, "Middle America: Welcome to the Centre of the USA," *Independent,* May 19, 2006.

3. Susan Jacoby, *Freethinkers: A History of American Secularism* (New York: Metropolitan Books, 2004); Elaine Pagels, *Beyond Belief: The Secret Gospel of Thomas* (New York: Vintage Books, 2004).

4. Jacoby, *Freethinkers,* 1–11.

5. Ibid., 24. The Baptists supported Jefferson's candidacy for president, but they still believed in a Christian society and eventually, when they became mainstream in the nineteenth century, became orthodox in their beliefs. "Between 1630 and 1833," wrote William McLoughlin, "the Baptists went through the classical evolution from a dissenting sect to an established church." See William G. McLoughlin, *Soul Liberty: The Baptists' Struggle in New England, 1630–1833* (Hanover, N.H.: Brown University Press/University Press of New England, 1990), 2. An analysis of the views of Isaac Backus (1724–1806), a Baptist leader, and Thomas Jefferson is quite interesting in this regard (249–69).

6. Quoted in ibid., 34. For a recent account on how and why the Virginia Act came about and was enacted, see Feldman, *Divided by God,* 19–56.

7. Jacoby, *Freethinkers,* 25–26.

8. Quoted in ibid., 32. Washington's letter is still read every year at the Touro Synagogue in Newport, Rhode Island. See http://www.jewishvirtuallibrary.org/jsource/US-Israel/bigotry.html.

9. Bishop White is quoted in Meacham, *American Gospel,* 78.

10. Washington's troop address appears in the *Norton Anthology of American Literature,* 617; Thomas Paine, *The American Crisis, Number 1* (December 19, 1776). In *Paine: Collected Writings* (New York: Library of America, 1995), 91.

11. For a good account of the global influence of Thomas Paine, his role in shaping the modern world, and his tragic end, see Craig Nelson, *Thomas Paine: Enlightenment, Revolution, and the Birth of Modern Nations* (New York: Viking, 2006).

12. Thomas Paine, *The Age of Reason, Being an Investigation of True and Fabulous Theology,* in *Paine: Collected Writings,* 665–730, 731. Also, see Jacoby, *Freethinkers,* 58–65.

13. Adams and Paine are both quoted in *Paine: Collected Writings,* 416–21.

14. Jacoby, *Freethinkers,* 35–65.

15. Ibid., 118–19; also see 104–23.

16. Ibid., 124–28.

17. Quoted in ibid., 173.

18. Quoted in ibid., 184–85.

19. Ibid., 149–57.

20. Ibid., 191–93; Du Bois is quoted on page 192.

21. Ibid., 194–205.

22. The law, called the Indian Imprisonment Act, was drafted by the Massachusetts General Court in the wake of King Philip's War (1675–76). It was repealed by Mayor Thomas M. Menino of Boston on Wednesday, November 24, 2004, the day before Thanksgiving. See Katie Zezima, "Banned in Boston: American Indians, but Only for 329 Years," *New York Times,* November 25, 2004.

23. Quoted in Jacoby, *Freethinkers,* 219–20.

24. Walt Whitman, *Leaves of Grass and Other Writings,* ed. Michael Moon (New York: Norton, 2002), 634–35. The same passage, slightly abridged, is quoted in ibid., 214–15.

25. Jacoby, *Freethinkers,* 227–67.

26. Ibid., 268–91.

27. Ibid., 292–316, 340, 317–47.

28. Ibid., 348–56.

29. Henry David Thoreau, "Resistance to Civil Government" (1849), in *Norton Anthology of American Literature,* 1620–35.

30. Thoreau, *Walden, or Life in the Woods* (1854), in *Norton Anthology of American Literature,* 1635–1808.

31. Henry David Thoreau, "Slavery in Massachusetts" (1854) and "Life without Principle" (1863), in *Norton Anthology of American Literature,* 1808–32.

32. See a wonderful reflection on Thoreau's impact, including in France, in Thierry Paquot, "Désobéir . . . ," *Le Monde diplomatique* (January 2005): 32.

33. Andrew Delbanco, *The Real American Dream: A Meditation on Hope* (Cambridge, Mass.: Harvard University Press, 1999).

34. Ibid., 9–10.

35. Ibid., 103, 107, 111.

36. Quoted in ibid., 108–9.

37. Ibid., 45.

38. Ralph Waldo Emerson, "The Divinity School Address" (1838, 1841), in *Norton Anthology of American Literature,* 944–55.

39. Delbanco, *Real American Dream,* 51.

40. Elaine Pagels, *The Gnostic Gospels* (New York: Vintage Books, 1989 [1979]), xiii–xxxvi. For an account surrounding the incident of the discovery of "papyrus fragments" in Coptic script, see *The Nag Hammadi Library in English,* ed. James M. Robinson (New York: HarperCollins, 1990), 22–26. Karen L. King (author of a book titled *What Is Gnosticism?*) feels that the term covers up the similarities between the orthodox church and these fringe movements or, as Pagels calls them, "other Christianities." But heresy's impact derives precisely from its dissent from the mainstream, not from its radical difference. Atheists are not heretics to Christians; only "other" Christians are. For a lively scholarly debate on this issue, see Richard Byrne, "The End of Gnosticism?" *Chronicle of Higher Education,* May 5, 2006, A18–A22.

41. Pagels, *Gnostic Gospels,* 5, 26, 21.

42. Ibid., 28–47.

43. Quoted in ibid., 55–56. See 48–69 for the question of gender in the Gnostic Gospels.

44. See John Noble Wilford and Laurie Goodstein, "In Ancient Document, Judas Minus Betrayal," *New York Times,* April 7, 2006; Elaine Pagels, "The Gospel Truth," *New York Times,* April 8, 2006.

45. Quoted in Pagels, *Gnostic Gospels,* 74–75.

46. Quoted in ibid., 114.

47. Ibid., 119–41, 149.

48. Pagels, *Beyond Belief.*

49. Ibid., 3–73.

50. Ibid., 164, 185.

51. Yuri Stoyanov, *The Other God: Dualist Religions from Antiquity to the Cathar Heresy* (New Haven, Conn.: Yale Nota Bene/Yale University Press, 2000 [1994]), 21, 23, 156. Zaehner is quoted on page 21.

52. Haytham Manna, *Islam et hérésies: L'obsession blasphématoire* (Paris: Harmattan, 1997), 25–31, 22, 94.

53. Melhem Chokr, *Zandaqa et Zindiqs au second siècle de l'Hégire* (Damascus: L'Institut Français d'Études Arabes, 1993), 9–14.

54. Ibid., 15–26.

55. Quoted in *Leaving Islam: Apostates Speak Out,* ed. Ibn Warraq (Amherst, N.Y.: Prometheus Books, 2003), 67.

56. Chokr, *Zandaqu et Zindiqs au second siècle de l'Hégire,* 69–89; 153–70, 179.

57. Quoted in ibid., 140.

58. Sarah Stroumsa, *Freethinkers of Medieval Islam: Ibn al-Rāwandī, Abu Bakr al-Rāzī, and Their Impact of Islamic Thought* (Leiden: Brill, 1999), 9, 13. Also, see 1–19. Unless I am quoting directly from Stroumsa's text, I will avoid the use of diacritics to simplify spelling.

59. Ibid., 22, 43, 24, 27, 28.

60. Quoted in ibid., 43.

61. Ibid., 39–40, 46–50, 72–73, 79, 82–83, 84.

62. Quoted in Reynold Alleyne Nicholson, *Studies in Islamic Poetry* (London: Cambridge University Press, 1969 [1921]), 191.

63. Quoted in *Leaving Islam,* 69.

64. See Arthur J. Arberry's introduction to *The Spiritual Physick of Rhazes* (New York: Paragon Book Gallery, 1950), 8. Razi's guide to a healthy virtuous life is remarkable for its total reliance on reason.

65. Stroumsa, *Freethinkers of Medieval Islam,* 87–120.

66. *Min tarikh al-ilhad fi al-islam,* 263.

67. Quoted in Stroumsa, *Freethinkers of Medieval Islam,* 132.

68. Quoted in ibid., 130–31.

69. Manna, *Islam et heresies,* 24.

70. Stroumsa, *Freethinkers of Medieval Islam,* 133, 136.

71. Ibid., 142, 159, 166.

72. Ibid., 191–92, 172–73, 183, 241.

73. See *Philosophy in the Middle Ages: The Christian, Islamic, and Jewish Traditions,* ed. Arthur Hyman and James J. Walsh (New York: Harper and Row, 1967), 211–14, 237.

74. In Chokr, *Zandaqa et Zindiqs,* 8. I should note that one scholar, Mahmoud Ibrahim, in his detailed study of the historical context of this period, points out that the persecution of *zanadiqa* was a by-product of the social shift taking place, as a

landed aristocracy was displacing a commercial elite. See Mahmoud Ibrahim, "Religious Inquisition as Social Policy: The Persecution of the 'Zanadiqa' in the Early Abbasid Caliphate," *Arab Studies Quarterly* 16, no. 2 (spring 1994): 53–73.

75. Mohammed ʿAbed al-Jabri, *Arab-Islamic Philosophy: A Contemporary Critique,* trans. Aziz Abbassi (Austin: Center for Middle Eastern Studies, University of Texas, 1999), 1–7.

76. Ibid., 23, 26, 28, 38, 31.

77. Ibid., 55–56.

78. Quoted in ibid., 67.

79. Gould, "Nonoverlapping Magisteria," 16–22.

80. Al-Jabri, *Arab-Islamic Philosophy,* 67, 76, 85, 104–5.

81. Ibid., 125, 128–29.

82. Richard E. Rubenstein, *Aristotle's Children: How Christians, Muslims, and Jews Rediscovered Ancient Wisdom and Illuminated the Dark Ages* (Orlando: Harcourt, 2003).

83. Ibid., ix–46.

84. Ibid., 140–66.

85. Ibid., 209, 215, 237.

86. Ibid., 239–70.

87. Ibid., 293, 286, 288–89, 51.

88. Erik Reece, "Jesus without the Miracles," *Harper's* (December 2005): 33–41.

89. Ignaz Goldhizer, *Introduction to Islamic Theology and Law,* trans. Andras and Ruth Hamori (Princeton, N.J.: Princeton University Press, 1981), 147–48. The book was initially published in German in 1910.

90. Christopher Hart, "God Save the Heretic," *Sunday Times* (London), October 23, 2005.

91. See Abdellah Hammoudi, *A Season in Mecca: Narrative of a Pilgrimage* (New York: Hill and Wang, 2006), 19–38; "A History of Hajj Tragedies," *Guardian,* January 12, 2006. (There were no stampedes in the 2006–7 season, thanks to better planning and new construction. See Lee Keath, "Hajj Comes to a Close without Stampedes," *Washington Post,* January 2, 2007.) Faye Rapoport, "New Tower in Mecca Is Offering Shared Ownership for Muslims," *New York Times,* October 2, 2005; the Web site for Le Meridien Towers in Mecca at http://www.investorsprovident.com/meridienhotel towers.asp was last accessed on February 25, 2006.

92. Hassan M. Fattah, "The Price of Progress: Transforming Islam's Holiest Site," *New York Times,* March 8, 2007.

93. Hassan M. Fattah, "Ramadan Ritual: Fast Daily, Pray, Head to the Mall," *New York Times,* October 12, 2005.

94. See Global Ethic Foundation, *Declaration toward a Global Ethic,* at http://www .cpwr.org/resource/ethic.pdf.

95. Ian Fisher, "Benedict's First Encyclical Shuns Strictures of Orthodoxy," *New York Times,* January 26, 2006.

96. An official Vatican translation of Pope Benedict XVI's *Urbi et Orbi* was published in the *International Herald Tribune,* December 25, 2006.

97. Bellinzoni, *The Future of Christianity,* 15–16, 20, 38, 78, 169–82.

98. The World Institute for Development Economics Research of the United Nations University reported that in 2000, thirty-seven million people controlled "40 percent of the world's total net worth." Global disparities in wealth are happening among and within nations. See Eduardo Porter, "Study Finds Wealth Inequality Is Widening Worldwide," *New York Times,* December 6, 2006. If the world's wealth were equally distributed, "each person would have $20,500 of assets at their disposal." As it is now, half the world's adults have less than $2,200 in assets. See Chris Giles, "Half the World's Assets Held by 2% of Population," *Financial Times,* December 6, 2006.

99. Walter Gibbs, "Microcredit Pioneer Criticizes Globalization at Nobel Ceremony," *International Herald Tribune,* December 10, 2006; Serge Latouche, "Ecofascisme ou écodémocratie," *Le Monde diplomatique* (November 2005): 1, 26–27.

100. Souheila Al-Jadda, "Move Over, Barbie," *USA Today,* December 15, 2005. The Chinese-made doll was the rage among Moroccan girls in 2005–6. See Kenza Alaoui, "Fulah, la nouvelle poupée qui fait fureur," *Le Matin du Sahara et du Maghreb,* February 2, 2006.

INDEX

Abbasid empire, 67
'Abd al-Jabbar, 88
'Abd al-Malik, Hisham, 104, 206
'Abd al-Quddus, Salih ibn, 207
'Abd al-Wahhab, Mohammed ibn, 94
Abderraziq, Ali, 85
Abdu, Mohammed, 62, 84, 86, 87, 94, 107
Abidin-Algan, Emel, 245n.72
abortion, 120, 194, 253n.55
Abramoff, Jack, 161
absolutism: religious moderates as ineffective in struggle against, 46–47
Abu Abdallah al-Mahdi, 206
Abu al-'Atahiyya, 111
Abu Nuwwas, 83, 111
Abu 'Ubayda, 88
Abu Zayd, Nasr Hamid, 88–89
ACLU, 192
Act for Establishing Religious Freedom (Virginia, 1786), 185–86
Adams, Charles Francis, 16, 231n.36
Adams, John, 81, 113, 163–64, 173
Adams, Samuel, 188, 189
advertising: global spending on, 39
Afghani, Jamal al-Din al-, 62, 84, 94

Afghanistan: Christian convert in, treatment of, 137, 249n.67; constitution of Islamic Republic of, 114–15, 246n.1; *hudud* laws in, 137–38; Islamic democracy for, 136; Islamism implanted in, 94; regime change, 113–15, 118, 137–38, 146, 161; supremacy of Islam in, 114–15
Africa: Christian growth in, 41
African Americans: battle for justice, 159–60; Du Bois and, 190–91; freedom for, 156–57, 159; indignity among ghettoized and socially dispossessed, 34; religion as refuge for, 35; slavery and, 130, 151–52, 154, 155–56, 196
African Charter on Human and Peoples Rights (AfrCHR), 138
After Jihad (Feldman), 133, 137, 145
Age of Reason, The (Paine), 187–89
agrarian democracy, 156
agribusinesses, 23, 30
Ahmadinejad, Mahmoud, 29–30, 235n.25. *See also* Iran
Ahn, Christine, 23, 232n.8
Aid to Dependent Children, 161
Aisha, 104
akhbar, 104

Anouar Majid is founding chair and professor of English at the University of New England and the author of *Freedom and Orthodoxy: Islam and Difference in the Post-Andalusian Age, Unveiling Traditions: Postcolonial Islam in a Polycentric World,* and *Si Yussef,* a novel. He is cofounder and editor of *Tingis,* a Moroccan American magazine of ideas and culture.